The EVERYTHING®
Russian Practice Book

Dear Reader,

A Latin proverb claims that, with each new language, you live a new life." As always, the ancients got it right. Knowing a foreign language is more than just remembering vocabulary lists and grammar rules. Mastering a new language brings along a new perspective, a different way of thinking, and a fresh set of experiences. Learning a language is an exciting journey, which is as rewarding as the destination. I am happy to accompany you on this journey, my dear reader!

I have written this book and recorded the audio CD hoping that it will help you to master your Russian in several important ways. Completing the exercises will allow you to practice Russian grammar and vocabulary; listening to the audio CD will give you a chance to exercise your listening skills, training your ear to recognize Russian effortlessly. I have also included exercises that provide you with an opportunity to bring in your general knowledge and express it in Russian.

I hope that working through this book will not only be an educational experience for you, but also a fun one. Enjoy your journey through *The Everything® Russian Practice Book with CD*, and good luck!

Nina A. Wieda

The EVERYTHING® Series

Editorial

Publishing Director	Gary M. Krebs
Director of Product Development	Paula Munier
Associate Managing Editor	Laura M. Daly
Associate Copy Chief	Brett Palana-Shanahan
Acquisitions Editor	Lisa Laing
Development Editor	Larry Shea
Associate Production Editor	Casey Ebert
Language Editor	Ruth Sondermann

Production

Director of Manufacturing	Susan Beale
Associate Director of Production	Michelle Roy Kelly
Cover Design	Paul Beatrice
	Erick DaCosta
	Matt LeBlanc
Design and Layout	Heather Barrett
	Brewster Brownville
	Colleen Cunningham
	Jennifer Oliveira
Series Cover Artist	Barry Littmann

Visit the entire Everything® Series at *www.everything.com*

THE
EVERYTHING®
RUSSIAN PRACTICE
BOOK

Simple techniques to improve your speaking and writing skills

Nina Wieda

Adams Media
Avon, Massachusetts

To my mother, Alla Andreevna Tyurina

An Everything® Series Book.
Everything® and everything.com® are registered trademarks of F+W Publications, Inc.

Published by Adams Media, an F+W Publications Company
57 Littlefield Street, Avon, MA 02322 U.S.A.
www.adamsmedia.com

ISBN 10: 1-59337-724-X
ISBN 13: 978-1-59337-724-3

Printed in the United States of America.

J I H G F E D C B A

Library of Congress Cataloging-in-Publication Data

Wieda, Nina.
The everything Russian practice book with CD / Nina Wieda.
  p. cm. -- (Everything series)
Includes index.
ISBN-13: 978-1-59337-724-3
ISBN-10: 1-59337-724-X
1. Russian language--Textbooks for foreign speakers--English.
2. Russian language--Self-instruction I. Title.

PG2129.E5W54 2006
491.782'421--dc22

2006028205

This book is available at quantity discounts for bulk purchases.
For information, please call 1-800-289-0963.

Contents

cknowledgments

This book wouldn't have been possible without the support and encouragement of my husband John and my mother Alla Andreevna. Many thanks to them, and also to my five-month old daughter Nadia for being a wonderful working companion. Special thanks to my friend, Olga Livshin, who introduced me to this project.

Many warm thanks to Lisa Laing of Adams Media for being a great editor, to Julie Gutin for the wonderful technical editing; and to Dan Cantor of Notable Productions for the awesome job on the audio CD. My thanks extend to everybody at Adams Media for making this book a success.

And last but not least, I owe immense gratitude to all the teachers I have ever had for opening my horizons and feeding my passion for learning.

Top Ten Reasons to Practice Your Russian

1. You can freshen up all the Russian you knew, but haven't been using for a while.

2. You can spot out the gaps in your knowledge and fill them up.

3. Even if the material is fresh in your memory, you will benefit from practicing it yet another time! As the Russians say, *Povtoren'e – mat' uchen'ia*. (Repetition is the mother of learning.)

4. You will build up your Russian vocabulary.

5. You will feel more confident with cases, tenses, and aspects.

6. The Russian publications on the Internet will cease to be a mystery.

7. You will be able to order your borshch at a Russian restaurant in a grammatically correct way.

8. You can get even closer to reading your favorite Russian authors in the original!

9. You can show off your fluent Russian with the Russian speakers you meet.

10. You will make a huge step toward feeling at ease when visiting a Russian-speaking country.

Introduction

▶ BECOMING FLUENT IN a language takes more than just memorization. Each learned rule and vocabulary word has to start coming naturally, without requiring a mental effort. The only way to achieve this fluent stage is practice. This is exactly what this book will provide for you.

The Everything® Russian Practice Book offers you over 250 exercises to perfect your Russian. It is divided into convenient parts; each of them is devoted to a grammatical topic. Exercises range from simple ones—allowing you to review the basics of the Russian language—to those that give you a chance to try your hand at complex grammatical issues. The most demanding aspects of Russian grammar, such as cases, noun-adjective agreement, and various types of verb conjugations, have more exercises devoted to them to ensure that the reader gets enough practice with these tricky subjects.

Besides enhancing your knowledge of grammar, the exercises in *The Everything® Russian Practice Book* can also help you to refresh and expand your Russian vocabulary. Each sentence in the exercises is a fine sample of real conversational Russian as it is spoken by educated speakers. The best way to boost your vocabulary is to translate every word, phrase, and sentence you encounter in the book. While only a few of the exercises include translation in the instructions, it is in your best interests to translate as many sentences as you can. Even if an exercise concentrates on practicing a specific grammatical point, translating the sentences will help you grip the way this grammatical point plays into the context, and provide you with yet another chance to master your understanding of Russian.

For your convenience, this book comes with a short dictionary at the end, which should help you with the most common words and expressions. However, the exercises in *The Everything® Russian Practice Book* cover a wide vocabulary spectrum. If you want to benefit fully from the richness of Russian offered in this book, you need to use a big Russian-English dictionary. There are a number of decent dictionaries offered online. Enter "Russian-English online dictionary" in your search engine and browse through the results to find the dictionary you like.

As you have probably noticed, this book comes with an audio CD. This is a helpful feature, which favorably distinguishes *The Everything® Russian Practice Book* from many other Russian language books on the market. Listening to the audio components of the exercises will help you improve your listening comprehension, and will get you used to the sound of spoken Russian. Don't hesitate to listen to these tracks over and over. Even if at first all you hear is an incoherent mass of sounds, after a while you will start distinguishing words and phrases. Before you know it, Russian will sound familiar and understandable. Don't stop there. Go on listening to pick up the speaker's intonations and peculiarities of pronunciation. The best way to learn to speak the language is being exposed to its sounds.

And no matter what stage you are at, do not be afraid to take your language learning out into the world. Practicing your Russian in daily situations will not only set your grammar and vocabulary in stone, but will also bring you the satisfaction of knowing that you can function in the language. So, go for it and find a Russian neighborhood in the city nearest to you and start speaking! You may even find new friends this way. Good luck in your exploration of Russian, and in whatever ways you will choose to use your knowledge afterwards!

Part 1
Nouns: Introduction

Nouns are words that name someone or something (people, animals, objects, places, or concepts). Each Russian noun belongs to one of the three grammatical genders and changes according to number and case. In Part 1, practice recognizing the gender of Russian nouns.

Masculine Nouns

The Russian language does not have articles (like *the* or *a* in English, or *la* or *le* in French). Since you can't tell the gender of a noun by looking at its article, you have to look at the noun's ending. Russian masculine nouns end in consonants, as in *chelovek* (person); in *-j* (i kratkoe), as in *muzej* (museum); or *-'* (soft sign), as in *uchitel'* (teacher).

Exercise 1: Recognizing Masculine Nouns

In each of the following groups of words choose and circle the masculine noun.

1. *okno, komnata, stol*

2. *medvied', lisa, zmeia*

3. *tramvaj, ulitsa, taksi*

4. *devochka, mal'chik, devushka*

5. *komp'iuter, kniga, ruchka*

6. *svoboda, mir, druzhba*

7. *more, reka, okean*

8. *gitara, baraban, pianino*

9. *dvorets, statuia, Kreml'*

10. *vystavka, muzej, gallereia*

Exercise 2: Writing Down Masculine Nouns

TRACK 1

Listen to the speaker and repeat every word she pronounces. Then listen to the track again and write down every masculine noun. In the answer key, check your spelling.

Example:
Speaker: *vesna, chelovek*
Your answer: *chelovek*

1. ....

2. ....

3. ....

4. ....

5. ....

6. ....

7. ....

8. ....

9. ....

10. ....

Feminine Nouns

Russian feminine nouns end in vowels -*a*, -*ia*; or –' (soft sign). As you see, the ending -' (soft sign) is shared by both masculine and feminine nouns. The only way to distinguish them is to remember their gender. In case of doubt, opt for feminine: ¾ of the nouns ending in –' are feminine.

Exercise 3: What's the Gender?

Using the dictionary, translate each underlined noun and write if it is masculine (M) or feminine (F).

1. *V Moskve opiat' idiot <u>dozhd'</u>.* ....

2. *Moia <u>doch'</u> rodilas' v oktiabre.* ....

3. *<u>Uchitel'</u> – eto blagorodnaia professiia.* ....

4. *Gosudarstvennoe zhivotnoe Kanady – <u>los'</u>.* ....

5. *Segodnia ochen' tioplaia <u>noch'</u>.* ....

6. *Turisty liubiat Krasnuiu <u>ploshchad'</u>.* ....

7. *Peredajte, pozhalujsta, <u>sol'</u>!* ....

8. *Eio <u>mat'</u> rabotaet professorom.* ....

9. *On nichego ne umeet, dazhe zabit' <u>gvozd'</u>!* ....

10. *Govorit', chto tebia nikto ne ponimaet – eto takaia <u>poshlost'</u>.* ....

Exercise 4: She or He?

TRACK 2

Listen to the speaker read pairs of nouns that present a masculine and a feminine version of a certain profession or concept. Write down the feminine version.

Example:
Speaker: *prepodavatel' – prepodavatel'nitsa*
Your answer: *prepodavatel'nitsa*

1. ....

2. ....

3. ....

4. ....

5. ....

6. ....

7. ....

8. ....

9. ....

10. ....

Neuter Nouns

Neuter nouns in Russian end in vowels -*o* and -*e*. The most notable exception is *kofe* (coffee). In spite of its neuter ending, this noun is masculine.

Exercise 5: Where's the Neuter Noun?

Underline all the neuter nouns you can find in these sentences.

1. *Otkrojte, pozhalujsta, okno!*

2. *K etomu syru vino podhodit bol'she, chem pivo.*

3. *Pis'mo ot syna prishlo cherez mesiats.*

4. *My sideli v kafe i pili kofe.*

5. *Bol'she vsego ya liubliu more, solntse i leto.*

6. *Na ulitse kholodno; naden' pal'to.*

7. *Vse russkie devushki iz khoroshikh semej igrali na pianino i govorili na neskol'kikh inostrannykh iazykakh.*

8. *Nakonets on reshilsia priglasit' Lenu v kino.*

9. *Eto zdanie postroeno v stile barokko.*

10. *Ona voshla v kontsertnyj zal i zaniala svoio mesto.*

Special Endings

Some Russian noun endings are misleading. Nouns ending in -*mia*, e.g., *vremia* (time), *imia* (name), *znamia* (banner), or *plamia* (flame) are neuter.

A small group of Russian nouns has two genders: grammatical and actual. Some common nouns like *papa* (dad), *diadia* (uncle), *dedushka* (grandfather), and *muzhchina* (man) are feminine grammatically, but masculine actually, because they refer to male persons.

Exercise 6: Which Gender?

TRACK 3

Listen to the speaker and complete the phrases by adding nouns to the adjectives below. Mark the gender of each noun.

Example:
Speaker: *zolotoe kol'tso*
Your answer: *zolotoe kol'tso – neuter*

1. *dolgoe* ....

2. *moi* ....

3. *dorogoj* ....

4. *sinee* ....

5. *liubimyj* ....

6. *vashe* ....

7. *vysokij* ....

8. *beloe* ....

9. *dnevnoe* ....

10. *neznakomaia* ....

Animate and Inanimate Nouns

In Russian, it's important to know whether a noun is animate or inanimate because in the accusative case animate and inanimate masculine nouns decline differently. In Russian, not only people, but also animals are considered animate.

Exercise 7: Animate or Inanimate?

TRACK 4

Listen to the speaker. Write down the words she pronounces and mark them as animate (A) or inanimate (I).

Example:
Speaker: *devochka*
Your answer: *devochka – animate*

1. ....

2. ....

3. ....

4. ....

5. ....

6. ....

7. ....

8. ....

9. ....

10. ....

Proper Nouns

Proper nouns are words that name specific people, organizations, or places, e.g., Mary, Red Cross, and New York. In Russian, just like in English, proper nouns are capitalized. Please note that, unlike in English, months and days of the week are not capitalized in Russian.

Exercise 8: Trivial Pursuit

Choose one of the following proper names to answer the questions.
Rim, Tchaikovsky, Konstantinopol', Gagarin, Vatikan, Avstraliia, Everest, Tolstoj, Bajkal, Indiia

1. *Kto napisal balet "Lebedinoe ozero?"* ....

2. *Kto byl pervym chelovekom v kosmose?* ....

3. *Kakoj gorod – stolitsa Italii?* ....

4. *Kakoj gorod iavliaetsia odnovremenno i gosudarstvom?* ....

5. *Kto napisal roman "Vojna i mir?"* ....

6. *Kakaia gora – samaia vysokaia v mire?* ....

7. *V kakoj strane nakhoditsia gorod Deli?* ....

8. *Kakoe ozero samoe glubokoe v mire?* ....

9. *Kakoj kontinent – samyj malen'kij?* ....

10. *Kak ran'she nazyvalsia Stambul?* ....

Exercise 9: Completing Phrases

TRACK 5

Listen to the speaker and complete the phrases with proper nouns.

Example:
Speaker: *stolitsa Anglii London*
Your answer: *stolitsa Anglii <u>London</u>*

1. *stolitsa Rossii —* ....

2. *poet i pisatel'* ....

3. *avtor baleta "Romeo i Dzhul'etta"— kompozitor* ....

4. *kosmicheskaia stantsiia* ....

5. *drevnij moskovskij* ....

6. *samaia dlinnaia reka Evropy* ....

7. *avtor romana "Lolita" — Vladimir* ....

8. *planeta* ....

Review

In this section, see how comfortable you are with important properties of Russian nouns. Check your answers using the key at the back of the book. If you find mistakes, go back to corresponding sections and review them.

Exercise 10: Telling the Gender

TRACK 6

Listen to the speaker and write down the nouns she pronounces. Mark the gender of each noun.

Example:
Speaker: *televizor*
Your answer: *televizor – M (masculine)*

1. ....

2. ....

3. ....

4. ....

5. ....

6. ....

7. ....

8. ....

9. ....

10. ....

Exercise 11: What Kind of Noun?

Evaluate each underlined noun based on the three characteristics: whether it's animate (A) or inanimate (I), whether it's a proper noun (P) or not (nP), and indicate what its grammatical gender is [M—masculine; F—feminine; N—neuter].

1. _Chelovek_ – eto zvuchit gordo ....

2. Vy znaete, kto eta _devushka_? ....

3. Na stole stoiala krasivaia _vaza_. ....

4. Moia _koshka_ liubit moloko. ....

5. _Samoliot_ pribyvaet v 10 chasov utra. ....

6. Mne podarili chiornyj kozhanyj _portfel'_. ....

7. Mnogie schitaiut, chto _London_ – teatral'naia stolitsa mira.

    ....

8. "_Kasablanka_" – eto klassika amerikanskogo kino. ....

9. _Iguana_ stala modnym domashnim zhivotnym. ....

10. _Dedushka_ prishel domoj pozdno. ....

Part 2

Declension of Nouns

There are six cases in the Russian language. Each case has its own meaning, and each case is used with specific verbs and prepositions. Russian nouns have different endings in all cases. In this chapter, practice declining singular and plural nouns in all the six cases.

The Nominative Case of Nouns

Nouns in the Nominative case describe the subject of the sentence. In the sentence, "A cat jumped on the table," the word "cat" is the subject. In Russian, "cat" will be translated by a noun in the Nominative case. The Nominative form of nouns is the easiest to produce; it's the form you find in dictionaries.

Exercise 1: Finding the Noun in Nominative

Read these sentences and underline the nouns in the Nominative case. You might have to translate the sentences to find who the actor of the sentence is.

1. *Molodoj muzhchina voshiol v pod'ezd.*

2. *Motsart rodilsia v 18 veke.*

3. *Eta devushka prekrasno poiot.*

4. *Moia babushka prozhila do sta let.*

5. *Moskva rastiot kazhdyj den'.*

6. *V etot den' emu pozvonila ego mat'.*

7. *"Lunnuiu sonatu" napisal Betkhoven.*

8. *Eto leto zapomnilos' mne nadolgo.*

9. *Nastupil tioplyj vecher.*

10. *Poshiol dozhd'.*

Exercise 2: Completing Sentences

TRACK 7

The sentences below are missing nouns naming the subject. Listen to the speaker and complete the sentences with nouns in the Nominative case.

Example:
Speaker: *Mal'chik pozvonil domoj.*
Your answer: ***Mal'chik*** *pozvonil domoj.*

1. .... *upala so stola.*

2. *Na nego laiala bol'shaia* ....

3. .... *opiat' opozdal na lektsiiu.*

4. *Eta* .... *pishet sinimi chernilami.*

5. .... *dukhov raznosilsia po vsej kvartire.*

6. .... *neozhidanno ostanovilas'.*

7. *Ko mne prishli* ....

8. .... *govorit za sebia.*

9. *Molodoe* .... *vybiraet rok muzyku.*

10. *Opiat' idiot* ....

The Nominative Plural of Nouns

In the plural form Russian nouns change their endings.

Table 2-1

Masculine noun endings in Nominative plural			
Nominative singular	Example	Nominative plural	Example
all consonants except zh, ch, sh, shch	televizor	-y	televizory
zh, ch, sh, shch	borshch	-i	borshchi
-'	stroitel'	-i	stroiteli
-j	geroj	-i	geroi

Table 2-2

Feminine noun endings in Nominative plural			
Nominative singular	Example	Nominative plural	Example
-a	komnata	-y	komnaty
-ia	nedelia	-i	nedeli
-iia	delegatsiia	-ii	delegatsii
-'	veshch'	-i	veshchi

Table 2-3

Neuter noun endings in Nominative plural			
Nominative singular	Example	Nominative plural	Example
-o	oblako	-a	oblaka
-e	obaianie	-ia	obaianiia

A number of Russian neuter nouns do not change in plural. Many of these nouns are borrowings from other languages, e.g., *kino* (movie theater), *shosse* (highway).

Some Russian nouns form irregular plurals. For instance, a small group of commonly used Russian nouns retained archaic plural endings, e.g., *doch'* (daughter) – *docheri*. These endings are archaic because they are not used to produce plurals of nouns anymore. Since these nouns are used often, they have retained their old endings. Most Russian words, however, have more contemporary endings. Neuter nouns ending in *-mia* form their plural by adding the ending *-mena*. For example: *imia* (name) – *imena*. Two common words derive their plural from a different root: *rebionok* (child) – *deti*; *chelovek* (person) – *liudi*.

Exercise 3: Making It Plural

TRACK 8

Listen to the speaker and write down the words she pronounces. Then make them plural.

Example:
Speaker: *ulitsa*
Your answer: ***ulitsa–ulitsy***

1. ....

2. ....

3. ....

4. ....

5. ....

6. ....

7. ....

8. ....

9. ....

10. ....

Exercise 4: Changing the Neuter Noun

Some Russian nouns, e.g., *radio*, do not change in plural. Underline the neuter noun in each sentence and, if possible, change it to plural. Write the plural forms.

1. *Nochnoe pole v lunnom svete bylo neobychajno krasivo.* ....

2. *Zdes' zharko, snimajte pal'to.* ....

3. *V dome gorelo tol'ko odno okno.* ....

4. *Ozero Bajkal – samoe glubokoe ozero v mire.* ....

5. *Oni liubili sidet' v kafe na naberezhnoj.* ....

6. *V vozraste shesti let ona uzhe igrala na pianino.* ....

7. *Za obedom oni obychno p'iut moldavskoe vino.* ....

8. *Liudi so vsego Sovetskogo Soiuza priezzhali otdykhat' na Chiornoe more.* ....

9. *Davaj poedem domoj na metro.* ....

10. *Biuro zakryto na pereryv.* ....

Exercise 5: Plural or Singular?

Change the singular nouns to plural, and the plural nouns to singular. When in doubt whether a certain noun is singular or plural, consult a dictionary.

1. *avtomobili* ....

2. *derevnia* ....

3. *rubli* ....

4. *televizory* ....

5. *zhizn'* ....

6. *samoliot* ....

7. *okna* ....

8. *gore* ....

9. *muzei* ....

10. *roial'* ....

Exercise 6: Forming Irregular Plurals

All the nouns in this exercise form irregular plurals. Write their plural forms.

1. *syn* ....

2. *den'* ....

3. *drug* ....

4. *stul* ....

5. *brat* ....

6. *uchitel'* ....

7. *mat'* ....

8. *vremia* ....

9. *pasport* ....

10. *direktor* ....

The Accusative Case of Nouns

Nouns in the Accusative case name the direct object in a sentence. For instance, in the sentence "A boy likes ice cream," "boy" is the actor, and "ice cream" is the direct object. In Russian, "boy" will be translated by a noun in the Nominative case, and "ice cream" will be translated by a noun in the Accusative case. Use the Accusative case with verbs, such as *smotret'* (to watch), *slushat'* (to listen), *liubit'* (to like, to love), *zhdat'* (to wait for), and *iskat'* (to look for).

Masculine nouns behave differently in the Accusative case depending on whether they are animate or inanimate. Inanimate nouns do not change their ending while animate nouns do.

Table 2-4

Animate masculine noun endings in Accusative singular			
Nominative	**Example**	**Accusative**	**Example**
a consonant	*brat*	-a	*brata*
-'	*voditel'*	-ia	*voditelia*
-j	*muzej*	-ia	*muzeia*

Table 2-5

Feminine noun endings in Accusative singular			
Nominative	Example	Accusative	Example
-a	sestra	-u	sestru
-ia	pesnia	-iu	pesniu
-'	mysh'	-'	mysh'

Singular neuter nouns do not change in the Accusative case.

Exercise 7: Putting Nouns in the Accusative

Complete the sentences by putting the nouns in parentheses in the Accusative case. Then translate the sentences.

1. *Ia slyshu krasivuiu* .... *. (muzyka)*

....

2. *My sideli i smotreli na* .... *. (gorod)*

....

3. *Davajte priglasim na den' rozhdeniia* .... *. (Olia)*

4. *On vstal, chtoby zakryt'* .... *. (okno)*

....

5. *Vy znaete etogo* .... *? (chelovek)*

....

6. *Ty uzhe videl Krasnuiu* .... *? (ploshchad')*

....

7. *Kak zovut tvoego* ....? *(uchitel')*

....

8. *Etot malysh ochen' liubit svoiu* .... *(babushka)*

....

9. *Pozovite vashu* .... *(sobaka)*

....

10. *Bol'she vsekh kurortov mira ia liubliu Chiornoe* ....
    (more)

....

Exercise 8: Completing Sentences

TRACK 9

The sentences below lack the nouns naming direct object. Listen to the speaker and complete the sentences with the nouns in the Accusative case. Then provide the nominative form of each noun.

Example:
Speaker: *Babushka pozvala vnuka.*
Your answer: *Babushka pozvala <u>vnuka.</u>* ***(vnuk)***

1. *Etu* .... *zovut Tat'iana Petrovna.* ....

2. *Moj otets sam sdelal etot* ....

3. *Ty segodnia uzhe kormil svoiu* ....? ....

4. *Ia vchera prochitala zamechatel'nuiu* ....

5. *Chto vy budete est',* .... *ili borshch?* ....

6. *Vy ne videli zdes' malen'kogo* ....? ....

7. *Na ulitse ona vstretila svoiu* ....

8. *Terpet' ne mogu* ....

9. *Studenty vnimatel'no slushali* ....

10. *Ty kogda-nibud' videl* .... *Bajkal?* ....

The Accusative Plural of Nouns

All inanimate nouns in Accusative plural, regardless of gender, have the same endings as in Nominative plural. Animate nouns, on the other hand, have different endings depending on what their endings were in Nominative singular.

Table 2-6

Masculine noun endings in Accusative plural			
Nominative singular	**Example**	**Accusative plural**	**Example**
a consonant	*volk*	⁻*ov*	*volkov*
⁻*'*	*stroitel'*	⁻*ej*	*stroitelej*
⁻*j*	*geroj*	⁻*ev*	*geroev*

Table 2-7

Feminine noun endings in Accusative plural			
Nominative singular	**Example**	**Accusative plural**	**Example**
⁻*a*	*aktrisa* (no ending)	zero ending	*aktris*
⁻*ia*	*Nadia*	⁻*'*	*Nad'*
⁻*iia* or ⁻*eia*	*zmeia*	⁻*j*	*zmej*
⁻*'*	*loshad'*	⁻*ej*	*loshadej*

Since almost all the neuter nouns are inanimate, their Accusative plural is the same as their Nominative plural. (See Table 2-3.)

Exercise 9: Putting Nouns in Accusative Plural

TRACK 10

Listen to the speaker and write down the words. Then put the words in Accusative plural. Remember the difference between inanimate and animate nouns.

Example:
Speaker: *korova*
Your answer: *korova* – ***korov***

1. ....

2. ....

3. ....

4. ....

5. ....

6. ....

7. ....

8. ....

9. ....

10. ....

Exercise 10: Completing Sentences

Complete the sentences by putting the animate nouns in parentheses in Accusative plural. Then translate the sentences.

1. *On mnogo chital russkikh* .... *(pisatel')*

   ....

2. *Na etoj vystavke mozhno vstretit' izvestnykh* ....
   (khudozhnitsa)

   ....

3. *My prishli v zoopark, chtoby uvidet' belykh* ....
   (medved')

   ....

4. *On znal vsekh* .... *v gorode. (direktor)*

   ....

5. *Ona stoiala u vkhoda v kinoteatr i zhdala*
   svoikh .... *(podruga)*

   ....

6. *Ty chasto naveshchaesh svoikh* ....? *(tiotia)*

   ....

7. *V romane "Miortvye dushi" Gogol' opisyvaet obyknovennykh*
   .... *(obyvatel')*

   ....

8. *Ia ochen' liubliu* .... *(sobaka)*

   ....

9. *On rabotal na pochte i lichno znal mnogikh* ....
   (pochtal'on)

....

10. *Mnogie prikhodiat v kino, tol'ko chtoby posmotret' na liubimykh*
    .... *(aktrisa)*

....

The Dative Case of Nouns

Nouns in the Dative case name the indirect object in a sentence. In the sentence, "A boy gave a flower to a girl," "a boy" is the actor, "a flower" is the direct object, and "a girl" is the indirect object. In Russian, "a boy" is translated by a noun in the Nominative case, "a flower" is translated by a noun in the Accusative case, and "a girl" is translated by a noun in the Dative case.

The name of the case, "dative," comes from the Latin verb meaning "to give." Remember to use the Dative case when you are talking about giving things to someone. The Dative case is also used when talking about telling or showing things to someone. (You can think about it as "giving information" to someone.) Other common verbs that require the use of the Dative case are *zvonit'* (to call) [think about it as "giving someone a call"]and *pomogat'* (to help) [think about it as "giving someone a hand].

Table 2-8

Masculine noun endings in Dative singular			
Nominative	Example	Dative	Example
a consonant	*drug*	-u	*drugu*
-'	*pisatel'*	-iu	*pisateliu*
-j	*muzej*	-iu	*muzeiu*

Table 2-9

Feminine noun endings in Dative singular			
Nominative	**Example**	**Dative**	**Example**
-a	zhena	-e	zhene
-ia	zemlia	-e	zemle
-'	ploshchad'	-i	ploshchadi

Commonly used exceptions are the nouns *mat'* (mother) – *materi*, and *doch'* (daughter) – *docheri*.

Table 2-10

Neuter noun endings in Dative singular			
Nominative	**Example**	**Dative**	**Example**
-o	pis'mo	-u	pis'mu
-e	more	-iu	moriu

Exercise 11: Dative Endings

Put the following nouns in the Dative case.

1. *moloko* ....

2. *roza* ....

3. *devochka* ....

4. *avtobus* ....

5. *avtomobil'* ....

6. *simfoniia* ....

7. *noch'* ....

8. *volia* ....

9. *more* ....

10. *mat'* ....

Exercise 12: Telling the Case

Mark the case of each underlined noun as Dative (D) or Nominative (N).

1. *Mat' dala <u>synu</u> yabloko.* ....

2. *Professor dal <u>studentu</u> zadanie.* ....

3. *<u>Mariia</u> daiot uroki muzyki.* ....

4. *Mne vchera pozvonil moj <u>sosed</u>.* ....

5. *Ya chasto zvoniu <u>podruge</u>.* ....

6. *<u>Muzyka</u> pomogaet Lene rasslabit'sia.* ....

7. *My dali etoj <u>pesne</u> smeshnoe nazvanie.* ....

8. *Dajte kusok torta <u>Mashe</u>.* ....

9. *<u>More</u> daiot cheloveku zariad bodrosti.* ....

10. *Etot mal'chik pomogaet svoej <u>babushke</u>.* ....

Exercise 13: Completing Sentences

Complete each sentence with the noun in the parenthesis. If necessary, put the noun in the Dative case.

1. *Ty uzhe dal* .... *moloko? (koshka)*

2. *Misha rasskazal* .... *smeshuiu istoriiu. (drug)*

3. *Eta* .... *ochen' liubit chitat'. (devochka)*

4. *Pozvoni, pozhalujsta,* .... *! (sosed)*

5. *Ya pokazala* .... *dorogu. (puteshestvennik)*

6. *Eta* .... *igraet v teatre i kino. (aktrisa)*

7. .... *napisal eto stikhotvorenie v rannej iunosti.*
   (poet)

8. *Misha dal* .... *kliuchi. (sestra)*

9. *Pervogo sentiabria deti prinosiat tsvety* ....
   (uchitel')

10. *Militsioner pomog* .... *najti Bol'shoj teatr. (turist)*

The Dative Plural of Nouns

All Russian nouns, regardless of gender, have the endings -am or -iam in Dative plural.

Table 2-11

Masculine noun endings in Dative plural			
Nominative singular	Example	Dative plural	Example
a consonant	dom	¯am	domam
¯'	stroitel'	¯iam	stroiteliam
¯j	geroj	¯iam	geroiam

Table 2-12

Feminine noun endings in Dative plural			
Nominative singular	Example	Dative plural	Example
¯a	ruka	¯am	rukam
¯ia	bania	¯iam	baniam
¯'	sol'	¯iam	soliam

Table 2-13

Neuter noun endings in Dative plural			
Nominative singular	Example	Dative plural	Example
¯o	iskusstvo	¯am	iskusstvam
¯e	svidanie	¯iam	svidaniiam

All plural forms of *chelovek* (person) and *rebionok* (child) are formed from their irregular plural Nominative forms *liudi* (people) and *deti* (children).

Exercise 14: Dative Plural Nouns

Complete each sentence with the noun in parenthesis. Remember to put the nouns in Dative plural.

1. *Na 8 marta muzhchiny dariat* .... *tsvety.* *(zhenshchina)*

2. *Ekskursovod rasskazal* .... *legendu. (turist)*

3. *Pozvonite* ....! *(roditel')*

4. *Prezident vruchil* .... *medali. (geroj)*

5. *Khoroshaia muzyka pomogaet* .... *stat' znamenitymi. (fil'm)*

6. *Konstitutsiia daiot* .... *pravo na svobodu slova. (chelovek)*

7. *Stiuardessa prinesla* .... *vodu. (passazhir)*

8. *Publika dolgo aplodirovala* .... *(aktior)*

9. *On vsegda daval ulichnym* .... *den'gi. (muzykant)*

10. *Uchitel' pokazal* .... *novyj fil'm. (rebionok)*

Exercise 15: Answering Questions

TRACK 11

Listen to the speaker. Then answer the questions below. You can answer either in full sentences or give one-word answers. A hint: *komu* means "to whom."

Example:
Speaker: *Prodavets pokazyvaet pokupateliam tovary.*
Question: *Komu prodavets pokazyvaet tovary?*
Your answer: *Pokupateliam.* OR *Prodavets pokazyvaet tovary pokupateliam.*

1. *Komu v Rossii priniato govorit' komplimenty?*

   ....

2. *Komu v Rossii redko dariat tsvety?*

   ....

3. *Komu dolzhny pomogat' vnuki?*

   ....

4. *Komu mat' dala konfety?*

   ....

5. *Komu kassir daiot sdachu?*

   ....

6. *Komu dlia zdorov'ia daiut sol' ?*

   ....

7. *Komu ia daiu moloko?*

   ....

8. *Komu ekskursovod pokazal starinnyj zamok?*

....

9. *Komu voditel' pomog vyjti na ostanovke?*

....

10. *Komu chasto zvoniat uchitelia?*

....

The Prepositional Case of Nouns

The Prepositional case is most often used to describe location. As the name indicates, it is always used with a preposition. The most common prepositions used with the Prepositional case are *v* (on, at), *na* (on, at), and *o* (about).

Table 2-14

Masculine noun endings in Prepositional singular			
Nominative	Example	Prepositional	Example
a consonant	*stul*	-e	*stule*
-'	*dozhd'*	-e	*dozhde*
-j	*roj*	-e	*roe*

Table 2-15

Feminine noun endings in Prepositional singular			
Nominative	Example	Prepositional	Example
-a	*strana*	-e	*strane*
-ia	*dolia*	-e	*dole*
-'	*dver'*	-i	*dveri*

Table 2-16

Neuter noun endings in Prepositional singular			
Nominative	Example	Prepositional	Example
ˉo	steklo	ˉe	stekle
ˉe	more	ˉe	more
ˉie	svidanie	ˉii	svidanii

Exercise 16: Putting Nouns in Prepositional

Put the following nouns in the Prepositional case.

1. stadion ....

2. pochta ....

3. ploshchad' ....

4. dom ....

5. zdanie ....

6. pole ....

7. avtobus ....

8. konervatoriia ....

9. okno ....

10. vishnia ....

Exercise 17: A Working Family

TRACK 12

Listen to the speaker and answer the questions about where different family members work. A hint: *gde* means "where."

Example:
Speaker: *Zhena rabotaet v redaktsii.*
Question: *Gde rabotaet zhena?*
Your answer: *Zhena rabotaet v redaktsii.*

1. *Gde rabotaet mama?*

....

2. *Gde rabotaet papa?*

....

3. *Gde rabotaet babushka?*

....

4. *Gde rabotaet dedushka?*

....

5. *Gde rabotaet tiotia?*

....

6. *Gde rabotaet diadia?*

....

7. *Gde rabotaet sestra?*

....

8. *Gde rabotaet brat?*

....

Exercise 18: Natural Wonders

Complete each sentence with one of the following nouns: *Antarktika, Amerika, Evropa, Afrika, okean, Aziia, Avstraliia, Rossiia.* Remember to put each noun in the Prepositional case and match it with the meaning of the sentence.

1. *Niagarskij vodopad nakhoditsia v* ....

2. *Zhirafy zhivut v* ....

3. *Kity zhivut v* ....

4. *Kenguru zhivut v* ....

5. *Pingviny zhivut v* ....

6. *Ozero Bajkal nakhoditsia v* ....

7. *Gory Al'py nakhodiatsia v* ....

8. *Everest nakhoditsia v* ....

The Prepositional Plural of Nouns

Table 2-17

Masculine noun endings in Prepositional plural			
Nominative singular	**Example**	**Prepositional plural**	**Example**
a consonant	*most*	¯*akh*	*mostakh*
-'	*rubl'*	¯*iakh*	*rubliakh*
-j	*boj*	¯*iakh*	*boiakh*

Table 2-18

Feminine noun endings in Prepositional plural			
Nominative singular	**Example**	**Prepositional plural**	**Example**
-a	ulitsa	-akh	ulitsakh
-ia	sem'ia	-iakh	sem'iakh
-'	rol'	-iakh	roliakh

Table 2-19

Neuter noun endings in Prepositional plural			
Nominative singular	**Example**	**Prepositional plural**	**Example**
-o	plecho	-akh	plechakh
-e	rastenie	-iakh	rasteniiakh

Exercise 19: *Making It Prepositional Plural*

TRACK 13

Listen to the speaker and write down the words. Then put them in Prepositional plural and complete the "preposition + noun" phrases.

Example:
Speaker: *dvor*
Your answer: *dvor; vo dvorakh*

1. .... ; *na* ....

2. .... ; *na* ....

3. .... ; *v* ....

4. .... ; *na* ....

5. .... ; *na* ....

6. .... ; *v* ....

7. .... ; *na* ....

8. .... ; *na* ....

9. .... ; *v* ....

10. .... ; *v* ....

Exercise 20: Where Does This Happen?

Choose the best noun from the list to complete each sentence. Remember to put the nouns in Prepositional plural and use the preposition *v* or *na*.

gorod, muzej, universitet, teatr, ofis, stadion, biblioteka, ferma, okean, ostrov

1. *V futbol igraiut* ....

2. *Vystavki khudozhnikov prokhodiat* ....

3. *Doma stroiatsia* ....

4. *Parakhody plavaiut* ....

5. *Spektakli staviat* ....

6. *Liudi rabotaiut* ....

7. *Studenty uchatsia* ....

8. *Fermery vyrashchivaiut ovoshchi* ....

9. *Liudi chitaiut knigi* ....

10. *Vse liubiat otdykhat'* ....

The Genitive Case of Nouns

Nouns in the Genitive case are used to talk about possession, quantity, or absence of something. The meaning of a noun in the Genitive case can be usually translated with the help of the preposition "of." In the phrase "a cup of tea," the word "tea" is translated into Russian by a noun in the Genitive: *chashka chaia*. For quantities, Genitive singular is used when talking about substances, such as tea, water, salt, sugar, etc., i.e. *kilogramm sakhara* (a kilo of sugar). The Genitive is also used with objects that can be counted after numbers 2, 3, and 4, i.e., *dva doma* (two houses); *tri kvartiry* (three apartments); *chetyre dereva* (four trees).

The Genitive case is also used to talk about the absence of something. In the phrase "there is no water here," the word "water" is translated into Russian with the noun in the genitive case: *zdes' net vody*.

The other major use of the Genitive is to express possession. The noun naming the possessor has to be in the Genitive. The phrase "a boy's book" is translated into Russian as *kinga mal'chika*, where the noun *mal'chik* (boy) is in the Genitive. Since the Genitive is associated with the use of the preposition "of," it might be easier to remember this pattern if you rephrase "a boy's book" as "a book of a boy." Although this phrase is not exactly proper English, it's still possible to understand what it means. Putting your phrases this way will help you remember how to say it in Russian. To name the author of something, also use the genitive case: *poeziia Bajrona*.

Table 2-20

Masculine noun endings in Genitive singular			
Nominative	Example	Genitive	Example
a consonant	*student*	ˉa	*studenta*
ʼ	*uchitel'*	ˉia	*uchitelia*
j	*muzej*	ˉia	*muzeia*

Table 2-21

Feminine noun endings in Genitive singular			
Nominative	Example	Genitive	Example
-a	roza	-y	rozy
-ia	pesnia	-i	pesni
-'	noch'	-i	nochi

Table 2-22

Neuter noun endings in Genitive singular			
Nominative	Example	Genitive	Example
-o	okno	-a	okna
-e	more	-ia	moria
-mia	vremia	-meni	vremeni

Exercise 21: Describing Supplies

Use the pairs of nouns to make up meaningful phrases as in the example. Remember to put the word naming the substance in the Genitive case.
Example: butylka, voda
Your answer: **butylka vody**

1. kilogram, sakhar ....

2. bokal, vino ....

3. tarelka, sup ....

4. stakan, moloko ....

5. lozhka, sol' ....

6. butylka, sok ....

7. *polkilo, miaso* ....

8. *litr, benzin* ....

9. *kilogram, maslo* ....

10. *korobka, pechen'e* ....

Exercise 22: Urban Landscape

TRACK 14

Listen to the speaker read the sentences about the existence of something. For example: *Zdes' est' dom.* (There is a house here.) Oppose the speaker. Write a sentence stating that there is no such object here: *Zdes' net doma.* (There is no house here.) Remember to put the noun following *net* in the Genitive case.

Example:
Speaker: *Zdes' est' dom.*
Your answer: *Zdes' net doma.*

1. ....

2. ....

3. ....

4. ....

5. ....

6. ....

7. ....

8. ....

9. ....

10. ....

THE EVERYTHING RUSSIAN PRACTICE BOOK

Exercise 23: Whose Is This?

Match each object from the list with a person. Remember to put the nouns naming possessors in the Genitive case. The first phrase is done for you.

miach, pistolet, gitara, mashina, samoliot, komp'iuter, kniga, molotok

1. *futbolist:*   *miach*   *futbolista*

2. *muzykant:* ....

3. *professor:* ....

4. *voditel':* ....

5. *programmist:* ....

6. *pilot:* ....

7. *militsioner:* ....

8. *stroitel':* ....

Exercise 24: Who's the Author?

Put each name in parenthesis in the Genitive to indicate that the person is the author of that masterpiece. Note the Russian spelling of the famous names. Hint: Both first and last names of the author have to be changed. The first phrase is done for you.

1. *"Rekviem"* (Amadej Motsart):
   "Rekviem" Amadeia Motsarta

2. *"Lunnaia sonata"* (Liudvig van Betkhoven):

....

3. *roman "Tom Sojer" (Mark Tvejn):*

   ....

4. *"Dialogi" (Sokrat):*

   ....

5. *roman "Proshchaj, oruzhie" (Ernest Kheminguej):*

   ....

6. *roman "Velikij Getsbi" (Skot Fitszheral'd):*

   ....

7. *philosophiia (Seneka):*

   ....

8. *p'esa "Chajka" (Anton Chekhov):*

   ....

9. *roman "Evgenij Onegin" (Aleksandr Pushkin):*

   ....

10. *kartina "Chiornyj kvadrat" (Kazemir Malevich):*

    ....

The Genitive Plural of Nouns

The Genitive plural is used to talk about quantity or absence of countable objects.

Table 2-23

Masculine noun endings in Genitive plural			
Nominative singular	**Example**	**Genitive plural**	**Example**
all consonants except zh, ch, sh, shch	stol	-ov	stolov
-zh, -ch, -sh, -shch	borshch	-ej	borshchej
-'	stroitel'	-ej	stroitelej
-j	geroj	-ev	geroev

Table 2-24

Feminine noun endings in Genitive plural			
Nominative singular	**Example**	**Genitive plural**	**Example**
-a	komnata	zero ending (no ending)	komnat
-ia	nedelia	-'	nedel'
-iia	konstitutsiia	-ij	konstitutsij
-'	sol'	-ej	solej

Table 2-25

Neuter noun endings in Genitive plural			
Nominative singular	**Example**	**Genitive plural**	**Example**
-o	mesto	zero ending (no ending)	mest
-e	more	-ej	morej
-ie	obshchezhitie	-ij	obshchezhitij

Nouns that form irregular plurals in the Nominative case use the same irregular stems to form the Genitive plural. For example: *doch'* (daughter, nom. sing.), *docheri* (daughters, nom. pl.), *docherej* (daughters, gen. pl.).

Exercise 25: A Happy Bunch

Translate the phrases using the nouns in parentheses and one of the following words: *mnogo* (a lot of), *gruppa* (group), *neskol'ko* (several), *korobka* (box), *buket* (bouquet). Remember that some nouns form irregular Genitive plurals.

1. a group of students (*student*) ....

2. a lot of mistakes *(oshibka)* ....

3. a bouquet of roses *(roza)* ....

4. several tourists *(turist)* ....

5. a box of candy *(konfeta)* ....

6. a lot of friends *(drug)* ....

7. a box of crackers *(kreker)* ....

8. a bouquet of tulips *(tiul'pan)* ....

9. several buildings *(zdanie)* ....

10. a group of writers *(pisatel')* ....

Exercise 26: Contradicting the Speaker

TRACK 15

Listen to the speaker and contradict her using the "*net* + noun in gen. pl." construction.

Example:
Speaker: *V nebe – oblaka.*
Your answer: *V nebe net oblakov.*

1. *V biblioteke* ....

2. *Na ulitse* ....

3. *V metro* ....

4. *V universitete* ....

5. *V shkole* ....

6. *V muzee* ....

7. *V ofise* ....

8. *V restorane* ....

9. *V kvartire* ....

10. *V okeane* ....

The Instrumental Case of Nouns

Nouns in the Instrumental case name the instrument by which an action is carried out. For instance, in the sentence *Ia pishu ruchkoj* (I am writing with a pen), the noun *ruchka* (pen) is in the Instrumental case. In Russian, no preposition is used, unlike in English. Compare: *pishu ruchkoj* versus "writing with a pen."

After the preposition *s* (with), the Instrumental has the meaning "together with." For example: *Masha poshla v kino s Lenoj.* (Masha went to the movies together with Lena. OR Lena and Masha went to the movies.) Note that Russian uses the construction "X in Nominative + preposition *s* + Y in Instrumental" where English uses "X and Y". For instance, compare: "Mom and Dad went to work" and *Mama s papoj poshli na rabotu.* There are also a number of verbs that require the use of the Instrumental case. The most often used are *rabotat'* (to work [as]), *stanovit'sia* (to become), *gordit'sia* (to be proud of), *byt'* (to be), *zanimat'sia* (to be taking up [an activity]), and *interesovat'sia* (to be interested in).

Table 2-26

Masculine noun endings in Instrumental singular			
Nominative	**Example**	**Instrumental**	**Example**
a consonant	*gorod*	-om	*gorodom*
-'	*prepodavatel'*	-em	*prepodavatelem*
-j	*boj*	-em	*boem*

Table 2-27

Feminine noun endings in Instrumental singular			
Nominative	**Example**	**Instrumental**	**Example**
-a	*stena*	-oj	*stenoj*
-ia	*vishnia*	-ej	*vishnej*
-'	*noch'*	-iu	*noch'iu*

Table 2-28

Neuter noun endings in Instrumental singular			
Nominative	**Example**	**Instrumental**	**Example**
-o	*koleso*	-om	*kolesom*
-e	*gore*	-em	*gorem*
-mia	*vremia*	-menem	*vremenem*

Exercise 27: How Is It Done?

Complete each sentence by choosing a matching noun from the list. Remember to put the nouns in the Instrumental case.

lozhka, vilka, ruka, poezd, samoliot, avtobus, nozh, ruchka

1. *Ia pishu* ....

2. *Misha edet v Moskvu* ....

3. *Sup ediat* ....

4. *On uletel v Parizh* .... *"Aeroflota."*

5. *Ia em makarony* ....

6. *Olia rezhet kolbasu* ....

7. *Zhenshchina pokazyvaet na zdanie* ....

8. *Petia ezdit na rabotu* ....

Exercise 28: Paraphrasing

TRACK 16

You remember that Russians use the preposition *s* (with) to describe groups of people. Listen to the speaker and paraphrase the sentences she is saying according to this model:

Example:
Speaker: *Misha i Kolia poshli v kino.*
Paraphrase: *Misha s Kolej poshli v kino.*

1. .... *poekhali v Moskvu.*

2. .... *poshli v teatr.*

3. .... *risuiut.*

4. .... *poshli v shkolu.*

5. .... *igraiut v futbol.*

6. .... *poshli na progulku.*

7. .... *voshli v shkolu.*

8. .... *zashli v muzej.*

Exercise 29: Reading the Story

Read the text and fill in the blanks with the appropriate nouns from the list. The nouns are given in their dictionary form, so remember to put them in the correct case.

professiia, inzhener, balerina, khudozhnik, kosmonavt, balet, iskusstvo

Kogda Dashe bylo 10 let, ona interesovalas'

.... *Kak vse russkie devochki, ona khotela*

byt' .... *A eio brat Seriozha, kak vse russkie*

mal'chiki, khotel stat' .... *Proshlo 10 let, i*

Dasha stala .... *Ona rabotaet na bol'shom*

zavode i ochen' gorditsia svoej .... *A*

Seriozha nachal zanimat'sia .... *On stal*

.... , *i chasto pishet kartiny na temu baleta.*

The Instrumental Plural of Nouns

Table 2-29

Masculine noun endings in Instrumental plural			
Nominative singular	**Example**	**Instrumental plural**	**Example**
a consonant	*port*	⁻ami	*portami*
⁻'	*pisatel'*	⁻iami	*pisateliami*
⁻j	*muzej*	⁻iami	*muzeiami*

Table 2-30

Feminine noun endings in Instrumental plural			
Nominative singular	**Example**	**Instrumental plural**	**Example**
⁻a	*gostinitsa*	⁻ami	*gostinitsami*
⁻ia	*petlia*	⁻iami	*petliami*
⁻'	*svekrov'*	⁻iami	*svekroviami*

Table 2-31

Neuter noun endings in Instrumental plural			
Nominative singular	**Example**	**Instrumental plural**	**Example**
⁻o	*plecho*	⁻ami	*plechami*
⁻e	*more*	⁻iami	*moriami*

Exercise 30: Putting It in Instrumentals

Complete each sentence with the word in parenthesis. Remember to put the nouns in Instrumental plural.

1. *Pro takikh govoriat: "On stoit na zemle obeimi* ...." *(noga)*

2. *Roditeli vsegda gordiatsia svoimi* .... *(rebionok)*

3. *Futbolisty chasto otbivaint miach* .... *(golova)*

4. *Renuar pisal* .... *(kraska)*

5. *On derzhal sumku obeimi* .... *(ruka)*

6. *Byvshie druz'ya stali* .... *(vrag)*

7. *On vstal na travu* .... *(botinok)* (fleeting *o*)

8. *On svobodno vladeet tremia inostrannymi* .... *(iazyk)*

Review

In this section, practice using all six cases both in singular and in plural. If a certain case causes a problem, go back to the section devoted to this case and review the rules and the exercises.

Exercise 31: Which Case?

Complete each sentence with the words in parentheses. Remember to use the appropriate case and number. Then translate the sentences.

1. *Ivan kupil doroguiu* .... *(kartina)* .... *(Renuar).*

   ....

2. *Mama stoiala na* .... *(kukhnia) i meshala* ....
   (borshch) dereviannoj .... *(lozhka).*

   ....

3. *Za vremia turpoezdki gruppa* .... *(turist) videla* ....
   (Moskva), ... *(Vladimir), i* .... *(reka Volga).*

   ....

4. *Dedushka sidel na* .... *(divan) i chital* ....
   (gazeta).

   ....

5. *V* .... *(zoopark) deti videli* .... *(medved'),*
   .... *(lisa), i* .... *(slon).*

   ....

6. *Biznesmen podpisal* .... *(kontrakt) i otoslal ego* ....
   (partnior).

   ....

7. .... (Nina) s .... (Nadia) guliali v .... (park).

....

8. Vadim pozvonil .... (kollega) i poprosil prislat' .... (kontrakt).

....

Exercise 32: A Story about Dasha

TRACK 17

Listen to the speaker read the text. Then complete the sentences below using the information you learned from the text. Remember to put the nouns in the appropriate cases.

1. Etu .... zovut Dasha.

2. Dasha zhiviot v .... Novorossijske.

3. Dasha zhiviot ne v ...., a v bol'shoj ....

4. Dasha liubit svoiu ....

5. Dasha uchitsia v ....

6. Dasha khochet stat' ....

7. Dasha liubit chitat' ....

8. Lena – podruga ....

9. Lena zhiviot v ....

10. Dasha pishet pis'ma ....

Exercise 33: Translating into Russian

Translate the sentences into Russian. Use the verbal forms given in parentheses.

1. I am writing a letter to Grandma. *(pishu)*

   ....

2. Andrej and Olia live in Moscow. *(zhivut)*

   ....

3. I like theater, music, and books. *(liubliu)*

   ....

4. My brother wanted to become a teacher. *(khotel)*

   ....

5. A professor is helping students to translate a short story. *(pomogaet; perevodit')*

   ....

6. I often call my friend. *(zvoniu)*

   ....

7. Dasha sent Lena a book of poems by Pushkin. *(poslala)*

   ....

8. Dasha and Lena are going by bus. *(edut)*

   ....

Part 3

Pronouns

Pronouns are words that replace nouns in sentences. They are used to avoid repeating the same nouns. In this part, you will practice using different types of pronouns.

Pronouns in the Nominative Case

Pronouns such as "I," "she," or "we" are called personal pronouns. In Russian, personal pronouns change according to case. When used in the Nominative case, personal pronouns act as subjects of the sentence.

Table 3-1

Russian personal pronouns in Nominative	
I	ia
you (singular/informal)	ty
he	on
she	ona
it (neuter)	ono
we	my
you (plural and/or formal)	vy
they	oni

In Russian there are two ways to say "you." When you address a single person, use *ty*. When you address a group of people, use *vy*. *Vy* is also the correct way to address someone you are on formal terms with. *Ty* is reserved for family, friends, and children.

Exercise 1: How to Address?

Choose whether to use *ty* or *vy* when addressing these people.

1. your mother ....

2. a group of your colleagues ....

3. one of your colleagues ....

4. your cousin   ....

5. a waiter   ....

6. your grandmother   ....

7. a doctor   ....

8. your friend   ....

Exercise 2: Rewriting Sentences

Rewrite each sentence. Replace each subject noun with an appropriate personal pronoun.

1. *Ivan rabotaet v redaktsii.*

   ....

2. *Moi roditeli zhivut v Moskve.*

   ....

3. *Eto kafe nazyvaetsia "Skazka."*

   ....

4. *Moj drug i ia sobiraemsia poiti v kino.*

   ....

5. *Natasha igraet na skripke.*

   ....

6. *Ty i tvoia sobaka vchera byli v parke?*

   ....

7. *Moskovskoe metro zakryvaetsia v chas nochi.*

....

8. *Eti konfety ochen' sladkie.*

....

Exercise 3: Completing the Sentences

TRACK 18

Listen to the speaker. Complete the following sentences, replacing the nouns read by the speaker with appropriate pronouns.

Example:
Speaker: *Masha liubit chitat'.*
Your answer: ***Ona** liubit chitat'.*

1. .... *poshiol domoj.*

2. .... *pozvonila pozdno.*

3. .... *prigotovleno iz ryby.*

4. .... *pribyli v gostinitsu.*

5. .... *pojdiom v kino.*

6.. *budete na vecherinke?*

7. .... *uekhali v otpusk.*

8. .... *rabotaet na pochte.*

Pronouns in the Accusative Case

In the Accusative case, Russian pronouns change as indicated in the table that follows.

Table 3-2

Russian personal pronouns in the Accusative case	
Nominative	**Accusative**
ia	menia
ty	tebia
on	ego
ona	eio
ono	ego
my	nas
vy	vas
oni	ikh

Exercise 4: Rewriting Sentences

Rewrite the sentences replacing the underlined words or phrases naming the direct object with pronouns in the Accusative case.

1. *Olia vstretila <u>druga</u>.*

   ....

2. *Ia nikogda ne videla <u>reku Volgu</u>.*

   ....

3. *Vy chitali etu knigu?*

....

4. *Ia chasto naveshchaiu moikh roditelej.*

....

5. *Menia i moiu zhenu priglasili v gosti.*

....

6. *Ia ne videla vchera tebia i tvoikh druzej.*

....

7. *Etikh khudozhnikov nazyvali "peredvizhnikami."*

....

8. *Etogo cheloveka zovut Vasilij Petrov.*

....

Exercise 5: Choosing the Correct Case

Complete the sentences with the pronouns in parentheses. Depending on the role of the pronoun in the sentence, either leave it in the Nominative case or put it in the Accusative. Translating the sentences will help you to choose the appropriate case.

1. .... *idiot v kino. (ona)*

....

2. *Ty videl* .... *po televizoru? (ona)*

....

3. *Vy znaete* .... *? (on)*

....

4. .... *rabotaiut s moim muzhem. (oni).*

....

5. .... *nazyvaiut luchshimi druz'iami. (my)*

....

6. .... *segodnia prekrasno vygliadite. (vy)*

....

7. *Ia vstretila* .... *na ulitse. (on)*

....

8. .... *davno nikto ne videl. (oni)*

....

Exercise 6: Completing Sentences

TRACK 19

Listen to the speaker. Complete the following sentences, replacing the nouns read by the speaker with appropriate pronouns. Remember to put the pronouns in the Accusative case.

Example:
Speaker: *Studenty slushaiut <u>gida</u>.*
Your answer: *Studenty slushaiut **ego**.*

1. *Misha liubit* ....

2. *Lena uvidela* ....

3. *Turisty smotriat* ....

4. *Ia prinesu* ....

5. *Khoziajka prigotovila* ....

6. *Militsioner ostanovil* ....

7. *Vy videli vchera* .... ?

8. .... *prigotovil novyj povar.*

Pronouns in the Dative Case

In the Dative case, Russian pronouns change as indicated in the table that follows.

Table 3-3

Russian personal pronouns in the Dative case	
Nominative	**Dative**
ia	*mne*
ty	*tebe*
on	*emu*
ona	*ej*
ono	*emu*
my	*nam*
vy	*vam*
oni	*im*

When used after prepositions, the Dative pronouns *emu*, *ej*, and *im* gain the consonant *n-* at the beginning of the word: *nemu*, *nej*, and *nim*.

Exercise 7: Rewriting Sentences

Rewrite each sentence replacing the underlined word or phrase naming the indirect object with a pronoun in the Dative case.

1. *Natasha pozvonila <u>mame</u>.*

   ....

2. *Olia podarila <u>drugu</u> knigu.*

   ....

3. <u>*Tebe i tvoej sestre*</u> *prihsla posylka.*

   ....

4. <u>*Molodomu cheloveku*</u> *chasto zvonili devushki.*

   ....

5. <u>*Nashim sosediam*</u> *prinosiat gazety kazhdyj den'.*

   ....

6. <u>*Mne i moemu bratu*</u> *podarili sobaku.*

   ....

7. <u>*Etoj devushke*</u> *20 let.*

   ....

8. *Napishite pis'mo <u>babushke</u>.*

   ....

Exercise 8: Choosing the Correct Case

Complete the sentences with the pronouns in parentheses. Depending on the role of the pronoun in the sentence, either leave it in the Nominative case or put it in the Dative case. Translating the sentences will help you choose the correct case. A hint: remember that after prepositions, some pronouns gain the consonant *n-* at the beginning.

1. *My prishli k* .... *(ona)*

    ....

2. .... *liubish' chitat'? (ty)*

    ....

3. .... *nravitsia eta kniga? (ty)*

    ....

4. *My chasto khodim k* .... *v gosti. (ona)*

    ....

5. *Peredajte* .... , *pozhalujsta, sol'. (ia)*

    ....

6. .... *zhivut v tsentre goroda. (oni)*

    ....

7. *K* .... *priekhali gosti iz Sibiri. (oni)*

    ....

8. .... *nravitsia zdes' zhit'. (my)*

    ....

Exercise 9: Completing Sentences

TRACK 20

Listen to the speaker. Complete the following sentences, replacing the nouns [in the Dative case] read by the speaker with appropriate pronouns. Remember to put the pronouns in the Dative case.

Example:
Speaker: *Sobaka nesiot trost' <u>khoziainu</u>.*
Your answer: *Sobaka nesiot trost' **emu**.*

1. *Vera pozvonila* ....

2. *Podari etu knigu* ....

3. .... *eta muzyka ne nravitsia.*

4. *Mal'chik pomogaet* ....

5. .... *, navernoe, kholodno.*

6. *Nadia pokazala* .... *gorod.*

7. *Rasskazhi* .... *novosti.*

8. *Pokazhi* .... *dorogu.*

Pronouns in the Prepositional Case

In the Prepositional case, Russian pronouns change as indicated in the table that follows.

Table 3-4

Russian personal pronouns in the Prepositional case	
Nominative	**Prepositional**
ia	mne
ty	tebe
on	niom
ona	nej
ono	niom
my	nas
vy	vas
oni	nikh

Exercise 10: Rewriting Sentences

Rewrite the sentences replacing the underlined words or phrases with pronouns in the Prepositional case.

1. *Kniga lezhit na <u>stole</u>.*

   ....

2. *My liubim otdykhat' na <u>Chiornom more</u>.*

   ....

3. Druz'ia sideli v kafe i razgovarivali o _Lene._

....

4. Moj kosheliok v _etoj sumke._

....

5. Na vystavke oni razgovarivali o _khudozhnikakh-impressionistakh._

....

6. Ia chasto dumala o _tebe_ i obo _mne._

....

7. Na _devushke_ bylo krasnoe plat'e.

....

8. V _etom gorode_ zhivut liudi raznykh natsional'nostej.

....

Exercise 11: Choosing the Correct Case

Complete the sentences with the pronouns in parentheses. Depending on the role of the pronoun in the sentence, either leave it in the Nominative case or put it in the Prepositional case. Translating the sentences will help you choose the appropriate case.

1. .... zanimaetsia muzykoj. (on)

....

2. Lena vsegda dumaet o .... (oni)

....

3. *Vam rasskazyvali chto-nibud' o* .... *? (my)*

....

4. *Davajte pogovorim o* .... *. (ona)*

....

5. *Na* .... *opasno ezdit'. (on)*

....

6. .... *igraem na pianino. (my)*

....

7. *O* .... *khodiat legendy. (vy)*

....

8. .... *tantsuet v Bol'shom teatre. (ona)*

....

Exercise 12: Choosing the Correct Pronoun

TRACK 21

Listen to the speaker. Complete the following sentences, replacing the nouns read by the speaker with appropriate pronouns. Remember to put the pronouns in the Prepositional case.

Example:
Speaker: *Na <u>stadione</u> igraiut v futbol.*
Your answer: *Na **niom** igraiut v futbol.*

1. *V* .... *malo smysla.*

2. *Nam nado pogovorit' o* .... *.*

3. *Na* .... *davno nikto ne igraet.*

4. *On podumal o* ....

5. *Etot pisatel' napisal vse svoi rasskazy o* ....

6. *V* .... *zhivut moi znakomye.*

7. *Na* .... *rastiot vinograd.*

8. *My vchera razgovarivali o* ....

Pronouns in the Genitive Case

In the Genitive case, Russian pronouns change as indicated in the table that follows.

Table 3-5

Russian personal pronouns in the Genitive case	
Nominative	**Genitive**
ia	menia
ty	tebia
on	ego
ona	eio
ono	ego
my	nas
vy	vas
oni	ikh

When used after prepositions, the Genitive pronouns *ego*, *eio*, and *ikh* gain the consonant *n-* at the beginning of the word: *nego*, *neio*, and *nikh*.

Exercise 13: Rewriting Sentences

Rewrite the sentences replacing the underlined words or phrases with pronouns in the Genitive case. Remember that after prepositions, some pronouns gain the consonant *n-* at the beginning.

1. *Deti proveli leto u <u>svoej tioti</u>.*

   ....

2. *<u>Leny</u> segodnia net.*

   ....

3. *U nas sovsem net <u>kofe.</u>*

   ....

4. *Turisty ostanovilis' okolo <u>pamiatnika</u>.*

   ....

5. *Davajte vstretimsia u <u>Ivana</u> doma.*

   ....

6. *V etikh lesakh net <u>dikikh zhivotnykh.</u>*

   ....

7. *Eto mashina <u>brata</u>.*

   ....

8. *Eto gazon <u>nashikh sosedej</u>.*

   ....

Exercise 14: Choosing the Correct Case

Complete the sentences with the pronouns in parentheses. Depending on the role of the pronoun in the sentence, either leave it in the Nominative case or put it in Genitive. Translating the sentences will help you choose the appropriate case.

1. *U* .... *vsegda khoroshee nastroenie. (oni)*

....

2. .... *skoro poedu vo Frantsiiu. (ia)*

....

3. .... *nikogda net doma. (on)*

....

4. .... *ne bylo na etoj vecherinke. (my).*

....

5. *U* .... *est' bilety? (vy)*

....

6. .... *liubim puteshestvovat'. (my)*

....

7. *Okolo* .... *vsegda vrashchaiutsia liudi. (ona)*

....

8. *U* .... *prekrasnye sposobnosti. (on)*

....

Exercise 15: Phone Conversations

TRACK 22

Imagine that you are answering the phone. The person on the other end of the line is asking to talk to a certain person. Using pronouns in Genitive, tell them that that person, or persons, is not there at the moment. The first sentence has been done for you.

1. *Eio net.*

2. ....

3. ....

4. ....

5. ....

6. ....

7. ....

8. ....

Pronouns in the Instrumental Case

In the Instrumental case, Russian pronouns change as indicated in the table that follows.

Table 3-6

Russian personal pronouns in the Instrumental case	
Nominative	Instrumental
ia	mnoj
ty	toboj
on	im
ona	ej

Table 3-6

Russian personal pronouns in the Instrumental case	
ono	im
my	nami
vy	vami
oni	imi

When used after prepositions, Instrumental pronouns *im*, *ej*, and *imi* gain the consonant *n-* at the beginning of the word: *nim*, *nej*, and *nimi*.

Exercise 16: Rewriting Sentences

Rewrite the sentences replacing the underlined words or phrases with pronouns in the Instrumental case. Remember that after prepositions some pronouns gain the consonant *n-* at the beginning.

1. *Lena ochen' zainteresovalas' <u>etim molodym chelovekom</u>.*

   ....

2. *Vy chasto vidites' so <u>svoimi druz'iami</u>?*

   ....

3. *Moia dochka druzhit s <u>etoj devochkoj.</u>*

   ....

4. *Gid zajmiotsia <u>turistami</u>.*

   ....

5. *Ty risuesh' <u>etim karandashom</u>?*

   ....

6. *Prikhodite v gosti s <u>drugom.</u>*

   ....

7. *Ia chasto razgovarivaiu s <u>roditeliami</u> po telefonu.*

   ....

8. *On uvlioksia <u>muzykoj</u>.*

   ....

Exercise 17: Choosing the Correct Case

Complete the sentences with the pronouns in parentheses. Depending on the role of the pronoun in the sentence, either leave it in the Nominative case or put it in Instrumental. Translating the sentences will help you choose the correct case.

1. *Masha razgovarivala s* .... *po telefonu. (ona)*

   ....

2. .... *razgovarivali ochen' gromko. (my)*

   ....

3. *Kogda on byl molodym, devushki chasto* .... *uvleka-lis'. (on)*

   ....

4. *Vy pojdiote s* .... *v teatr? (my)*

   ....

5. .... igraet v futbol. (on)

....

6. Vasia igraet s .... v shakhmaty. (on)

....

7. .... uvlekaetsia iskusstvom. (ona)

....

8. On uvlekaetsia .... (ona)

....

Exercise 18: Completing Sentences

TRACK 23

Listen to the speaker. Complete the following sentences, replacing the nouns read by the speaker with appropriate pronouns. Remember to put the pronouns in the Instrumental case.

Example:
Speaker: *My chasto razgovarivaem s <u>sosedkoj</u>.*
Your answer: *My chasto razgovarivaem s **nej**.*

1. *Ia pogovoriu s* ....

2. *Ia idu v kino s* ....

3. *Vadim liubit sporit' s* ....

4. *My khotim vstretit'sia s* ....

5. *My chasto razgovarivaem s* ....

6. *Moj brat edet v otpusk s* ....

7. *On vsegda prikhodit s* ....

8. *Viktor khochet pogovorit' s* ....

Reflexive Pronouns

The reflexive pronoun *sebia* means "self." It is used when the subject of the sentence is also its direct or indirect object. *Sebia* can be used in all cases except for Nominative. Note that in English, the word "self" cannot be the subject of the sentence either.

Sebia does not change according to number or gender, but it changes according to case.

Table 3-7

Declension of the reflexive pronoun *sebia*	
Nominative	
Accusative	*sebia*
Dative	*sebe*
Prepositional	*sebe*
Genitive	*sebia*
Instrumental	*soboj*

Exercise 19: Using Reflexive Pronouns

Circle the sentences that require the use of the reflexive pronoun.

1. He bought flowers for Lena.

2. They bought a present for themselves.

3. She saw herself in the mirror.

4. He saw children.

5. She congratulated herself.

6. We congratulated the winner.

7. She went on vacation with Chris.

8. They took a dog along.

Exercise 20: Completing Sentences

Complete the sentences with reflexive pronouns.

1. *Ona kupila* .... *mashinu.* (for herself)

2. *Volodia vzial s* .... *syna.* (along; literally: with himself)

3. *On liubil smotret'* .... *po televizoru.* (himself)

4. *Oni prigotovili* .... *uzhin.* (for themselves)

5. *On nazyval* .... *velikim kompozitorom.* (himself)

6. *Ulitka nosit svoj domik na* .... (itself)

7. *Ona vsegda nakhodila v* .... *mnogo nedostatkov.* (herself)

8. *Vy mozhete gordit'sya* .... (yourself)

Exercise 21: Translating Sentences

Translate these sentences into Russian.

1. He is proud of himself.

   ....

2. She made herself a present.

   ....

3. The dog saw itself in the mirror.

   ....

4. They bought a house for themselves.

   ....

5. Can you hear yourself?

   ....

6. I bought myself flowers.

   ....

7. They saw themselves on TV.

   ....

8. He considered himself lucky.

   ....

Demonstrative Pronouns

The demonstrative pronouns *etot* (this), *tot* (that), and *takoj* (such) change according to gender, number, and case. They decline like adjectives.

Exercise 22: Declining etot

Decline the masculine singular form of the pronoun *etot*.

1. Nominative: *etot*

2. Accusative: ....

3. Dative: ....

4. Prepositional: ....

5. Genitive: ....

6. Instrumental: ....

Exercise 23: Declining ta

Decline the feminine singular form of the pronoun *tot*.

1. Nominative: *ta*

2. Accusative: ....

3. Dative: ....

4. Prepositional: ....

5. Genitive: ....

6. Instrumental: ....

Exercise 24: Declining takie

Decline the plural form of the pronoun *takoj*.

1. Nominative: *takie*

2. Accusative: ....

3. Dative: ....

4. Prepositional: ....

5. Genitive: ....

6. Instrumental: ....

Exercise 25: Translating Phrases

Translate the following phrases into Russian using demonstrative pronouns.

1. this house   ....

2. that woman   ....

3. these letters   ....

4. such book   ....

5. such a beautiful day   ....

6. those people   ....

7. such prices   ....

8. this hotel   ....

Exercise 26: Completing Sentences

Complete the sentences with the demonstrative pronouns in parentheses. Remember to put the pronouns in the appropriate gender, number, and case.

1. *Ia nikogda ne videla* .... *dozhdia.* (such)

2. *Vy znaete* .... *cheloveka?* (this)

3. *Moia mashina von* .... , *belaia.* (that)

4. .... *dni luchshe provodit' na svezhem vozdukhe.* (such)

5. .... *kvartira byla luchshe, chem novaia.* (that)

6. *V* .... *pogodu ia liubliu chitat'.* (such)

7. .... *frukty ochen' vkusnye.* (these)

8. .... *kraskami trudno risovat'.* (these)

Possessive Pronouns

The Russian possessive pronouns *moj* (my), *tvoj* (your—singular, informal), *nash* (our), and *vash* (you—plural, formal) agree with the nouns they describe in gender, number, and case. They have the same endings as adjectives. The possessive pronouns *ego* (his), *eio* (her), *ego* (its), and *ikh* (their) do not change.

Exercise 27: Completing Sentences

Complete the sentences with the possessive pronouns in parentheses. Remember to put the pronouns in the appropriate gender, number, and case.

1. *Eto* .... *mashina.* (my)

2. *Ia ne pomniu* .... *imia.* (your, formal)

3. *Gde zhivut* .... *roditeli?* (your, informal)

4. .... *dom stoit u moria.* (our)

5. *V etom dome zhiviot* .... *sestra.* (his)

6. .... *kniga stala ochen' populiarnoj.* (her)

7. .... *kvartira na vtorom etazhe.* (their)

8. .... *deti khodiat v shkolu.* (her)

Exercise 28: Completing Sentences

Complete the sentences with the phrases in parentheses. Remember to put the pronouns in the appropriate gender, number, and case

1. *Ia liubliu* .... (my city)

2. *Ia guliaiu s* .... (my dog)

3. *Kak proshiol* ....? (your vacation, formal)

4. *Vy znaete* ....? (his sister)

5. *My poedem na* .... (her car)

6. *Eto* .... (their children)

7. *U menia net* .... (your number, informal)

8. *My kupili tsvety* .... (for our [male] teacher)

Exercise 29: Completing Sentences

TRACK 24

Listen to the speaker. Complete the following sentences, replacing the possessive nouns read by the speaker with appropriate possessive pronouns.

Example:
Speaker: *Eto telefon <u>moej podrugi</u>.*
Your answer: *Eto **eio** telefon.*

1. *Eto* .... *mashina.*

2. *Eto* .... *dacha.*

3. *Eto* .... *kniga.*

4. *Eto* .... *pal'to.*

5. *Eto* .... *diski.*

6. *Eto* .... *podarki.*

7. *Eto* .... *dom.*

8. *Eto* .... *tarelka.*

Reflexive Possessive Pronoun svoj

If the subject of the sentence is the same as the possessor in that sentence, you have to use the reflexive possessive pronoun *svoj* (one's own). This rule is optional for first and second persons, but is mandatory for the third person. For instance, "I am reading my book" can be translated with either the possessive pronoun *moj* or with the reflexive possessive pronoun *svoj: Ia chitaiu moiu knigu* or *Ia chitaiu svoiu knigu*. On the other hand, "She is reading her book" can be translated only with the reflexive possessive pronoun *svoj: Ona chitaet svoiu knigu*. Otherwise, using *eio (Ona chitaet eio knigu)* will change the meaning of the sentence: she is reading a book that belongs to some other woman.

The reflexive possessive pronoun *svoj* agrees with the nouns it describes in gender, number, and case.

Exercise 30: Completing Sentences

Complete the sentences with the appropriate form of the pronoun *svoj*.

1. *Ona sela v* .... *mashinu.*

2. *On chasto razgovarival so* .... *roditeliami.*

3. *Oni zanimalis'* .... *delami.*

4. *Lena zapisala* .... *nomer telefona.*

5. *More imeet* .... *nepovtorimyj zapakh.*

6. *Turisty dostali* .... *fotoapparaty.*

7. *Moj drug uekhal na* .... *dachu.*

8. *Nadia sidela na* .... *liubimoj skamejke.*

Exercise 31: Who Has What?

Read the sentences. In each group, complete the second sentence with either a possessive pronoun or a reflexive possessive pronoun, depending on the information you learned from the first sentence.

1. *U Leny est' sobaka. Natasha guliaet s* .... *sobakoj.*

2. *U Vadima est' mashina. Vadim edet na* .... *mashine.*

3. *U moikh roditelej est' dacha. Moi roditeli uekhali na* .... *dachu.*

4. *U moikh sosedej est' dzhakuzi. Ia sizhu v* .... *dzhakuzi.*

5. *U Nadi est' samoliot. Nadia letaet na* .... *samoliote.*

6. *U Very est' mototsikl. Vera ezdit na* .... *mototsikle.*

7. *U Oli est' televizor. Natasha smotrit* .... *televizor.*

8. *U Ivana est' koshka. Andrei kormit* .... *koshku.*

Interrogative Pronouns

The Russian interrogative pronouns *kto* (who) and *chto* (what) change according to case. The interrogative pronouns *kakoj* (which, what kind) and *chej* (whose) change according to gender, number, and case.

Table 3-8

Declension of interrogative pronouns *kto* and *chto*		
Nominative	kto	chto
Accusative	kogo	chto
Dative	komu	chemu
Prepositional	kom	chiom
Genitive	kogo	chego
Instrumental	kem	chem

In questions, verbs agreeing with *kto* are used in masculine, and verbs agreeing with *chto* are used in neuter: *Kto napisal? Chto upalo?*

Table 3-9

Gender and plural forms of the interrogative pronouns *kakoj* and *chej*		
Masculine	*kakoj*	*chej*
Feminine	*kakaia*	*ch'ia*
Neuter	*kakoe*	*ch'io*
Plural	*kakie*	*ch'i*

The Interrogative pronouns *kakoj* and *chej* are declined like adjectives.

Exercise 32: Changing the Pronouns

Match the interrogative pronouns *kakoj* and *chej* with the nouns listed.

1. *dozhd'*　......................................　......................................

2. *strana*　......................................　......................................

3. *stol*　......................................　......................................

4. *ploshchad'*　......................................　......................................

5. *druz'ia*　......................................　......................................

6. *telefon*　......................................　......................................

7. *veshchi*　......................................　......................................

8. *plat'e*　......................................　......................................

Exercise 33: Asking Questions

Ask questions about the following phrases. If it's a regular adjective, ask *Kakoj*? If it's a possessive adjective or a possessive pronoun, ask *Chej*? Remember to agree the interrogative pronouns with each noun's gender and number.

1. *bol'shoe okno*

....

2. *moia rabota*

....

3. *krasivyj sobo*

....

4. *tvoio pis'mo*

....

5. *dorogie podarki*

....

6. *ikh deti*

....

7. *maminy knigi*

....

8. *vashe imia*

....

Exercise 34: Who or What?

Ask questions to get the underlined words in each sentence as the response. Remember to use each interrogative pronoun in the appropriate case.

1. *My podarili podarok <u>babushke</u>.*

   ....

2. *Ia uvidela <u>Lenu</u>.*

   ....

3. *Roditeli gordiatsia svoim <u>synom</u>.*

   ....

4. *Mal'shik risuet <u>solntse</u>.*

   ....

5. *Ona boitsia <u>grozy</u>.*

   ....

6. *Ia pozvonil <u>vrachu</u>.*

   ....

7. *Oni risuiut <u>karandashom</u>.*

   ....

8. *Ona poshla v pokhod s <u>druz'iami</u>.*

   ....

Exercise 35: Asking Questions

TRACK 25

Listen to the speaker. Ask questions to the sentences read by the speaker using interrogative pronouns *kto* or *chto*. Remember to agree the verbs with the interrogative pronouns.

Example:
Speaker: *Za oknom stoit derevo.*
Your answer: *Chto stoit za oknom?*

1. ....

2. ....

3. ....

4. ....

5. ....

6. ....

7. ....

8. ....

Indefinite Pronouns

Russian indefinite pronouns are formed by adding the particle *-to* or *-nibud'* to the interrogative pronouns. These two particles produce different kinds of indefinite pronouns. Adding the particle *-to* produces specific indefinite pronouns, when the object is specific, but unknown. For instance: *Kto-to zvonil* (somebody called). Adding the particle *-nibud'* produces unspecific indefinite pronouns, when the object is unknown and unspecific. For instance: *Kto-nibud' zvonil?* (Has anybody called?)

The first part of the indefinite pronouns changes according to case and/ or gender and number, like the interrogative pronouns from which they were produced. The particles *-to* and *-nibud'* do not change.

Exercise 36: *Something or Someone*

TRACK 26

Listen to the speaker. Change the sentences she is reading using indefinite pronouns *chto-to* or *kto-to,* depending on whether the noun is animate or not. Remember to agree the gender of the verb with the indefinite pronouns. Write down the sentences. The first sentence has been done for you.

1. *Na stole lezhalo chto-to.*

2. ....

3. ....

4. ....

5. ....

6. ....

7. ....

8. ....

Exercise 37: Something Indefinite

TRACK 27

Listen to the speaker. Complete the sentences below, replacing the missing nouns with Indefinite pronouns in the appropriate case. The first sentence has been done for you.

1. *Ya videla **kogo-to**.*

2. *My videli* ....

3. *Gid rasskazyvaet legendu* ....

4. *Ya chasto pishu pis'ma* ....

5. *Vadim dumaet o* ....

6. *Kolia dumaet o* ....

7. *Ania interesuetsa* ....

8. *Ania khochet stat'* ....

Exercise 38: Specific or Unspecific?

Rewrite the sentences, replacing the possessive pronouns or adjectives with indefinite pronouns. In statements, use specific indefinite pronouns (e.g., *kakoj-to*). In questions, use unspecific indefinite pronouns (e.g., *kakoj-nibud'*). Remember to put the pronouns in the appropriate cases.

1. *Eto moia kniga.*

....

2. *On uvidel beloe zdanie.*

....

THE EVERYTHING RUSSIAN PRACTICE BOOK

3. *Vy chitaete istoricheskie romany?*

....

4. *Pozvonite eio roditeliam.*

....

5. *Vy znaete moj adres?*

....

6. *Ona liubit klassicheskuiu muzyku?*

....

7. *U vas est' ego telefon?*

....

8. *Na stole stoiala belaia chashka.*

....

Negative Pronouns

The Russian negative pronouns are formed by adding *ni-* to the interrogative pronouns. The only exception— *nichto* (nothing)— formed according to the general rules, is considered archaic. A more widely used word for "nothing" is *nichego*.

Remember the rule of double negation. In sentences with negative pronouns, verbs and adverbs also have to be negative: *Nikto nichego ne sdelal* (No one did a thing).

Negative pronouns decline like interrogative pronouns from which they are produced.

Exercise 39: Producing Negative Pronouns

Form negative pronouns from the following interrogative pronouns. Translate the negative pronouns into English.

1. *kto*   ....

2. *kakoj*   ....

3. *chej*   ....

4. *chto*   ....

5. *kakaja*   ....

6. *ch'i*   ....

7. *kakie*   ....

8. *ch'io*   ....

Exercise 40: Being Negative

Rewrite the sentences replacing the underlined words with negative pronouns. Remember the rule of double negation.

1. *Devushka napisala pis'mo.*

    ....

2. *Eto moj telefon.*

    ....

3. *Professor napisal knigu.*

    ....

4. *Na stole lezhit <u>iabloko</u>.*

....

5. *Mne nraviatsia <u>bol'shie</u> sobaki.*

....

6. *<u>Turist</u> zashiol v gostinitsu.*

....

7. *<u>Pis'mo</u> prishlo po pochte.*

....

8. *On liubit <u>narodnye</u> pesni.*

....

Relative Pronouns

The Russian relative pronoun *kotoryj* can be translated as "which," "that," or "who." It is used to join two simple sentences into a complex one. *Kotoryj* is used to refer both to animate and inanimate objects. It changes according to gender, number, and case. The gender and number of the pronoun *kotoryj* is determined by the noun it replaces in the first part of the sentence. The case of *kotoryj* is determined by its position in the second part of the sentence.

Exercise 41: Declining kotoryj

Complete the sentences with the correct form of *kotoryj*.

1. *Vot devushka,* .... *zhiviot v moiom pod 'ezde.*

2. *Vot dom, v* .... *ya zhivu.*

3. *Eto liudi, s* .... *my vmeste rabotaem.*

4. *Vot to kafe, v* .... *my vstretilis'.*

5. *Eto sportsmen,* .... *vyigral sorevnovanie.*

6. *Vot kniga,* .... *ia napisal.*

7. *Eto vrach,* .... *ty dolzhen pozvonit'.*

8. *Eto mashina,* .... *vodit moj drug.*

Exercise 42: Making Complex Sentences

Join the two sentences into one complex sentence with *kotoryj*. Remember to use *kotoryj* in the appropriate gender, number, and case.

1. *Po ulitse shiol molodoj chelovek. Etot molodoj chelovek rabotaet v banke.*

   ....

2. *Na stsenu vyshla aktrisa. Eta aktrisa igrala v fil'me "S liogkim parom."*

   ....

3. *V dver' postuchala sosedka. Eta sosedka zhiviot naprotiv.*

   ....

4. *Mne pozvonil drug. Etot drug zhiviot v Parizhe.*

   ....

5. *Ia napisala knigu. Eta kniga stala izvestnoj.*

   ....

6. *Lena poteriala sumku. Etu sumku ej podarila eio mama.*

   ....

7. *My nashli khoroshee kafe. V etom kafe podaiut otlichnyj chaj s travami.*

   ....

8. *Moj drug napisal roman. Etot roman sdelal ego bogatym.*

   ....

Review

In this section, practice using all the different kinds of pronouns. If you face difficulties with a particular type of pronoun, go back to the section devoted to this type and go over the exercises again.

Exercise 43: A Story about Dasha

TRACK 28

Listen to the speaker read the text. Using the information you learned from the text, complete the sentences below with appropriate pronouns.

1. *Dasha zhiviot s* ....

2. .... *rabotaet v muzee.*

3. .... *zakryvaetsia rano.*

4. *Posle raboty Dasha vstrechaet* ....

5. .... *i dut v kino ili v kafe.*

6. *V kafe Dasha i Olia vstrechaiutsia s* ....

7. *Oni razgovarivaiut o* ....

8. *Druz'ia ochen' liubiat* ....

Exercise 44: Reading Chekhov

These sentences with pronouns are from the short story *Dama s sobach-koj* ("Lady With a Lapdog") by Anton Chekhov. Translate the sentences into English, paying special attention to the case of the pronouns.

1. *I potom on vstrechal eio v gorodskom sadu i na skvere . . .*

   ....

2. *Emu ne bylo eshchio soroka, no u nego byla uzhe doch' dvenadtsati let . . .*

   ....

3. *V ego naruzhnosti . . . bylo chto-to privlekatel'noe . . .*

   ....

4. *No pri vsiakoj novoj vstreche s interesnoiu zhenshchinoj etot opyt kak-to uskol'zal iz pamiati.*

   ....

5. *Eio vyrazhenie, pokhodka . . . govorili emu, chto ona iz poriadochnogo obshchestva, . . . chto ej skuchno zdes'.*

   ....

6. *Ona nichego ne otvetila.*

   ....

7. *Gurov otrezal sebe lomot' i stal est' ne spesha.*

   ....

8. *I vot ia stala poshloj, driannoj zhenshchinoj, kotoruiu vsiakij mozhet prezirat'.*

   ....

Exercise 45: Translating into Russian

Translate these sentences into Russian. Pay careful attention to gender, number, and case of the pronouns. Remember that before prepositions, some pronouns gain the consonant *n-*.

1. Which skirt will you wear?

   ....

2. Her parents are proud of her.

   ....

3. He and I went to school together.

   ....

4. He is 44.

   ....

5. Whose children are these?

   ....

6. Bring the book that your sister gave you.

   ....

7. She called her sister.

   ....

8. They bought themselves a present.

   ....

Part 4

Adjectives

Adjectives are words that describe nouns. In Russian, adjectives agree with the nouns they describe in gender, number, and case. That means that an adjective's ending depends on the grammatical form of the noun it describes, and changes when the noun's case or number changes. In this chapter, you will find out all about adjectives, and you will learn how to make adjective-noun agreements.

Adjective-Noun Agreement in the Nominative Case

Russian adjectives, like Russian nouns, consist of a stem and an ending. The stem is the part of the word that does not change. Ending is the part of the word that changes according to gender, number, and case. The adjectives you find in dictionaries are singular masculine adjectives in the Nominative case. In order to agree this adjective with feminine, neuter, plural nouns, or nouns in cases other than Nominative, you have to change its ending.

In Nominative singular, Russian masculine adjectives end in *-yj*, *-ij*, or *-oj*. Feminine adjectives end in *-aia* or *-iaia*. Neuter adjectives end in *-oe* or *-ee*. In Nominative plural, all adjectives have the endings *-ye* or *-ie*.

Exercise 1: Changing the Adjective

Make the adjectives feminine, neuter, and then plural.

1. *goluboj* ....

2. *sil'nyj* ....

3. *pravyj* ....

4. *vesiolyj* ....

5. *goriachij* ....

6. *poslednij* ....

7. *ryzhij* ....

8. *smeshnoj* ....

Exercise 2: Agreeing Adjectives with Nouns

Use each adjective in parenthesis and make it agree with the noun. Remember that in Russian, like in English, adjectives precede nouns.

1. .... *kniga (khoroshij)*

2. .... *chelovek (molodoj)*

3. .... *okno (bol'shoj)*

4. .... *muzhchina (khudoj)*

5. .... *gorod (chistyj)*

6. .... *plat'e (sinij)*

7. .... *devushka (vysokij)*

8. .... *ploshchad' (tsentral'nyj)*

9. .... *den' (korotkij)*

10. .... *noch' (letnij)*

Exercise 3: Geography

Combine adjectives from Group 1 with nouns from Group 2 to form famous geographical and architectural proper names. You may use the same word several times. There are as many as ten famous proper names consisting of these words. How many can you figure out? Remember to agree adjectives with nouns.

Group 1.   *chiornyj, belyj, krasnyj, zhioltyj, tikhij, baltijskij, miortvyj, mramornyj, kitajskij*

Group 2.   *ploshchad', more, okean, stena*

1. ....

2. ....

3. ....

4. ....

5. ....

6. ....

7. ....

8. ....

9. ....

10. ....

Exercise 4: Recognizing Plural Adjectives

TRACK 29

Listen to the speaker and complete the phrases by writing down the plural adjectives. At the end of each phrase, write down the masculine singular form of the used adjective.

Example:
Speaker: _dobrye_ liudi
Your answer: **_dobrye_ liudi; _dobryj_**

1. .... zimy; ....

2. .... deti; ....

3. .... avtobusy; ....

4. .... ulitsy; ....

5. .... *tsvety;* ....

6. .... *nochi;* ....

7. .... *podarki;* ....

8. .... *pis'ma;* ....

9. .... *glaza;* ....

10. .... *pesni;* ....

Adjectives in the Accusative Case

Masculine and neuter adjectival endings in the Accusative case depend on whether a noun is animate or inanimate. If a noun is inanimate, endings in the Accusative coincide with those in the Nominative. If the noun is animate, the endings change.

Table 4-1

Masculine animate adjectival endings in Accusative		
Nominative singular	**Accusative singular**	**Accusative plural**
-oj	-ogo	-ykh or -ikh
-yj	-ogo	-ykh
-ij	-ego	-ikh

Table 4-2

Feminine adjectival endings in Accusative		
Nominative singular	**Accusative singular**	**Accusative plural**
-aia	-uiu	ykh or -ikh
-iaia	-iuiu	-ikh

Since there are almost no animate neuter nouns, Accusative neuter endings are the same as Nominative neuter endings.

Exercise 5: Completing Sentences

Use each adjective in parenthesis and make it agree with the noun. Remember that in Russian, like in English, adjectives precede nouns.

1. *Ya vstretil* .... *cheloveka. (umnyj)*

2. *Daj pochitat'* .... *knigu! (interesnyj)*

3. *Ia uvidel na ulitse* .... *druga. (staryj)*

4. *Nadia liubit slushat'* .... *muzyku. (klassicheskij)*

5. *Ona napisala muzhu* .... *pis'mo. (dlinnyj)*

6. *Naden' svoio* .... *plat'e. (liubimyj)*

7. *My pojmali* .... *rybu. (bol'shoj)*

8. *Oni kupili* .... *stol. (novyj)*

9. *Vy kogda-nibud' videli* .... *slona? (afrikanskij)*

10. *On chitaet* .... *zhurnal. (tolstyj)*

Exercise 6: Answering Questions

TRACK 30

Listen to the speaker and give one-word answers to the questions below. Then write down the dictionary form of the used adjectives. A hint: *kakoj / kakaia / kakoe / kakie* mean "What kind" in regards to masculine/feminine/ neuter/plural nouns respectively.

Example:
Speaker: *Eto gor'kaia pravda.*
Question: *Kakaia eto pravda?*
Your answer: *gor'kaia; gor'kij*

1. *Kakaia eto roza?*

   .... ; ....

2. *Kakoi eto mal'chik?*

   .... ; ....

3. *Kakaia v etom godu osen'?*

   .... ; ....

4. *Kakoe u Natashi plat'e?*

   .... ; ....

5. *Kakoj dozhd' idiot letom?*

   .... ; ....

6. *Kakie medvedi zhivut v moskovskom zooparke?*

   .... ; ....

7. *Kakie frukty prodavali na rynke?*

   .... ; ....

8. *Kakoj borshch gotovit mama?*

   .... ; ....

9. *Kakie rasskazy liubit chitat' Dasha?*

.... ; ....

10. *Kakoj eto kusok torta?*

.... ; ....

Exercise 7: Changing Phrases

Change the adjective + noun phrases in Nominative singular to Accusative singular. To review the Accusative endings of nouns, consult Tables 2-4 to 2-7. Remember the difference between adjectives describing animate and inanimate nouns!

1. *belaia majka*

....

2. *vkusnyj obed*

....

3. *zhioltyj tiul'pan*

....

4. *amerikanskiy turist*

....

5. *Krasnaia ploshchad'*

....

6. *dereviannyj stol*

....

7. *vysokaia temperatura*

   ....

8. *iuzhnoe more*

   ....

9. *polnaia luna*

   ....

10. *gornoe ozero*

    ....

Adjectives in the Dative Case

Table 4-3

Masculine adjectival endings in Dative		
Nominative singular	**Dative singular**	**Dative plural**
‑oj	‑omu	‑ym or ‑im
‑yj	‑omu	‑ym
‑ij	‑emu	‑im

Table 4-4

Feminine adjectival endings in Dative		
Nominative singular	**Dative singular**	**Dative plural**
‑aia	‑oj	‑ym or ‑im
‑iaia	‑ej	‑im

Table 4-5

Neuter adjectival endings in Dative		
Nominative singular	Dative singular	Dative plural
ˉoe	ˉomu	ˉym or ˉim
ˉee	ˉemu	ˉim

Exercise 8: Putting It in Dative

Put the phrases in Dative case. For noun endings in Dative, consult Tables 2-8 to 2-13.

1. *molodoj uchitel'* ....

2. *bol'shoj sad* ....

3. *starinnyj dvorets* ....

4. *drevniaia tserkov'* ....

5. *glavnyj prospect* ....

6. *sinee plat'e* ....

7. *dorogaia gostinitsa* ....

8. *starshij brat* ....

9. *tioploe more* ....

10. *zolotoe kol'tso* ....

Exercise 9: Completing Sentences

Complete the sentences with the adjectives in parentheses. Remember to put the adjectives in the Dative case. To find out which case and number to use, look at the noun with which the adjective has to agree.

1. *Professor chitaet lektsiiu* .... *studentam. (novyj)*

2. *Gid pokazyvaet dvorets* .... *turistam. (amerikan- skij)*

3. *Sasha zvonit* .... *bratu. (liubimyj)*

4. *Misha dal edu* .... *sobake. (chiornyj)*

5. *Babushka rasskazala* .... *vnuku skazku. (malen'kij)*

6. *Zhurnal "Zdorov'e" pomogaet* .... *roditeliam. (molodoj)*

7. *Eta gazeta daiot* .... *chitateliam skidku. (novyj)*

8. *John prislal otkrytku svoemu* .... *drugu. (russkij)*

Adjectives in the Prepositional Case

Table 4-6

Masculine adjectival endings in Prepositional		
Nominative singular	Prepositional singular	Prepositional plural
ˉoj	ˉom	ˉykh or ˉikh
ˉyj	ˉom	ˉykh
ˉij	ˉem	ˉikh

Table 4-7

Feminine adjectival endings in Prepositional		
Nominative singular	Prepositional singular	Prepositional plural
-aia	-oj	-ykh or -ikh
-iaia	-ej	-ikh

Table 4-8

Neuter adjectival endings in Prepositional		
Nominative singular	Prepositional singular	Prepositional plural
-oe	-om	-ykh or -ikh
-ee	-em	-ikh

Exercise 10: Telling Where

Choose one of these adjectives to complete the sentences below. Remember to put the adjectives in the correct case, gender, and number.

vostochnyj, tropicheskij, russkij, mirovoj, Tikhij, drevnij, ital'ianskij, Chiornyj

1. *Pitstsu mozhno zakazat' v* .... *restorane.*

2. *Boston nakhoditsia na* .... *poberezhe' SShA.*

3. *V* .... *sem'yakh chasto gotoviat borshch.*

4. *My chasto otdykhaem na* .... *ostrovakh.*

5. *Gavajskie ostrova raspolozheny v* .... *okeane.*

6. *Turisty liubiat byvat' v* .... *Kremle.*

7. *Gorod Odessa nakhoditsia na* .... *more.*

8. *Roman Khemingueia "Proshchaj, oruzhie" rasskazyvaet o Pervoj*

.... *vojne.*

Exercise 11: Describing Locations

TRACK 31

Listen to the speaker read the phrases. Write down the phrases. Then put them in Prepositional. Remember to use the appropriate preposition: *v* or *na*. To review noun endings in Prepositional, consult Tables 2-14 to 2-19.

Example:
Speaker: *khoroshij fil'm*
Your answer: *khoroshij fil'm – v khoroshem fil'me*

1. ....

2. ....

3. ....

4. ....

5. ....

6. ....

7. ....

8. ....

9. ....

10. ....

Adjectives in the Genitive Case

Table 4-9

Masculine adjectival endings in Genitive		
Nominative singular	**Genitive singular**	**Genitive plural**
-oj	-ogo	-ykh or -ikh
-yj	-ogo	-ykh
-ij	-ego	-ikh

Table 4-10

Feminine adjectival endings in Genitive		
Nominative singular	**Genitive singular**	**Genitive plural**
-aia	-oj	-ykh or -ikh
-iaia	-ej	-ikh

Table 4-11

Neuter adjectival endings in Genitive		
Nominative singular	**Genitive singular**	**Genitive plural**
-oe	-ogo	-ykh or -ikh
-ee	-ego	-ikh

Exercise 12: Is There or Not?

TRACK 32

Listen to the speaker and answer the questions using the Genitive. Remember that *est'* means "there is." To review noun endings in Genitive, consult Tables 2-20 to 2-25.

Example:
Speaker: *V tundre est' severnye oleni. A v stepi?*
Your answer: *V stepi <u>net severnykh olenej</u>.*

1. *V Moskve* ....

2. *V Kalifornii* ....

3. *V Rossii* ....

4. *V Tekhase* ....

5. *V Los Andzhelese* ....

6. *Na ekvatore* ....

7. *V Venetsii* ....

8. *V Moskve* ....

Exercise 13: *Making It Genitive*

Complete the phrases by using the words in parentheses and putting them in Genitive. Then translate the phrases into English. Note that there are phrases both in singular and in plural in the parentheses.

1. *muzyka* .... *(izvestnyj kompozitor)*

....

2. *kartina* .... *(znamenityj khudozhnik)*

....

3. *pesni* .... *(ital'ianskie ispolniteli)*

....

4. *doma* .... *(molodye iuristy)*

....

5. *ulitsy* .... *(novye goroda)*

....

6. *geroi* .... *(liubimye knigi)*

....

7. *rubashka* .... *(starshij brat)*

....

8. *telefon* .... *(milaia devushka)*

....

Adjectives in the Instrumental Case

Table 4-12

Masculine adjectival endings in Instrumental		
Nominative singular	**Instrumental singular**	**Instrumental plural**
ˉoj	ˉym	ˉymi or ˉimi
ˉyj	ˉym	ˉymi
ˉij	ˉim	ˉimi

Table 4-13

Feminine adjectival endings in Instrumental		
Nominative singular	**Instrumental singular**	**Instrumental plural**
ˉaia	ˉoj	ˉymi or ˉimi
ˉiaia	ˉej	ˉimi

Table 4-14

Neuter adjectival endings in Instrumental		
Nominative singular	**Instrumental singular**	**Instrumental plural**
ˉoe	ˉym	ˉymi or ˉimi
ˉee	ˉim	ˉimi

Exercise 14: Completing Sentences

Complete the sentences with the adjectives in parentheses. Remember to use adjective-noun agreement.

1. *Vadim stanet* .... *nachal'nikom. (bol'shoj)*

2. *Nadia poshla v kino s* .... *podrugami. (liubimyj)*

3. *Olia khotela stat'* .... *pevitsej. (opernyj)*

4. *Etot khudozhnik pishet kartiny* .... *kraskami. (maslianoj)*

5. *Turisty osmotreli gorod s* .... *ekskursovodom. (otlichnyj).*

6. *Vika zanimaetsia* .... *gimnastikoj. (khudozhest-vennyj)*

7. *Okhotnik pobedil l'va* .... *rukami. (golyj)*

8. *Anna interesuetsia* .... *literaturoj. (russkij)*

Exercise 15: Answering Questions

TRACK 33

Listen to the speaker and answer the questions. Give as many details as you can; remember to include adjectives in your answers. A hint: the word *chem* is used to ask question about nouns in Instrumental. It can be translated into English as "with what" or simply "what," depending on the verb used. To review Instrumental noun endings, see Tables 2-26 to 2-31.

Example:
Speaker: *Volodia interesuetsia bol'shim tennisom.*
Question: *Chem interesuetsia Volodia?*
Your answer: *Volodia interesuetsia bol'shim tennisom.*

1. *Chem risuet devochka?*

    ....

2. *Chem pishet mal'chik?*

    ....

3. *Chem risuet khudozhnik?*

    ....

4. *Chem zanimaetsia Tom?*

....

5. *Chem interesuetsia Sveta?*

....

6. *S chem sidit v parke Nadia?*

....

7. *Chem devushka ukrashaet komnatu?*

....

8. *Chem interesuetsia Alla?*

....

Short Forms of Adjectives

The short form of Russian adjectives is much less common than the long form. The use of a short form makes the quality named by the adjective sound temporary. For example, the adjective *bol'noj* (ill) in its long form is used to describe an ill person. The short form of the same adjective, *bolen*, is used to describe someone who is experiencing a temporary illness. For the majority of adjectives, this subtle difference in meaning has been lost. Today, using an adjective's short form makes the phrase sound elevated, and even bookish.

There are some instances, however, when a short form has to be used. The most common of them are *zakryt* (closed), *otkryt* (open), *bolen* (temporarily ill), *svoboden* (free; vacant), *zaniat* (busy; occupied).

Remember that short adjectives can't be used before a noun, only after a noun. Short forms of adjectives do not change according to cases.

Table 4-15

Endings of short forms of adjectives			
Masculine	**Feminine**	**Neuter**	**Plural**
no ending	*-a*	*-o*	*-y*

Exercise 16: Paraphrasing

TRACK 34

Listen to the speaker read sentences with long forms of adjectives. Paraphrase the sentences so as to use short forms of adjectives. Remember to change the word order. The first sentence has been done for you.

1. *Mir prekrasen.*

2. ....

3. ....

4. ....

5. ....

Exercise 17: Using Short Adjectives

Translate the following sentences into Russian using short forms of adjectives.

1. The library is closed.

....

2. The seats are occupied.

....

3. Are you free today?

....

4. The store is open.

....

5. He is ill today.

....

6. Anna is busy.

....

7. This compartment *(kupe)* is vacant.

....

8. All the windows are closed.

....

Possessive Adjectives

There are two ways to express possession: by using the Genitive case (see section on the Genitive case in Part 2) and by forming possessive adjectives.

Table 4-16

Possessive adjective formation for masculine nouns			
Noun ending	**Example**	**How to form a possessive**	**Example**
a consonant	⁻ov	*Anton*	*Antonov*
⁻ʲ ⁻j	⁻ev	*Igor'*	*Igorev*

Feminine nouns, regardless of the ending, form possessives by adding *-in*; e.g., *mama* (mom) — *mamin (mom's)*.

Remember that the gender in question is grammatical, not actual. Thus, *dedushka* (grandfather) describes a male person. However, the grammatical gender of the word *dedushka* is feminine; therefore, *-in* has to be used to form a possessive: *dedushkin*. (To review nouns like *dedushka*, see the section on "Special Endings" in Part 1.)

Possessive adjectives agree with the nouns they describe.

Table 4-17

Possessive adjective endings in Nominative singular			
Masculine	**Feminine**	**Neuter**	**Plural**
zero ending	*-a*	*-o*	*-y*

In all other cases, possessive adjectives have the same endings as regular adjectives.

Exercise 18: Whose Is This?

Russian possessive adjectives are most often formed from proper nouns. Form possessive adjectives from these proper names.

1. *Valia*   ....

2. *Misha*   ....

3. *Sergej*   ....

4. *Seriozha*   ....

5. *Masha*   ....

6. *Oleg*   ....

7. *Irina*   ....

8. *Liosha*   ....

Exercise 19: Paraphrasing the Possessives

In the phrases below, possession is expressed by the use of the Genitive case. Change the phrases so that possession is expressed by possessive adjectives.

1. *kniga Vadima*   *Vadimova*   *kniga*

2. *dom Nadi* ....

3. *zhurnal papy* ....

4. *plat'e mamy* ....

5. *ochki dedushki* ....

6. *telefon Oli* ....

7. *adres Sashi* ....

8. *vaza babushka* ....

Comparative Degree of Adjectives

To form the comparative form of an adjective, add *-ee* to the adjective stem: *bystr-ij – bystr-ee.* There are two ways to make a comparative sentence:

Pattern #1: noun 1 in Nominative + comparative adjective + noun 2 in Genitive— *Parizh teplee Moskvy.*

Pattern #2: noun 1 in Nominative + comparative adjective + comma + *chem* + noun 2 in Nominative—*Parizh teplee, chem Moskva.*

Exercise 20: Forming Comparatives

Form comparatives from these adjectives.

1. *svetlyj* ....

2. *krasivyj* ....

3. *novyj* ....

4. *milyj* ....

5. *dostupnyj* ....

6. *nezhnyj* ....

7. *vesiolyj* ....

8. *staryj* ....

Exercise 21: Paraphrasing Comparatives

TRACK 35

Listen to the speaker compare different objects using Pattern #2. Write down the information, paraphrasing the sentences according to Pattern #1. The first sentence has been done for you.

1. *Moskva kholodnee Novorossijska.*

2. ....

3. ....

4. ....

5. ....

6. ....

7. ....

8. ....

Superlative Degree of Adjectives

There are two ways to form the superlative degree of adjectives in Russian. The first way is taking an adjective's stem and adding the suffix *-ejsh-* + a regular adjectival ending: *sil'nyj* (strong) – *sil'nejshij* (the strongest). Superlative adjectives formed this way sound a little bookish. The second way is using the construction *samyj* (most) + the regular form of the adjective: *samyj sil'nyj* (the strongest). The word *samyj* changes like a regular adjective. This is the preferred superlative form in conversational Russian.

Exercise 22: Forming Superlatives

Paraphrase these phrases with superlative adjectives using the word *samyj*. The first one has been done for you.

1. *krasivejshij*   *samyj*   *krasivyj*

2. *umnejshij*   ....

3. *dobrejshij*   ....

4. *schastlivejshij* ....

5. *novejshij*   ....

6. *chistejshij*   ....

7. *milejshij*   ....

8. *strojnejshij*   ....

Exercise 23: Translating Phrases

Translate the following phrases into Russian.

1. the smartest kid

2. the most expensive gift

3. the most popular song

4. the oldest tradition

5. the most experienced (opytnyj) teacher

6. the most delicious cake

7. the warmest coat

8. the fastest car

Irregular Comparisons and Superlatives

A rather large group of common Russian adjectives from irregular comparatives and superlatives. The most common ones are *khoroshij* (good) – *luchshe* (better) – *luchshij* (the best), and *plokhoj* (bad) – *khuzhe* (worse) – *khudshij* (the worst).

Exercise 24: What Is Better?

Complete each sentence the comparative form of the adjective in parenthesis.

1. *Leto* .... *zimy.* (better)

2. *Kvartira* .... *mashiny.* (more expensive)

3. *Okean* .... *moria.* (farther)

4. *Baraban* .... *skripki.* (louder)

5. *Konfety* .... *pechen'ia.* (cheaper)

6. *Golos Mishi* .... , *chem golos Very.* (worse)

7. *Reka Volga* .... , *chem reka Nil.* (shorter)

8. *Sobaka* .... , *chem slon.* (smaller)

Exercise 25: Answering Questions

TRACK 36

Listen to the speaker ask you questions and answer them. The first question has been answered for you.

1. *Chicago men'she Moskvy.*

2. ....

3. ....

4. ....

5. ....

6. ....

7. ....

8. ....

Review

In this section, practice using different types of adjectives in all the six cases. If a topic causes a problem, go back to the section devoted to this subject and review the rules and the exercises.

Exercise 26: Completing Sentences

Complete the sentences with the adjectives in parentheses and agree them with the nouns. Then translate the sentences.

1. *My zhiviom na* .... *(prekrasnyj) planete s*

   .... *(zelionyj) lesami i* ....

   (goluboj) oziorami.

   ....

2. *Uchitel' vruchil priz* ....

   (samyj talantlivyj) ucheniku.

   ....

3. *Olia liubim nosit'* .... *(krasnyj) rubashku i*

   .... *(sinij) briuki.*

   ....

4. *Gruppa* .... *(russkij) turistov posetila*

   .... *(drevnij) khramy* ....

   (solnechnyj) Ispanii.

   ....

5. *Oni vstretilis' v* ....

   (samyj romantichnyj) gorode v mire – Parizhe.

   ....

THE EVERYTHING RUSSIAN PRACTICE BOOK

6. *Ania chasto pishet* .... *(dlinnyj) pis'ma*

.... *(amerikanskij) podruge.*

....

7. *Ia liubliu kupat'sia v* .... *(chistyj) vode*

.... *(gornyj) ozior.*

....

8. *Vera segodnia* .... *(bolen), a apteka*

.... *(zakryt).*

....

Exercise 27: A Story about Dasha

TRACK 37

Listen to the speaker read the text. Then complete the sentences below using the information you learned from the text. Remember to put the adjectives in the appropriate cases.

1. *Dasha zhiviot v* .... *klimate.*

2. *Zimoj Dasha nosit* .... *kurtku.*

3. .... *liubimyj sviter -* ....

4. *V* .... *mesiatsy Dasha nosit* .... *plat'ia.*

5. *Dasha guliaet v* .... *parke.*

6. *Dasha chitaet v parke, esli ona ne ochen'* ....

7. *V parke Dasha chitaet* .... *knigi.*

8. *Eto knigi* .... *pisatelej.*

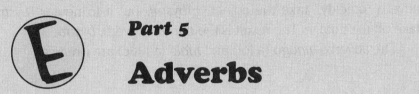

Part 5

Adverbs

Adverbs modify verbs or, in other words, give details about how something is done. Words like "still," "already," and "here" are adverbs. In this part, you will practice forming regular adverbs and use irregular ones.

Adverbs of Manner

Most adverbs describe the manner in which something is done. For instance, *On krasivo tantsuet.* (He dances beautifully.) In English, most adverbs end in "-ly"; in Russian, most adverbs end in *-o*.

To form an adverb of manner, take the neuter form of the adjective and take off the final *-e*. For instance, to form the Russian equivalent of the adverb "quickly," take the adjective *bystrij,* put it in neuter (*bystroe),* and take off the final *-e.* The result is the correct adverb, *bystro.*

The adverbs *mnogo* (a lot) and *malo* (a little) are irregular.

Exercise 1: Forming Adverbs

Form adverbs from these adjectives.

1. *vkusnyj* ....

2. *kholodnyj* ....

3. *medlennyj* ....

4. *gratsioznyj* ....

5. *effektivnyj* ....

6. *umelyj* ....

7. *khoroshij* ....

8. *vesiolyj* ....

Exercise 2: Writing Adverbs

TRACK 38

Listen to the speaker read adjectives. Produce an adverb from each adjective and write it down.

Example:
Speaker: *goriachij*
Your answer: *goriacho*

1. ....

2. ....

3. ....

4. ....

5. ....

6. ....

7. ....

8. ....

Comparative Degree of Adverbs

The comparative degree of adverbs is formed the same way as the comparative degree of adjectives: change the adverb's ending (*-o*) to *-ee*. For example: *bystro* (quickly) –*bystree* (more quickly).

Some adverbs have irregular comparative forms: *khorosho* (well) – *luchshe* (better), *plokho* (badly) –*khuzhe* (worse), *mnogo* (a lot) –*bol'she* (more), *malo* (a little) –*men'she* (less).

There are two ways to use comparative adverbs in a sentence.

Pattern #1. noun 1 in Nominative + verb 1 + comparative adverb + noun 2 in Genitive— *Boris begaet bystree Ivana.* (Boris runs faster than Ivan.)

Pattern #2. noun 1 in Nominative + verb 1 + comparative adjective + comma + *chem* + noun 2 in Nominative—*Boris begaet bystree, chem Ivan.* (Boris runs faster than Ivan.)

Exercise 3: Making a Comparison

Using the nouns, verbs, and adverbs given, form sentences with comparative adverbs. The first sentence has been done for you.

1. *olen'/ cherepakha / begaet / bystro*
   Olen' begaet bystree, chem cherepakha.

2. *del'fin / sobaka / plavaet / gratsiozno*

   ....

3. *chelovek / obez'iana / govorit / khorosho*

   ....

4. *mashina / velosiped / ezdit / medlenno*

   ....

5. *povar / mama / gotovit / vkusn*

   ....

6. *ptitsy / ryby / poiut / gromko*

   ....

7. *futbolist / shakhmatist / igraet / agressivno*

   ....

8. *koala / obez'iana / dvigaetsia / energichno*

   ....

Superlative Degree of Adverbs

The superlative degree of an adverb consists of the comparative form followed by *vsekh* if you mean "than anybody else," or *vsego* if you mean "than anything else."

Exercise 4: Doing It the Best

Complete the sentences using the phrases in parentheses. Remember to distinguish between the meaning "than anyone else" and the meaning "than anything else."

1. *Moia sestra risuet* ....
   (better than anything else)

2. *Kolia igraet v futbol* ....
   (more energetically than anyone else)

3. *Isidora Dunkan tantsevala* ....
   .... (more beautifully than anybody else)

4. *Ia govoriu po-anglijski* ....
   .... (faster than anything else)

5. *My znaem etogo uchitelia* ....
   .... (worse than anybody else)

6. *Karuzo poiot* .... (louder than anybody else)

7. *Natasha liubit morozhennoe* ....
   .... (more than anything else)

8. *Kostia opiat' el* .... (less than anybody else).

Adverbs of Place

As opposed to adverbs of manner, Russian adverbs of place, such as "here," "outside," and "where to" are not formed from adjectives. They do not end in *-o* or *-e*, and they have neither comparative, nor superlative form.

In Russian, you need to use different adverbs for "where," "here," and "there," depending on whether the subject of the sentences is moving in the direction named by the adverb, or is stationary. If the subject is moving, you need to use motion adverbs *kuda* (where to), *siuda* (here, this way), and *tuda* (that way). For instance, the Russian equivalent of the question "Where do you live?" requires the regular adverb *gde: Gde ty zhiviosh'?* The question "Where are you going?" requires a motion adverb *kuda: Kuda ty idiosh'?*

Exercise 5: Where Did It Happen?

TRACK 39

Listen to the speaker read adverbs of place, and write down their antonyms (opposites).

Example:
Speaker: *vnutri*
Your answer: *snaruzhi*

1. ....

2. ....

3. ....

4. ....

5. ....

6. ....

Exercise 6: Where or Where to?

Depending on the meaning of the sentence, complete it with either a regular or a motion adverb.

1. .... *Vy rabotaete?* (where)

2. *Idi* .... (here)

3. .... *ia zhivu.* (here)

4. .... *ty edesh' v otpusk?* (where)

5. *Ia ne liubliu* .... *khodit'.* (there)

6. .... *nakhoditsia biblioteka.* (there)

7. .... *idiot etot avtobus?* (where)

8. *Zavtra* .... *priedet populiarnaia rok-gruppa.* (here)

Adverbs of Time

Like adverbs of place, Russian adverbs of time are not formed from adjectives, and do not end in -o or -e.

Exercise 7: Giving Details about Time

Read the sentences. Depending on the meaning of the first sentence, complete the second sentence with one of the adverbs of time from the list.

kogda (when), *togda* (then), *dolgo* (for a long time), *davno* (a long time ago), *nedavno* (recently), *uzhe* (already), *eshchio* (yet, still)

1. *On rabotal v shkole 55 let. On rabotal v shkole* ....

2. *V poslednij raz ia byla v Parizhe v 1979 godu. V poslednij raz ia byla v Parizhe* ....

3. *Vchera ia nachala novuiu knigu. Ia* .... *nachala novuiu knigu.*

4. *Cherez 10 minut Lena ujdiot s raboty. Lena* .... *na rabote.*

5. *V 2000 godu mne bylo 20 let.* .... *mne bylo 20 let.*

6. *On uezzhaet zavtra.* .... *on uezzhaet?*

7. *Vchera ia vstretil starogo druga.* .... *ia vstretil starogo druga.*

8. *Oni sideli v restorane 4 chasa. Oni* .... *sideli v restorane.*

Review

In this section, practice using different types of adverbs. If you face difficulties with a particular type of adverb, go back to the section devoted to this type and go over the exercises there.

Exercise 8: A Story about Dasha

TRACK 40

Listen to the speaker read the text. Complete the sentences below with adverbs based on the information you learned from the text.

1. *Dasha* .... *risuet.*

2. *Dasha pishet kartiny* ....

3. *Dasha zakanchivaet kartiny* ....

4. *Dasha podpisyvaet svoi kartiny* ....

   ....

5. *Dasha* .... *ne prodala ni odnoj svoej kartiny.*

6. *Dasha nadeetsya prodat' svoi kartiny*
   .... *i* ....

Exercise 9: Reading Chekhov

These sentences with adverbs are taken from the short story *Dama s sobachkoj* ("Lady With a Lapdog") by Anton Chekhov. Translate the sentences into English, paying special attention to the adverbs.

1. *Ego zhenili rano, . . .*

   ....

2. *Ona mnogo chitala, . . .*

   ....

3. *Izmeniat' ej on nachal uzhe davno, izmenial chasto, . . .*

   ....

4. *Emu kazalos', chto on dostatochno nauchen gor'kim opytom . . .*

   ....

5. *V obshchestve muzhchin emu bylo skuchno, . . .*

   ....

6. *On laskovo pomanil k sebe shpitsa . . .*

   ....

7. *Vremia idiot bystro . . .*

   ....

8. *Eto tol'ko priniato govorit', chto zdes' skuchno.*

....

Exercise 10: Translating into Russian

Translate these sentences into Russian, paying special attention to the adverbs.

1. He came early.

....

2. She hasn't called yet.

....

3. Lena writes beautifully.

....

4. He knows math worse than his brother.

....

5. Where is he going?

....

6. He slept for a long time.

....

7. You speak Russian very well.

....

8. She draws the best in her class.

....

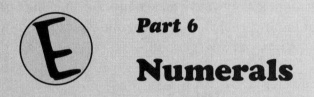

Part 6
Numerals

When talking about numbers, quantities, dates, or time, you need to use numerals. In Russian, numerals change according to case. Some Russian numerals also change according to number. In this part, practice using different kinds of numerals.

Cardinal Numerals

Numerals that name the quantity of something—one hour, ten people, twenty-four cats, or one hundred seventy-two years—are called cardinal numerals.

In Russian, numbers one and two change according to the gender of the noun which quantity the numeral states. In the case of the numeral 2, if the group consists of a feminine noun and a masculine one, then the masculine numeral is used. For instance: *muzhchina* (man) and *zhenshchina* (woman) are described as *dva cheloveka* (two people).

Table 6-1

Numeral 1 in all three genders	
Masculine	*odin*
Feminizne	*odna*
Neuter	*odno*

Table 6-2

Numeral 2 in all three genders	
Masculine	*dva*
Feminine	*dve*
Neuter	*dva*

With numeral 1 nouns are used in the Nominative singular. With numerals 2, 3, and 4 nouns are used in the Genitive singular. With numerals 5 to 20 nouns are used in the Genitive plural. With numerals 21 and larger, the case of the noun depends on the last digit of the number. Thus, after the numeral 21 the noun has to be in the Nominative singular because the last digit of the number is 1: *dvadtsat' odin den'* (21 days). After the numeral 32, the Genitive singular has to be used because the last digit of the number is 2: *tridtsat' dva turista* (32 tourists). After the numeral 45 the Genitive plural has to be used because the last digit of the number is 5: *sorok piat' domov* (45 houses). When a number ends in 0, the Genitive plural has to be used: *piat'desiat shtatov* (50 states), sto *vosem'desiat dollarov* (180 dollars).

Exercise 1: Recognizing Numerals

TRACK 41

Listen to the speaker. Write down the cardinal numerals she is reading.

1. ....

2. ....

3. ....

4. ....

5. ....

6. ....

7. ....

8. ....

9. ....

10. ....

11. ....

12. ....

13. ....

14. ....

15. ....

Exercise 2: One or Two?

Write out the numerals in the following phrases. Pay special attention to the gender of the nouns.

1. 2 .... *devushki*

2. 2 .... *okna*

3. 1 .... *slovo*

4. 1 .... *restoran*

5. 2 .... *stula*

6. 1 .... *dom*

7. 2 .... *koshki*

8. 1 .... *sobaka*

9. 2 .... *mashiny*

10. 1 .... *iubka*

Exercise 3: Planning a Party

Imagine that you are planning a party and stocking up on supplies. Using the numbers and the nouns below, make your shopping list. Write out the numbers, and remember to put the nouns in the appropriate case depending on the numeral.

1. 40, *buterbrod*

   ....

2. 15, *arbuz*

   ....

3. 44, *iabloko*

   ....

4. 12, *tarelka*

   ....

5. 22, *stakan*

   ....

6. 31, *banan*

   ....

7. 33, *apel'sin*

   ....

8. 35, *mandarin*

   ....

Exercise 4: Age and Time

Translate the following sentences into Russian.

1. Lena is 25 years old.

   ....

2. I waited 4 hours.

   ....

3. I've lived here for 2 years.

   ....

4. My son is 3 months old.

   ....

5. My brother is 1 year old.

   ....

6. He slept for 8 hours.

   ....

7. The movie is 42 minutes long.

   ....

8. Wait 5 minutes.

   ....

Ordinal Numerals

Ordinal numerals indicate the position of an object in an order or a sequence. Russian ordinal numerals agree with the objects they describe in gender, number, and case. They decline as adjectives.

Exercise 5: Recognizing Numerals

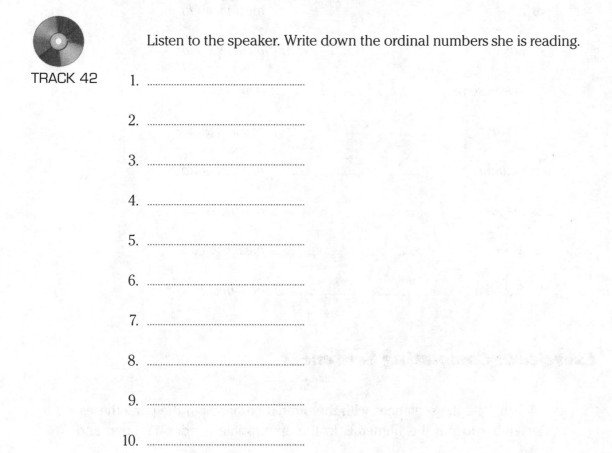

TRACK 42

Listen to the speaker. Write down the ordinal numbers she is reading.

1. ....

2. ....

3. ....

4. ....

5. ....

6. ....

7. ....

8. ....

9. ....

10. ....

Exercise 6: Days and Months

Complete the sentences below with appropriate ordinal numerals. A hint: Russian week starts with Monday.

1. *Ianvar'* .... *mesiats goda.*

2. *Piatnitsa* .... *den' nedeli.*

3. *Mart* .... *mesiats goda.*

4. *Iiul'* .... *mesiats goda.*

5. *Voskresen'e* .... *den' nedeli.*

6. *Dekabr'* .... *mesiats goda.*

7. *Oktiabr'* .... *mesiats goda.*

8. *Sreda* .... *den' nedeli.*

9. *Maj* .... *mesiats goda.*

10. *Subbota* .... *den' nedeli.*

Exercise 7: Completing Sentences

Complete the sentences with the ordinal numerals in the parentheses. Remember to put the numerals in the appropriate gender, number, and case.

1. *Moiu* .... *sobaku zvali Kutia.* (first)

2. *Ikh* .... *syn stal diplomatom.* (fourth)

3. *Oni kupili sebe* .... *kvartiru.* (second)

4. *Ia ochen' liubliu* ....

.... *simfoniiu Motsarta.* (forty first)

5. *Eto moj* .... *visit v Moskvu.* (tenth)

6. *Segodnia na obed* .... *bliudo – shokoladnyj tort.*
(third)

7. *On chasto slushal* .... *simfoniiu Chajkovskogo.*
(fifth)

8. *Eta zhenshchina–*.. *zhena izvestnogo pisatelia.*
(eleventh)

Collective Numerals

In order to refer to a group consisting of up to seven people, you can use collective numerals. A choice of a collective numeral depends on the number of people in the group.

Table 6-3

Collective numerals	
two people	*dvoe*
three people	*troe*
four people	*chetvero*
five people	*piatero*
six people	*shestero*
seven people	*semero*

Exercise 8: How Many?

TRACK 43

The sentences below are lacking the subjects. Listen to the speaker and complete the sentences with appropriate collective numerals.

Example:
Speaker: *Lena i Vika zhivut v etom dome.*
Your answer: <u>*Dvoe*</u> *zhivut v etom dome.*

1. .... *sidiat v stolovoj.*

2. .... *prishli v kino.*

3. .... *priekhali na Kavkaz.*

4. .... *poselilis' v gostinitse.*

5. .... *ostanovilis' u nas doma.*

6. .... *priekhala na kurort.*

7. .... *sideli v parke.*

8. .... *otdykhali v Italii.*

Review

In this section, practice using different types of numerals. If you face difficulties with a particular type of numeral, go back to the section devoted to this type and go over the exercises there.

Exercise 9: A Story about Dasha

TRACK 44

Listen to the text read by the speaker, and complete the sentences with the appropriate numerals.

1. *UDashiest'* .... *sobakai* .... *koshki.*

2. *Eto dashina*.. *sobaka.*

3. *Dashinu koshku* .... *zvali Pushinka.*

4. *Pushinka prozhila* .... *goda.*

5. *Dasha otmechala Den' Rozhdeniia svoej koshki* .... *maia.*

6. *U Dashi takzhe bylo* .... *rybok i* .... *khomiachka.*

Exercise 10: Making up Phrases

Match an appropriate noun from the first group with a numeral from the second to form meaningful phrases. Write out the numerals. Remember to put the nouns in the appropriate case. You may use the same numeral twice.

Example: *piat'desiat' shtatov (Ameriki)*
Group 1:
mushketior, mesiats, chas, storona sveta, den' nedeli, vremia goda
Group 2:
3, 4, 7, 12, 24

1. ....

2. ....

3. ....

4. ....

5. ....

6. ....

Exercise 11: Translating from Russian

Translate the following sentences into English, paying special attention to the numerals.

1. *U nego dva syna i dve dochki.*

    ....

2. *On zakonchil desiatyj klass.*

    ....

3. *Kuda idiot avtobus nomer vosem'?*

    ....

4. *Ia voz'mu odnu korobku konfet i odin paket kofe.*

    ....

5. *V komnate sideli dvoe.*

    ....

6. *Ia zvonila chetyri raza, a on – piat' raz.*

    ....

7. *U nas v ofise dvesti sorok tri sotrudnika.*

    ....

8. *On zanial pervoe mesto na konkurse.*

    ....

Part 7

Verbs: Introduction

Verbs are words that name actions. The Russian language is extremely rich in verbs, which change according to person, number, and tense. Verbs can also be modified by adding prefixes, that slightly change the meaning of the verbs. In this part, you will practice using different types of verbs.

Infinitives

Russian verb infinitives end in *-t'*, e.g., *chitat'* (to read), *smotret'* (to draw), *liubit'* (to love). A small group of infinitives end in other letter combinations, e.g., *moch'* (to be able) and *idti* (to walk).

Exercise 1: Finding Infinitives

Read the sentences and underline the infinitives.

1. *On brosil kurit'.*

2. *Turisty probovali govorit' po-russki.*

3. *My liubim smotret' fil'my.*

4. *Edinstvennoe, chto emu nado – eto begat' po ulitse.*

5. *Moi brat'ia uekhali lovit' rybu.*

6. *Pomogi mne, pozhalujsta, nesti sumku.*

7. *A vy dumaete, rastit' detej legko?*

8. *Emu pora vesti dochku v detskij sad.*

Exercise 2: Recognizing Infinitives

TRACK 45

Listen to the speaker read various verbal forms. Write down only verb infinitives.

Example:
Speaker: *uznavat', risuesh'*
Your answer: ***uznavat'***

1. ....

2. ....

3. ....

4. ....

5. ....

6. ....

7. ....

8. ....

9. ....

10. ....

Exercise 3: Writing Infinitives

In each sentence, find the verb and write down its infinitive form along with its translation.

1. *Moj drug igraet na skripke.*

   ....

2. *Ona idiot v magazin.*

   ....

3. *Deti risuiut solntse.*

   ....

4. *Moia sem'ia zhila v etom dome.*

   ....

5. *My budem otdykhat' v Sochi desiat dnej.*

   ....

6. *Vy chasto zvonite v Moskvu?*

   ....

7. *Segodnia oni ostaiutsia doma.*

   ....

8. *Anfisa khorosho uchitsia.*

   ....

Conjugating -e Verbs

In the present tense, the Russian language has two sets of verb endings: -e-conjugation verbs, also called *first-conjugation verbs*, and -*i*-conjugation verbs, also called *second-conjugation verbs*. In this section, review -*e*-conjugation verb endings and practice using them.

Table 7-1

Present tense verb endings for -e-conjugation verbs			
Person and number	**Ending**	**Example**	**Translation**
First person singular	-iu	chitaiu	I read/am reading
Second person singular	-esh'	chitaesh'	you (singular; informal) read/are reading
Third person singular	-et	chitaet	he/she/it reads/is reading
First person plural	-em	chitaem	we read/are reading
Second person plural	-ete	chitaete	you (plural; formal) read/are reading
Third person plural	-iut	chitaiut	they read/are reading

Exercise 4: Conjugating -e verbs

Conjugate each -*e* verb so that it agrees with the subject. The first task has been done for you.

1. *oni / kashliat'*
   oni kashliaiut

2. *my / imet'*

3. *vy / sprashivat'*

....

4. *ia / slushat'*

....

5. *ona / igrat'*

....

6. *my / znat'*

....

7. *ty / letat'*

....

8. *oni / vyshivat'*

....

Exercise 5: Matching the Parts

Complete each sentence with one of the verb forms from the list. Remember to match the verb form with the subject of the sentence. You can use the same verb form more than once.

znaiu, znaesh', znaet, znaem, znaete, znaiut

1. *Moia sestra otlichno* .... *astronomiiu.*

2. *Moi druz'ia* .... *khoroshij restoranchik.*

3. *Ia* .... *pravdu.*

4. *Moj drug* .... *persidskij iazyk.*

5. *Ty* .... *etu devushku?*

6. *Vy ne* .... *, kotoryj chas?*

7. *My* .... *drug druga.*

8. *Ital'iantsy* .... *, kak naslazhdat'sia zhizn'iu.*

Exercise 6: Completing Sentences

Complete each sentence with the correct conjugation of the *-e* verb in parenthesis.

1. *Lena prekrasno* .... *na gitare. (igrat')*

2. *Vy* .... *ital'ianskij iazyk? (znat')*

3. *Ia* .... *nad knigoj. (rabotat')*

4. *Oni* .... *novuiu kvartiru. (pokupat')*

5. *My vsegda* .... *na voprosy. (otvechat')*

6. *V nashe vremia deti redko* .... *knigi. (chitat')*

7. *Ty khorosho* .... *matematiku? (ponimat')*

8. *Moi roditeli chasto* .... *v parke. (guliat')*

Conjugating -i Verbs

In this section, review -i-conjugation verbs, which are also called second-*conjugation verbs*, and practice using them.

Table 7-2

Present tense endings for -*i*-conjugation verbs			
Person and number	**Ending**	**Example**	**Translation**
First person singular	-iu	*stroiu*	I build/am building
Second person singular	-ish'	*stroish'*	you (singular; informal) build/are building
Third person singular	-it	*stroit*	he/she/it builds/is building
First person plural	-im	*stroim*	we build/are building
Second person plural	-ite	*stroite*	you (plural; formal) build /are building
Third person plural	-iat	*stroiat*	they build/are building

Exercise 7: Conjugating -i verbs

Conjugate each-*i* verb so that it agrees with the subject. The first task has been done for you.

1. *oni / varit'*
   oni variat

2. *my / gotovit'*

   ....

3. *vy / govorit'*

   ....

4. *ia / stroit'*

   ....

5. *ona / stoiat'*

   ....

6. *my / slyshat'*

   ....

7. *ty / lezhat'*

   ....

8. *oni / smotret'*

   ....

Exercise 8: Matching the Parts

Complete each sentence with one of the verb forms from the list. Remember to match the verb form with the subject of the sentence. You can use the same verb form more than once.

govoriu, govorish', govorit, govorim, govorite, govoriat

1. *Moj drug prekrasno* .... *po-ispanski.*

2. *My chasto* .... *po telefonu.*

3. *S kem ty* ....?

4. *Vy ochen' krasivo* ....

5. *Moi roditeli ne* .... *po-russki.*

6. *Ia chasto* .... *vo sne.*

7. *Moia sestra vsegda* .... *gromko.*

8. *Turisty* .... , *chto im ponravilos'.*

Exercise 9: Completing Sentences

Complete each sentence with the correct conjugation of the -*i* verb in parenthesis.

1. *Ty chasto* .... *televizor? (smotret')*

2. *Kogda on obychno* ....? *(zvonit')*

3. *Ia* .... *priiatnuiu muzyku. (slyshat')*

4. *Skol'ko* .... *eto pal'to? (stoit')*

5. *Segodnia vy* .... *obed? (gotovit')*

6. *Na etoj nedele oni* .... *varen'e. (varit')*

7. *Turisty* .... *na pliazhe. (lezhat')*

8. *Ia uzhe davno ne* .... *(kurit')*

Verbs with an Inserted Consonant -l-

Some Russian verbs whose stem ends in consonants *b, v, m, p,* or *f* gain an extra consonant *-l-* in the first person singular form. For example, the stem of the infinitive *liubit'* (to love) ends in a *-b-*. In the first person singular, an inserted consonant *-l-* appears: *liubliu* (I love). However, in the other forms this inserted consonant disappears again: *liubish'* (you [singular; informal] love), *liubit* (he/she/it loves), *liubim* (we love), *liubite* (you [plural, formal] love), *liubiat* (they love).

Exercise 10: Conjugating Verbs with an Inserted Consonant -l-

Conjugate each verb so that it agrees with the subject. Remember that the consonant *-l-* appears in the first person singular only. The first task has been done for you.

1. *ia / kupit'*
    ia kupliu

2. *my / kopit'*

....

3. *vy / terpet'*

....

4. *ia / kormit'*

    ....

5. *ona / toropit'*

    ....

6. *my / lovit'*

    ....

7. *ia / rubit'*

    ....

8. *oni / liubit'*

    ....

Exercise 11: Completing Sentences

Complete each sentence with the correct conjugation of the verb in parenthesis. Remember that the consonant *-l-* appears in the first person singular only.

1. *Dlia podniatiia dukha on* .... *drova. (rubit')*

2. *Po voskresen'iam ia* .... *rybu. (lovit')*

3. *Dver' sil'no* .... *. (skripet')*

4. *Mal'chik* .... *den'gi na velosiped. (kopit')*

5. *Ia* .... *puteshestvovat'. (liubit')*

6. *Na etoj nedele ia* .... *sebe iakhtu. (kupit')*

7. *Oni davno uzhe* .... *(terpet')*

8. *Chestno, ia ne* .... *(lukavit')*

Verbs with Consonant Mutation

Some Russian verbs whose stem ends in consonants *d, z, s,* and *t* undergo consonant mutation in the first person singular. For example, the stem of the verb *nosit'* (to carry) ends in an -*s*. In the first person singular, the final consonant of the stem changes to -*sh*-: *noshu* (I carry / am carrying). In the other forms, however, the original consonant -*s*- is restored: *nosish'* (you [singular; informal] carry / are carrying), *nosit* (he/she/it carries / is carrying); *nosim* (we carry / are carrying), *nosite* (you [plural; formal]) carry / are carrying); *nosiat* (they carry / are carrying).

Consult the following table to see what consonants replace the original ones in the first person singular. Remember that the mutation occurs in the first person singular only; in all other forms, the original consonant is restored.

Table 7-3

Consonant mutation in Russian verbs			
Final Stem consonant	**Example**	**Consonant after mutation**	**Example**
d⁻	*gladit'*	zh	*glazhu*
z⁻	*vozit'*	zh	*vozhu*
s⁻	*prosit'*	sh	*proshu*
st⁻	*svistet'*	shch	*svishchu*
t⁻	*letet'*	ch	*lechu*

Exercise 12: Conjugating Verbs with Consonant Mutation

Conjugate each verb with consonant mutation so that it agrees with the subject. Remember that the mutation occurs in the first person singular only. The first task has been done for you.

1. *ia / sidet'*
   ia sizhu

2. *my / kosit'*

   ....

3. *vy / katit'*

   ....

4. *ia / vozit''*

   ....

5. *ona / brodit'*

   ....

6. *my / krutit'*

   ....

7. *ia / krasit'*

   ....

8. *oni / chistit'*

   ....

Exercise 13: Matching the Parts

Complete each sentence with one of the verb forms from the list. Remember to match the verb form with the subject of the sentence.

sizhu, sidish', sidit, sidim, sidite, sidiat

1. *On vsegda* .... *v pervom riadu.*

2. *Gde ty obychno* .... *na lektsii?*

3. *Ia* .... *v parke i chitaiu knigu.*

4. *My* .... *na divane i smotrim televizor.*

5. *Moi druz'ia* .... *v restorane.*

6. *Vy* .... *na moiom meste.*

Exercise 14: Completing Sentences

Complete each sentence with the correct conjugation of the verb in parenthesis.

1. *Ia* .... *vas priekhat' k nam v gosti. (prosit')*

2. *On idiot po ulitse i* .... *(svistet')*

3. *Oni* .... *tovary iz Turtsii. (vozit')*

4. *Ia uzhe dva chasa* .... *po gorodu. (brodit')*

5. *Tom Sojer* .... *zabor ves' den'. (krasit')*

6. *Gde vy obychno* .... *na kontserte? (sidet')*

7. *Mal'chik* .... *zuby. (chistit')*

8. *Ia obychno* .... *dzhinsy i sviter. (nosit')*

Conjugating -ava / -ova Type Verbs

Some Russian verbs whose stems end in *-ova-* or *-ava-* have special conjugation patterns.

Table 7-4

Conjugation of the *-ava-* type verb *vstavat'* (to get up)	
Conjugation	**Translation**
vstaiu	I get up/am getting up
vstaiosh'	you (singular; informal) get up/are getting up
vstaiot	he/she/it gets up/is getting up
vstaiom	we get up/are getting up
vstaiote	you (plural; formal) get up/are getting up
vstaiut	they get up/are getting up

Table 7-5

Conjugation of the *-ova-* type verb *risovat'* (to draw)	
Conjugation	**Translation**
risuiu	I draw/am drawing
risuesh'	you (singular; informal) draw/are drawing
risuet	he/she/it draws/is drawing
risuem	we draw/are drawing
risuete	you (plural; formal) draw/are drawing
risuiut	they draw/are drawing

Exercise 15: Conjugating -ava- and -ova- Type Verbs

Conjugate each verb so that it agrees with the subject. The first task has been done for you.

1. *my / puteshestvovat'*
   my puteshestvuem

2. *vy / davat'*

   ....

3. *oni / sovetovat'*

   ....

4. *ia / uznavat'*

   ....

5. *ona / trebovat'*

   ....

6. *my / riskovat'*

   ....

7. *ty / vstavat'*

   ....

8. *oni / rekomendovat'*

   ....

Exercise 16: Matching the Parts

Complete each sentence with one of the verb forms from the list. Remember to match the verb form with the subject of the sentence.

uznaiu, uznaiosh', uznaiot, uznaiom, uznaiote, uznaiut

1. *Vy vsegda udachno* .... *dorogu.*

2. *Moia sobaka* .... *moi shagi.*

3. *Ty menia ne* .... *?*

4. *My vsio* .... *poslednimi.*

5. *Ia vas ne* ....

6. *Moi druz'ia* .... *vremia.*

Exercise 17: Completing Sentences

Complete each sentence with the correct conjugation of the verb in parenthesis.

1. *On slishkom chasto* .... *(riskovat')*

2. *Gde Vy obychno* .... *? (puteshestvovat')*

3. *Kak ty* .... *etot pribor? (ispol'zovat')*

4. *Oni* .... *povyshennogo vnimaniia. (trebovat')*

5. *Ia* .... *ne prodolzhat' igru. (sovetovat')*

6. *Po ponedel'nikam my* .... *sving. (tantsevat')*

7. *Vy* .... *etot kurort? (rekomendovat')*

8. *Ia* .... *ochen' pozdno. (vstavat')*

Irregular Verbs

A number of Russian verbs have irregular conjugation patterns. Here are the conjugation patterns of some common irregular verbs.

Table 7-6

Conjugation of the irregular verb *khotet'* (to want)	
Conjugation	**Translation**
khochu	I want
khochesh'	you (singular; informal) want
khochet	he/she/it wants
khotim	we want
khotite	you (plural; formal) want
khotiat	they want

Table 7-7

Conjugation of the irregular verb *moch'* (to be able)	
Conjugation	**Translation**
mogu	I am able
mozhesh'	you (singular; informal) are able
mozhet	he/she/it is able
mozhem	we are able
mozhete	you (plural; formal) are able
mogut	they are able

Table 7-8

Conjugation of the irregular verb *pisat'* (to write)	
Conjugation	**Translation**
pishu	I write/am writing
pishesh'	you (singular; informal) write/are writing
pishet	he/she/it writes/is writing
pishem	we write/are writing
pishete	you (plural; formal) write/are writing
pishut	they write/are writing

Exercise 18: Conjugating Irregular Verbs

Conjugate each irregular verb so that it agrees with the subject. The first task has been done for you.

1. *ty / khotet'*
   ty khochesh'

2. *vy / moch'*

   ....

3. *oni / pisat'*

   ....

4. *ia / iskat'*

   ....

5. *ona / plakat'*

   ....

6. *my / myt'*

....

7. *ty / pit'*

....

8. *oni / est'*

....

Exercise 19: Matching the Parts

Complete each sentence with one of the verb forms from the list. Remember to match the verb form with the subject of the sentence. You can use the same verbal form more than once. You don't have to use all of the given forms.

em, esh', est, edim, edite, ediat

1. *My vsegda* .... *v 5 chasov.*

2. *Ia ne* .... *klubniku.*

3. *Turisty* .... *v restorane.*

4. *Vy* .... *rybu?*

5. *Ona ne* .... *uzhe dva dnia.*

6. *Chto* .... *eto zhivotnoe?*

Exercise 20: Completing Sentences

Complete each sentence with the correct conjugation of the verb in parenthesis.

1. *Vse liudi* .... *nastoiashchuiu liubov'. (iskat')*

2. *My vsegda* .... *ruki pered edoj. (myt')*

3. *V Rossii govoriat, chto mal'chiki ne* .... *. (plakat')*

4. *Chto Vy* .... *? (pisat')*

5. *Ia bol'she ne* .... *zdes' rabotat'. (moch')*

6. *Chto ty* .... *morozhennoe ili konfety? (khotet')*

7. *Moj brat ne* .... *kofe. (pit')*

8. *Chto ty obychno* .... *na zavtrak? (est')*

Negation

In Russian, you have to use double negation (or, if the number of pronouns allows, even triple negation). If the verb of the sentence is negative, then all the pronouns in the sentence have to be negative as well. For example: *On nikogda nichego ne vidit.* (He never sees anything.)

Exercise 21: Being Negative

Make the following sentences negative. Remember to use double and triple negation.

1. *Ia vsio znaiu.*

   ....

2. *My nashli dorogu.*

   ....

3. *On vsegda zvonit.*

   ....

4. *Vy zdes' zhiviote?*

   ....

5. *Ia liubliu chitat' liubye knigi.*

   ....

6. *On dumaet obo vsiom.*

   ....

7. *Ona pishet knigu.*

   ....

8. *My mnogo rabotaem.*

   ....

Past Tense

To form the past tense of Russian verbs, start with the infinitive and take off the ending -*t'*. Then add the past tense endings as follows: add -*l* for masculine subjects, -*la* for feminine subjects, -*lo* for neuter subjects, and -*li* for plural subjects. For example, the past tense forms of *smotret'* (to watch) are *smotrel* (watched; masculine, singular), *smotrela* (watched; feminine, singular), *smotrelo* (watched; neuter, singular), and *smotreli* (watched; plural).

Exercise 22: Using Past Tense

Use each verb in the past tense so that it agrees with the subject. The first task has been done for you.

1. *on / liubit'*
   on liubil

2. *vy / khotet'*

   ....

3. *oni / znat'*

   ....

4. *ona / pomnit'*

   ....

5. *ono / shumet'*

   ....

6. *my / imet'*

   ....

7. *ona / tantsevat'*

....

8. *on / terpet'*

....

Exercise 23: Matching the Parts

Complete each sentence with one of the verb forms from the list. Remember to match the verb form with the subject of the sentence. You can use the same verbal form more than once.

zhil, zhila, zhilo, zhili

1. *A more* .... *svoej zagadochnoj zhizn'iu.*

2. *Ona ran'she* .... *v tom dome.*

3. *My togda* .... *v Moskve.*

4. *Vy tozhe ran'she* .... *u moria?*

5. *Do 17 let Ivan* .... *s roditeliami.*

6. *S nimi* .... *simpatichnaia koshka.*

7. *Etot starik* .... *odin.*

8. *Ona* .... *v samom krasivom gorode mira.*

Exercise 24: Completing Sentences

Complete each sentence with the correct past tense form of the verb in parenthesis.

1. *My dolgo* .... *po parku. (guliat')*

2. *Ona* .... *emu pis'ma kazhdyj den'. (pisat')*

3. *Deti* .... *v al'bome. (risovat')*

4. *Ozero* .... *vdali. (sverkat')*

5. *Pochtal'on* .... *v dver'. (postuchat')*

6. *Drug* .... *mne po telefonu. (pozvonit')*

7. *Lena* .... *podrugu na ulitse. (vstretit')*

8. *Mal'chik* .... *na skripke. (igrat')*

Exercise 25: Listening

TRACK 46

The sentences below are lacking verbs. Listen to the speaker and write down the verbs, changing them into the past tense.

Example:
Speaker: *Moj drug <u>smotrit</u> kino.*
Your answer: *Moj drug **smotrel** kino.*

1. *Ia chasto* .... *v Parizh.*

2. *Olia ochen'* .... *shokolad.*

3. *My* .... *v tennis.*

4. *Oni* .... *po-russki.*

5. *Professor i ego zhena* .... *v London.*

6. *Vy zdes'* .... ?

7. *Molodoj muzhchina* .... *ulitsu.*

8. *Samoliot* .... *v sem' chasov.*

Future Tense

There are two future tenses in Russian. The simple future tense is formed by conjugating perfective verbs. (This will be discussed below.) The compound future tense, (also called the continuous future or imperfect future), is formed with the conjugated form of the verb *byt'* (to be) followed by an infinitive of an imperfective aspect verb. For example: *ia budu chitat'.* (I will be reading.) The verb *byt'* agrees with the subject in person and number.

The continuous (imperfect) future describes actions that will be performed over a period of time or actions that do not necessarily imply completion.

Table 7-9

Conjugation of the verb *byt'* (to be)	
Person and number	**Form**
First person singular	*budu*
Second person singular	*budesh'*
Third person singular	*budet*
First person plural	*budem*
Second person plural	*budete*
Third person plural	*budut*

Exercise 26: Using Compound Future Tense

Use each verb in the compound future tense so that it agrees with the subject. The first task has been done for you.

1. *ia / rabotat'*
   Ia budu rabotat'

2. *vy / zhdat'*

   ....

3. *oni / uchit'*

   ....

4. *ona / spat'*

   ....

5. *Vy / zhit'*

   ....

6. *my / smotret'*

   ....

7. *ona / tantsevat'*

   ....

8. *oni / pet'*

   ....

Exercise 27: Matching the Parts

Complete each sentence with one of the compound future forms from the list. Remember to match the verb form with the subject of the sentence. You can use the same verb form more than once.

budu zhdat', budesh' zhdat', budet zhdat', budem zhdat', budete zhdat', budut zhdat'

1. *Ia .... na perone.*

2. *Moi druz'ia .... nas v kafe.*

3. *Skol'ko Vy .... ?*

4. *Ty .... ili pojdiosh' domoj?*

5. *Ona skazala, chto .... do utra.*

6. *My .... vas v gosti.*

7. *Moj brat .... tam svoiu devushku.*

8. *On .... pis'ma.*

Exercise 28: Completing Sentences

Complete each sentence with the compound future tense form of the verb in parenthesis.

1. *Ia .... v universitete. (prepodavat')*

2. *Ona .... aktrisoj. (rabotat')*

3. *My .... na Kavkaze. (otdykhat')*

4. *Chto vy .... posle kontserta? (delat')*

5. *Turisty* .... *v etom restorane. (obedat')*

6. *Papa* .... *uzhin. (gotovit')*

7. *Mama* .... *na konferentsii. (vystupat')*

8. *Koshka ne* .... *na divane. (spat')*

Exercise 29: Listening

TRACK 47

The sentences below are lacking verbs. Listen to the speaker and write down the verbs, changing them into the future imperfective tense.

Example:
Speaker: *Moia tiotia pishet rasskazy.*
Your answer: *Moia tiotia **budet pisat'** rasskazy.*

1. *My* .... *v kino.*

2. *Lena* .... *na pianino.*

3. *Moi roditeli* .... *na dache.*

4. *Vy* .... *po-russki?*

5. *Ty* .... *etogo cheloveka.*

6. *Ia* .... *zariadku kazhdyj den'.*

7. *Magazin* .... *v vosem' chasov.*

8. *My* .... *kazhdoe voskresen'e.*

Aspect: Imperfective and Perfective

Russian verbs have the category of aspect. Almost all Russian verbs come in pairs: a perfective verb and an imperfective verb. Often, both verbs are translated into English by the same word. For instance, the imperfective *chitat'* and the perfective *prochitat'* are translated into English by the same verb "to read." You need to look at the verbs in context to decide whether you need to use an imperfective or a perfective form.

Use perfective verbs when you need to name a single, specific, and complete action. You need to use perfective verbs when you want to concentrate on result and successful completion, rather than process. For instance, if you want to say that you will finish reading a book tomorrow, you can use the perfective verb *prochitat'*: *Zavtra ia prochitaiu knigu.* (Tomorrow, I'll read the book.)

Use imperfective verbs when you need to concentrate on the process rather than on completion, or when talking about repeated, incomplete, or unspecific actions. For example, if you want to say that you will spend time reading a book tomorrow, you can use the imperfective verb *chitat'*: *Zavtra ia budu chitat' knigu.* (Tomorrow I'll be reading the book.)

Exercise 30: Finding Perfective Pairs

Write down the perfective counterparts for these imperfective verbs.

1. *smotret'* ....
2. *slushat'* ....
3. *delat'* ....
4. *videt'* ....
5. *pokupat'* ....
6. *prodavat'* ....
7. *uznavat'* ....
8. *risovat'* ....

Exercise 31: Finding Imperfective Pairs

Write down the imperfective counterparts for these perfective verbs.

1. *priekhat'*   ....

2. *skazat'*   ....

3. *napisat'*   ....

4. *vyjti*   ....

5. *dat'*   ....

6. *vziat'*   ....

7. *zakonchit'*   ....

8. *otkryt'*   ....

Exercise 32: Listening

TRACK 48

The sentences below are lacking verbs. Listen to the speaker and write down the verbs, changing them from imperfective to perfective form. Translate the sentences.

Example:
Speaker: *Brat smotrit novyj fil'm.*
Your answer: *Brat* **posmotrit** *novyj fil'm.* (My brother will watch a new movie).

1. *Natasha* .... *knigu.*

    ....

2. *Rabochie* .... *zdanie.*

3. *Anna* .... *plat'e.*

4. *My* .... *dissertatsiiu.*

5. *Mal'chik* .... *dom.*

6. *Vy* .... *v gosti?*

7. *Voditel'* .... *eto pravilo.*

8. *Papa* .... *obed.*

Review

In this section, practice conjugating and using different types of verbs. If you face difficulties with a particular type of verb, go back to the section devoted to this type, and go over the exercises there.

Exercise 33: A Story about Dasha

Read the text, and complete the sentences with the correct grammatical forms of the verbs given in the parentheses.

Dasha .... (guliat') po parku. Ona ....

(sobirat') osennie list'ia. Dasha .... (iskat') samyj

krasivyj osennij listok.

"Ia tak .... (liubit') osen'," ....

(dumat') Dasha. Osen'iu list'ia .... (meniat')

tsvet. Deti .... (nachinat') khodit' v shkolu.

Ptitsy .... (puteshestvovat') na iug.

"Zhal', chto ia ne .... (moch') poekhat' na

iug", ... (vzdykhat') Dasha. Ona tozhe

.... (khotet') puteshestvovat'. "Kogda ia

.... (poletet') v tioplye strany?" ....

(govorit') Dasha. "Vmesto etogo, ia .... (sidet') v

skuchnom ofise". No Dasha uzhe .... (ezdit') v otpusk

v etom godu. Teper' ona ....

(rabotat') do sledui-ushchego goda.

Exercise 34: Reading Chekhov

These sentences are taken from the short story *Dama s sobachkoj* ("Lady
With a Lapdog") by Anton Chekhov. Translate the sentences into English,
paying special attention to the verbs.

1. *Kak Vy menia ispugali!*

   ....

2. *Ona vzglianula na nego i poblednela …*

   ....

3. *Anna Sergeevna i on liubili drug druga …*

....

4. *Golova ego uzhe nachinala sedet'.*

....

5. *On pri kazhdom shage pokachival golovoj i…postoianno klanialsia.*

....

6. *Veroiatno, eto byl muzh, kotorogo ona togda v Ialte…obozvala lakeem.*

....

7. *Vsio vremia, poka publika vkhodila i zanimala mesta, Gurov zhadno iskal glazami.*

....

8. *Chto zhe ia teper' noch'iu budu delat'?*

....

Exercise 35: Completing Sentences

The sentences below are lacking verbs. Complete each sentence with the appropriate verb form in parenthesis.

1. *Lena vchera* .... *mne podarok. (podarila, podarit)*

2. *Ia vsegda* .... *tut kofe. (pokupaiu, kupliu)*

3. *Zavtra nashi druz'ia* .... *. (rabotali, budut rabotat')*

4. *On stoial i zhdal, poka ona* .... *(pisala, napisala)*

5. *On nikogda nichego* .... *(ne zamechaet, zamechaet)*

6. *Ran'she ona* .... *v Bol'shom teatre. (tantsevala, tantsuet)*

7. *Vy uzhe vsio* .... *? (ne znaete, znaete)*

8. *Gde ty* .... *etot zamechatel'nyj sharf? (nakhodila, nashla)*

Exercise 36: Conjugating Verbs

Complete each sentence with the correct grammatical form of the verb in parenthesis.

1. *Ia vam* .... *tuda ne idti. (sovetovat')*

2. *Chto vy* .... *sobake na obed? (davat')*

3. *Kazhdoe utro ia* .... *svoiu rubashku. (gladit')*

4. *Ia chasto* .... *sebia na mysli, chto mne ochen' povezlo. (lovit')*

5. *Oni chasto* .... *drug drugu pis'ma. (pisat')*

6. *Vy* .... *pozvonit' zavtra? (moch')*

7. *My* .... *svoj gorod. (liubit')*

8. *Ona* .... *modnuiu odezhdu. (nosit')*

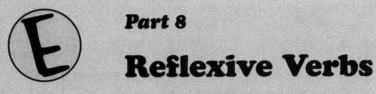

Part 8

Reflexive Verbs

Reflexive verbs are easily recognized by the particle *-sia* at the end of their infinitives. In this part, you will practice choosing between reflexive and nonreflexive verbs and using reflexive verbs in a sentence.

Reflexive Verb Conjugation

The infinitive of reflexive verbs ends in the particle *sia*, e.g., *kupat'sia* (to bathe oneself; to take a bath). These reflexive verbs retain this particle in all their forms. The particle has two forms: *-sia* after a consonant (including the soft sign) and *-s'* after a vowel sound. [See Table 8-1]

Apart from the particle *sia*, reflexive verbs conjugate like nonreflexive verbs.

Table 8-1
Conjugation of the reflexive verb *kupat'sia*
(to bathe oneself) and its past tense forms

Conjugation	Translation
ia kupa-iu-s'	I bathe
ty kupa-esh'-sia	you (singular, informal) bathe
on (ona, ono) kupa-et-sia	he (she, it) bathes
my kupa-em-sia	we bathe
vy kupa-ete-s'	you (plural; formal) bathe
oni kupa-iut-sia	they bathe
on kupa-l-sia	he bathed
ona kupa-la-s'	she bathed
ono kupa-lo-s'	it bathed
oni kupa-li-s'	they bathed

Exercise 1: Conjugating Reflexive Verbs

The sentences below are lacking verbs. Complete each sentence with the appropriate form of the reflexive verb in parenthesis. Watch out for the particle *-sia*!

1. *On chasto* .... *(ulybat'sia)*

2. *Ona* .... *vsego, chego khochet. (dobivat'sia)*

3. *Oni nikogda ne* .... *(rasstavat'sia)*

4. *Ia* .... *figurnym kataniem. (uvlekat'sia)*

5. *My* .... *vashej knigoj. (voskhishchat'sia)*

6. *Ty* .... *v shkole ili v institute? (uchit'sia)*

7. *Vy vsegda tut* .... *zakatom? (liubovat'sia)*

8. *Moj diadia* .... *v Chiornom more kruglyj god. (kupat'sia)*

Exercise 2: Scrambled Sentences

These sentences with reflexive verbs got scrambled up. Match the first half of each sentence with the second half from the list. A hint: to make the right match, watch for verb endings!

prosypaemsia rano
stesniaetsia zajti v gosti
ulybaius'
ubedites' v moej pravote
kataesh'sia na loshadi?
zanimaiutsia biznesom

1. *Moj drug …*

   ....

2. *Na fotografiiakh ia vsegda …*

   ....

3. *Vy skoro …*

   ....

4. *My …*

   ....

5. *Moi roditeli …*

   ....

6. *Ty chasto …*

   ....

Genuine Reflexive Verbs

A big group of reflexive verbs have the meaning of an action applied onto oneself. For example, *brit'* means "to shave [someone or something]". It requires a direct object. The corresponding reflexive verb *brit'sia* means "to shave [oneself]". It cannot be used with a direct object because the subject of the sentence is also the object of the action.

The way reflexive verbs were formed shows that this meaning of an action applied onto oneself is the primary one for reflexive verbs: the particle *-sia* is the remains of the reflexive pronoun *sebia* (oneself).

Exercise 3: Completing Sentences

Complete each sentence with one of the verbs parentheses. If the subject of the sentence is performing the action to him-, her-, -itself, use a reflexive verb. If the subject of the sentence is performing the action to somebody or something else, use a non-reflexive verb. Remember to put the verbs in the correct grammatical form.

1. *Devochka* .... *kotionka. (umyvat', umyvat'sia)*

2. *Etot molodoj chelovek* .... *ochen' modno. (odevat', odevat'sia)*

3. *Mat'* .... *rebionka. (kupat', kupat'sia)*

4. *Parikmakher* .... *klienta. (prichiosyvat', prichiosyvat'sia)*

5. *Ia* .... *kholodnoj vodoj. (umyvat', umyvat'sia)*

6. *Babushka* .... *vnuka. (odevat', odevat'sia)*

7. *Lena* .... *pered zerkalom. (prichiosyvat', prichiosyvat'sia)*

8. *Gosti* .... *v prikhozhej. (razdevat', razdevat'sia)*

Active Versus Passive Meaning

Many reflexive verbs are produced from non-reflexive verbs by adding the particle -*sia*. This transformation slightly changes the meaning of the verb—the non-reflexive verb maintains an active meaning, the meaning of an action performed by the subject of the sentence. On the other hand, a corresponding reflexive verb conveys a passive meaning—an action applied onto the subject of the sentence.

For example, the verb *zakryvat'* means "to close," as in *Direktor zakryl magazin.* (The manager closed the store.) The reflexive verb *zakryvat'sia* also translates into English as "to close,",but it can only be used when somebody else other than the subject of the sentence does the closing, e.g., *Magazin zakryvaetsia v vosem' chasov.* (The store closes at eight o'clock.) It is obvious that the store does not close itself; somebody else does the closing. That is why the reflexive verb can be used.

Exercise 4: Producing Reflexive Verbs

Translate the following non-reflexive verbs. Then produce reflexive verbs from them, and translate the verbs you have produced.

1. *nazyvat'*

   ....

2. *zakanchivat'*

   ....

3. *stroit'*

   ....

4. *nachinat'*

   ....

5. *otkryvat'* ....

....

6. *otrazhat'* ....

....

Exercise 5: Active or Passive?

Depending on whether the subject of the sentence or someone else is performing the action, choose either a reflexive or a non-reflexive verb to complete each sentence. Remember to put the verb in the appropriate form.

1. *Apteka* .... *v shest' utra. (otkryvat', otkryvat'sia)*

2. *Lena* .... *okno. (otkryvat', otkryvat'sia)*

3. *Etot muzej* .... *Ermitazh. (nazyvat', nazyvat'sia)*

4. *Liudi* .... *Sankt Peterburg "Piter." (nazyvat', nazyvat'sia)*

5. *Professor* .... *lektsiiu. (nachinat', nachinat'sia)*

6. *Fil'm* .... *v vosem' chasov. (nachinat', nachinat'sia)*

7. *Moia rabota* .... *v piat' chasov. (zakanchivat', zakanchivat'sia)*

8. *Pisatel'* .... *knigu. (zakanchivat', zakanchivat'sia)*

Exercise 6: Paraphrasing Sentences

Paraphrase the sentences below using reflexive verbs. The first sentence has been done for you.

1. *Nalogovaia politsiia zakryvaet restoran.*
   Restoran zakryvaetsia.

2. *Lektor nachinaet doklad.*

   ....

3. *Devochka otkryvaet glaza.*

   ....

4. *Chitatel' zakanchivaet stat'iu.*

   ....

5. *On nazval svoj otel' "Mechta."*

   ....

6. *Kompaniia "Dom" stroit eto zdanie uzhe desiat' let.*

   ....

7. *On otkroet novoe kafe zavtra.*

   ....

8. *My zakanchivaem etu banku kofe.*

   ....

Mutual Action

Another group of reflexive verbs produced from non-reflexive verbs have a meaning of reciprocity. For example, *vstrechat'* means "to meet [some-body]." The reflexive counterpart *vstrechat'sia* means "to meet [each other]," and can only be used to describe the action of a group of people.

Exercise 7: Is It Mutual?

Depending on whether the action is reciprocal or not, choose either a reflexive or a non-reflexive verb to complete the sentences below. Remember to put the verb in the appropriate form in each sentence.

1. *Kazhdyj den' ia* .... *etogo cheloveka na ulitse.* (*vstrechat'*, *vstrechat'sia*)

2. *Druz'ia* .... *v kafe kazhduiu subbotu.* (*vstrechat'*, *vstrechat'sia*)

3. *Lena* .... *menia s Mishej.* (*poznakomit'*, *poznakomit'sia*)

4. *My* .... *na vecherinke.* (*poznakomit'*, *poznakomit'sia*)

5. *Mat'* .... *syna v lob.* (*tselovat'*, *tselovat'sia*)

6. *Vliublionnye* .... *v metro.* (*tselovat'*, *tselovat'sia*)

7. *Ia* .... *Vaniu na pliazhe.* (*uvidet'*, *uvidet'sia*)

8. *Oni nakonets-to* .... *posle dolgoj razluki.* (*uvidet'*, *uvidet'sia*)

Exercise 8: Paraphrasing Sentences

TRACK 49

Listen to the speaker. Using the information you've learned, complete the sentences below using reflexive verbs.

Example:
Speaker: *Igor' vidit sestru kazhdoe voskresen'e.*
Your answer: *Igor' s sestroj <u>vidiatsia</u> kazhdoe voskresen'e.*

1. *Lena* .... *s Mishej.*

2. *Nina i Ivan* .... *u teatra.*

3. *Druz'ia* .... *na proshloj nedele.*

4. *Gosti* ....

5. *Olia i eio muzh* .... *v 2005.*

Other Reflexive Verbs

Besides the three groups discussed in the previous sections, there is also a number of reflexive verbs that have neither of the discussed meanings. These are always reflexive, and do not have a non-reflexive counterpart. These verbs have to be memorized.

Table 8-2

The most popular Russian verbs always used in the reflexive form	
nravit'sia	to like
smeiat'sia	to laugh
ulybat'sia	to smile
gordit'sia	to be proud of
boiat'sia	to be afraid of, to fear

Table 8-2

The most popular Russian verbs always used in the reflexive form	
sluchat'sia	to happen
stanovit'sia	to become
ostavat'sia	to remain, to stay
kazat'sia	to seem

The verbs *nravit'sia* (to like) and *kazat'sia* (to seem) require the use of a special construction. Much like in an English expression "it seems to me," "I", who is the actual subject of the sentence, is grammatically presented by a pronoun in the Dative case. In Russian, "it" is omitted: *mne kazhetsia* (it seems to me); *mne nravitsia* (I like).

In these constructions, the verb agrees in number with the grammatical subject of the sentence. In the sentence, *Mne nravitsia chaj* (I like tea), the verb is singular to agree with "tea." In the sentence, *Mne nraviatsia apel'siny* (I like oranges), the verb is plural to agree with "oranges."

Exercise 9: Completing Sentences

Complete the sentences with reflexive verbs. Refer to the Table 8-2 for the list of reflexive verbs to choose from. Remember to put the verbs in the appropriate grammatical form.

1. *Chto* ....? (happened)

2. *Moj syn* .... *vzroslym.* (is becoming)

3. *Mne* ...., *chto Vy ne pravy.* (seems)

4. *Moskvichi* .... *svoim gorodom.* (are proud of)

5. *Tebe* .... *eto bliudo?* (like)

6. *Ia zametila, chto Vy vsegda* .... (smile)

7. *On* .... *vysoty i sobak.* (is afraid of)

8. *Oni liubiat* .... (to laugh)

Exercise 10: Our Family's Tastes

TRACK 50

Listen to the speaker. Rewrite the sentences, using the verb *nravit'sia* instead of the verb *liubit'*. Remember that the verb *nravit'sia* requires the use of the Dative case. You are already given the actual subjects of the sentences in the Dative case.

Example:
Speaker: *Muzh liubit rabotat'.*
Your answer: *Muzhu nravitsia rabotat'.*

1. *Mame* ....

2. *Pape* ....

....

3. *Babushke* ....

4. *Dedushke* ....

5. *Bratu* ....

....

6. *Sestre* ....

7. *Nam* ....

....

8. *Mne* ....

....

Review

In this section, practice using different types of reflexive verbs. If you face difficulties with a particular group of reflexive verbs, go back to the section devoted to that group and go over the exercises there.

Exercise 11: A Story about Dasha

Read the text. Then complete the sentences with reflexive verbs from the list. Remember to put the verbs in the appropriate grammatical form.

prosypat'sia, zakryvat'sia, vstrechat'sia, smeiat'sia, sobirat'sia, otkryvat'sia, nachinat'sia, ulybat'sia, umyvat'sia, nravit'sia, gordit'sia, nazyvat'sia

Dasha .... *v vosem utra. Ona vstaiot,*

.... *, i* .... *na rabotu. Dasha rabotaet*

v ofise, kotoryj .... *"Mechta." Ofis* ....

v desiat' utra, no dashina rabota .... *ran'she. Tse-*

lyj den' dver' v dashin cabinet ne .... *. Dasha*

.... *klientam i* .... *ikh shutkam. Dashe*

.... *eio rabota. Ona* .... *tem, chto klienty*

eio liubiat. Kogda ofis .... *v 6 chasov, Dasha idiot v kafe.*

Tam ona .... *s druz'iami.*

Exercise 12: Completing the Sentences

The sentences below are lacking verbs. Complete each sentence with an appropriate verb from the parenthesis.

1. *Gosti* .... *v bassejne. (kupat', kupat'sia)*

2. *My* .... *v kafe. (vstrechat', vstrechat'sia)*

3. *Dedushka* .... *vnuka. (odevat', odevat'sia)*

4. *Biblioteka* .... *v 8 vechera. (zakryvat', zakryvat'sia)*

5. *Uchitel'* .... *urok. (nachinat', nachinat'sia)*

6. *Turisty* .... *vo vremia poezdki. (poznakomit', poznakomit'sia)*

7. *Devushka* .... *okno. (otkryvat', otkryvat'sia)*

8. *Podruga* .... *menia izvestnomu pisateliu. (predstavit', predstavit'sia)*

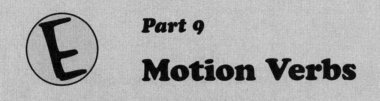

Part 9
Motion Verbs

The Russian language is especially rich in motion verbs. The single English verb "to go" can be translated into Russian by a dozen different motion verbs. In this part, you will practice using various motion verbs and distinguishing them from one another.

Moving on Foot Versus Moving by Vehicle

When it comes to Russian verbs, it makes a difference whether the subject is moving on foot or by a vehicle. In English, you can use the same verb "to go" to describe a car trip, a bus ride, or a walk. In Russian, you have to make a distinction.

When you talk about going somewhere by foot, use the imperfective verb *idti*.

Table 9-1

Conjugation of the imperfective motion verb *idti* (to go by foot) and its past tense forms	
Conjugation	**Translation**
ia idu	I go
ty idiosh'	you (singular, informal) go
on (ona, ono) idiot	he (she, it) goes
my idiom	we go
vy idiote	you (plural; formal) go
oni idut	they go
on shiol	he went
ona shla	she went
ono shlo	it went
oni shli	they went

The perfective form of the verb idti is *prijti* (to come by foot).

Table 9-2

Conjugation of the perfective motion verb *prijti* (to come by foot) and its past tense forms	
Conjugation	**Translation**
ia pridu	I will come
ty pridiosh'	you (singular, informal) will come
on (ona, ono) pridiot	he (she, it) will come
my pridiom	we will come
vy pridiote	you (plural; formal) will come
oni pridut	they will come
on prishiol	he came
ona prishla	she came
ono prishlo	it came
oni prishli	they came

When talking about going by vehicle—by car, by bus, by cab, or by train— use the imperfective verb *ekhat'*

Table 9-3

Conjugation of the imperfective motion verb *ekhat'* (to go by vehicle) and its past tense forms	
Conjugation	**Translation**
ia edu	I go
ty edesh'	you (singular, informal) go
on (ona, ono) edet	he (she, it) goes
my edem	we go
vy edete	you (plural; formal) go
oni edut	they go
on ekhal	he went

Table 9-3

Conjugation of the imperfective motion verb *ekhat'* (to go by vehicle) and its past tense forms	
ona ekhala	she went
ono ekhalo	it went
oni ekhali	they went

The perfective form of the verb *ekhat'* is *priekhat'* (to come be vehicle).

Table 9-4

Conjugation of the perf ective motion verb *priekhat'* (to come by vehicle) and its past tense forms	
Conjugation	**Translation**
ia priedu	I will come
ty priedesh'	you (singular, informal) will come
on (ona, ono) priedet	he (she, it) will come
my priedem	we will come
vy priedete	you (plural; formal) will come
oni priedut	they will come
on priekhal	he came
ona priekhala	she came
ono priekhalo	it came
oni priekhali	they came

Note that when talking about moving within the city limits, and when you don't want to specify how exactly you moved, you can always use the verbs *idti/prijti*, even if you travel by a vehicle. When talking about moving outside of the city limits, you always have to use the verbs *ekhat'/priekhat'*.

A common mistake is to use the verb *guliat'* (to take a walk) in the sense of "to walk." Please note that *guliat'* means "to take a walk for recreation," and cannot be used in a sentence such as "I walked to work." The best translation for this sentence would be *Ia shiol na rabotu peshkom.* (I went to work on foot.)

Exercise 1: Using the Verb idti

Complete each sentence with the correct form of the verb *idti*. Watch for the indicators of the past tense (such as the words "yesterday" or "last week") to know when to use the past tense verb form.

1. *Ia* .... *na rabotu.*

2. *Ia videla devushku, kotoraia* .... *po beregu moria.*

3. *Kuda vy* .... *?*

4. *Segodnia my* .... *v kino.*

5. *Vo skol'ko vy vchera* .... *na rabotu?*

6. *Lena* .... *v teatr.*

7. *Moi druz'ia* .... *na more.*

8. *Moj brat kupil apel'siny, kogda* .... *domoj.*

Exercise 2: Using the Verb prijti

Complete each sentence with the correct form of the verb *prijti*. Watch for the indicators of the past tense (such as the words "yesterday" or "last week") to know when to use the past tense verb forms.

1. *On* .... *vchera pozdno vecherom.*

2. *Zavtra my* .... *k vam v gosti.*

3. *V proshloe voskresen'e Lena* .... *domoj rano.*

4. *On* .... *v shest' chasov.*

5. *A kogda vy* .... *?*

6. *Ia segodnia ne* .... *na rabotu.*

7. *Vchera vrach ne* ....

8. *Moi druz'ia* .... *v kafe s opozdaniem.*

Exercise 3: Using the Verb ekhat'

Complete each sentence with the correct form of the verb *ekhat'*. Watch for the indicators of the past tense (such as the words "yesterday" or "last week") to know when to use the past tense verb forms.

1. *My* .... *na mashine.*

2. *Vchera my* .... *na avtobuse.*

3. *Misha* .... *v Moskvu.*

4. *Kuda vy* .... *v otpusk?*

5. *Ty tozhe* .... *na Kavkaz?*

6. *Moi roditeli* .... *vo Frantsiiu.*

7. *Zavtra ia* .... *v komandirovku.*

8. *Kogda vy* .... *domoj?*

Exercise 4: By Foot or by Vehicle?

Read the sentences and decide whether you need to use the verb *idti* or *ekhat'*. Then complete each sentence with the correct form of the verb.

1. *Misha* .... *na dachu.*

2. *Lena* .... *na rabotu peshkom.*

3. *My* .... *po parku.*

4. *Moi druz'ia* .... *otdykhat' na iug.*

5. *Segodnia vecherom ia* .... *v teatr.*

6. *Sejchas oni* .... *na metro.*

7. *My* .... *v kino.*

8. *Ty vsio eshchio* .... *na poezde?*

Exercise 5: Nonsense Sentences

These sentences don't make sense. Find out what's wrong with them and rewrite them using a different verb, so that the sentences make sense.

1. *Vika idiot v Moskvu.*

   ....

2. *Natasha edet peshkom.*

   ....

3. *My idiom na mashine.*

....

4. *Moj drug idiot v Chicago.*

....

5. *Vy idiote v otpusk na poezde ili na mashine?*

....

6. *Ia pojdu na taksi.*

....

Unidirectional and Multidirectional Verbs

In Russian, you have to use different verbs to describe unidirectional and multidirectional movement.

In the previous section, we discussed unidirectional verbs *idti* and *ekhat'*. These verbs are used when talking about one-way trips with a concrete destination, and trips still in progress. For example: *Kuda ty idiosh'?* (Where are you going?) – *Ia idu v magazin.* (I'm going to the store.)

In other situations, you need to use the multidirectional motion verbs: *khodit'* (to go by foot) and *ezdit'* (to go by vehicle). Use multidirectional verbs in the following situations.

1. To talk about a trip there and back in the past. *Ia khodila v magazin.* (I went to the store [and came back].)

2. To talk about repeated or regular trips. *Ia khozhu na rabotu peshkom.* (I walk to work.) *On khodit v teatr raz v nedeliu.* (He goes to the theater once a week.)

3. To talk about motion without concrete destination. *Ona ezdila po gorodu na mashine dva chasa.* (She drove around the city for two hours.)

When deciding whether to use a unidirectional or a multidirectional verb, watch for markers of repeated action, i.e., expressions such as *kazhdyj den'* (everyday) or *raz v mesiats* (once a month), and markers of duration, i.e., *dva dnia* (for two days), *desiat' let* (ten years).

Table 9-5

Conjugation of the multidirectional motion verb *khodit'* (to go by foot) and its past tense forms	
Conjugation	**Translation**
ia khozhu	I go
ty khodish'	you (singular, informal) go
on (ona, ono) khodit	he (she, it) goes
my khodim	we go
vy khodite	you (plural; formal) go
oni khodiat	they go
on khodil	he went
ona khodila	she went
ono khodilo	it went
oni khodili	they went

Table 9-6

Conjugation of the multidirectional motion verb *ezdit'* (to go by vehicle) and its past tense forms	
Conjugation	**Translation**
ia ezzhu	I go
ty ezdish'	you (singular, informal) go
on (ona, ono) ezdit	he (she, it) goes
my ezdim	we go
vy ezdite	you (plural; formal) go

Table 9-6

Conjugation of the multidirectional motion verb *ezdit'* (to go by vehicle) and its past tense forms	
oni ezdiat	they go
on ezdil	he went
ona ezdila	she went
ono ezdilo	it went
oni ezdili	they went

Exercise 6: Using the Verb khodit'

Complete each sentence with the correct form of the verb *khodit'*. Watch for the indicators of the past tense (such as the words for "yesterday" or "last week") to know when to use the past tense verb form.

1. *Moia doch'* .... *v shkolu.*

2. *My* .... *k nim v gosti kazhdyj den'.*

3. *Kuda Vy vchera* .... *?*

4. *Ia* .... *na balet.*

5. *Turisty* .... *po muzeiu tri chasa.*

6. *Moemu synu chetyrnadstsat' mesiatsev; on uzhe*
.... *.*

7. *Ty* .... *vchera na lektsiiu?*

8. *Lena* .... *po magazinam tselyj den'.*

Exercise 7: Using the Verb ezdit'

Complete each sentence with the correct form of the verb *ezdit'*. Watch for the indicators of the past tense (such as the words for "yesterday" or "last week") to know when to use the past tense verb form.

1. *Moj brat* .... *v Moskvy raz v mesiats.*

2. *Ia liubliu* .... *na poezde.*

3. *Kuda* .... *Lena v proshlom mesiatse?*

4. *Letom my* .... *na dachu.*

5. *Zimoj oni* .... *katat'sia na lyzhakh.*

6. *Ty chasto* .... *na Kavkaz?*

7. *Vy uzhe* .... *v otpusk v etom godu?*

8. *Studenty obychno* .... *na metro.*

Exercise 8: Completing Sentences

TRACK 51

Listen to the speaker read sentences with unidirectional verbs. Complete the sentences below, replacing unidirectional verbs with multidirectional ones so as to make them suitable to describe repeated actions.

Example:
Speaker: *Podrugi idut v kino.*
Your answer: *Podrugi **khodiat** v kino.*

1. *Lena* .... *v magazin.*

2. *Ia* .... *domoj.*

3. *Turisty* .... *v pokhod.*

4. *Vy* .... *na vecherinki?*

5. *My* .... *v gosti.*

6. *Ty* .... *na rabotu.*

7. *Anna* .... *v biblioteku.*

8. *Oni* .... *na kontsert.*

Exercise 9: Idti or khodit'?

Complete each sentence with either the verb *idti* or *khodit'*. Remember to put the verbs in the appropriate grammatical form.

1. *My* .... *na progulku kazhdyj den'.*

2. *Ia videla Ivana; on* .... *na rabotu.*

3. *My* .... *na futbol raz v mesiats.*

4. *Kuda ty sejchas* .... *?*

5. *Ia* .... *v etu shkolu tri goda.*

6. *On nervno* .... *po kvartire.*

7. *Vy* .... *peshkom ili edete na mashine?*

8. *Oni dolgo* .... *po parku.*

Exercise 10: **Ekhat' or ezdit'?**

Complete each sentence with either the verb *ekhat'* or *ezdit'*. Remember to put the verbs in the appropriate grammatical form.

1. *Kuda vy sejchas* .... ?

2. *Moi druz'ia skoro* .... *v otpusk.*

3. *Ona* .... *v London v proshlom godu.*

4. *Ia vstretila ego, kogda on* .... *v Moskvu.*

5. *Ona liubit* .... *po gorodu na mashine.*

6. *My vstretilis' v poezde; my oba* .... *v Budapesht.*

7. *My vsegda* .... *na metro.*

8. *Na rabotu ia* .... *na avtobuse.*

Other Modes of Transportation

In English, you can use the verb "to go" when you travel by car, by plane, or by boat. In Russian, however, you have to use different verbs to describe traveling by ground, by air, or by water.

When talking about going somewhere by ground transportation, use the verbs *ekhat'* (Table 9-3) and *ezdit'* (Table 9-6).

When talking about going by plane, use the unidirectional imperfective motion verb *letet'* (literally: to fly).

Table 9-7

Conjugation of the unidirectional motion verb *letet'* (to fly) and its past tense forms	
Conjugation	**Translation**
ia lechu	I fly
ty letish'	you (singular, informal) fly
on (ona, ono) letit	he (she, it) flies
my letim	we fly
vy letite	you (plural; formal) fly
oni letiat	they fly
on letel	he flew
ona lelela	she fllew
ono letelo	it flew
oni leteli	they flew

The perfective form of this verb is *priletet'* (to come by air). This verb conjugates like *letet'*. The multidirectional verb to use when talking about going by air is *letat'* (literally: to fly). This is a regular verb.

When talking about going by boat, use the unidirectional imperfective motion verb *plyt'* (literally: to swim, to float).

Table 9-8

Conjugation of the unidirectional motion verb *plyt'* (to swim, to float) and its past tense forms	
Conjugation	**Translation**
ia plyvu	I swim/float/go by boat
ty plyviosh'	you (singular, informal) swim/float/go by boat
on (ona, ono) plyviot	he (she, it) swims/floats/goes by boat
my plyviom	we swim/float/go by boat
vy plyviote	you (plural; formal) swim/float/go by boat
oni plyvut	they swim/float/go by boat
on plyl	he swam/floated/went by boat
ona plyla	she swam/floated/went by boat
ono plylo	it swam/floated/went by boat
oni plyli	they swam/floated/went by boat

The perfective form of this verb is *priplyt'*. This verb conjugates like *plyt'*. The multidirectional verb to use when talking about going by boat is, counterintuitively, *khodit'* (for the conjugation of this verb, see Table 9-5).

Exercise 11: By Ground, Air, or Water? (Unidirectional)

Complete each sentence with one of the unidirectional verbs: *ekhat'*, *letet'*, or *plyt'*. Remember to put the verbs in the appropriate grammatical form.

1. *Vy v pervyj raz* .... *po Volge?*

2. *On zavtra* .... *v Moskvu rejsom Aeroflota.*

3. *My poznakomilis', kogda* .... *na katere cherez bukhtu.*

4. *Ty* .... *na poezde ili* .... *na samoliote?*

5. *Etot parokhod* .... *v Turtsiiu.*

6. *Kuda* .... *etot avtobus?*

7. *Moia babushka v pervyj raz* .... *na samoliote, kogda ej bylo sem'desiat let.*

8. *Etot samoliot* .... *v London.*

Exercise 12: Ground, Air, or Water? (Multidirectional)

Complete each sentence with one of the unidirectional verbs: *ezdit'*, *letat'* or *khodit'*. Remember to put the verbs in the appropriate grammatical form.

1. *Etot parokhod* .... *po Missisipi.*

2. *On ne liubit* .... *na metro.*

3. *Dasha vsegda* .... *v komandirovku na samoliote.*

4. *Kater "Kometa"* .... *iz Novorossijska v Odessu kazhdye dva chasa.*

5. *Etot kruiznyj lajner* .... *na Bagamskie ostrova.*

6. *Kuda ty obychno* .... *v otpusk?*

7. *Ia vsegda* .... *na avtobuse.*

8. *Vy chasto* .... *na samoliote?*

Moving Objects

When talking about moving objects in Russian, you have to specify whether the object is carried or moved by vehicle. If the object is carried, use the unidirectional verb *nesti* (to carry/move manually) or a multidirectional verb *nosit'* (to carry/move manually). If the object is moved by a vehicle, use a unidirectional verb *vezti* (to move by vehicle) or a multidirectional verb *vozit'* (to move by vehicle).

Exercise 13: Moving Things

Choose the best motion verb to complete each sentence. Remember to put the verbs in the appropriate grammatical form.

1. *Sestra* .... *mne podarok iz Moskvy.*

2. *Ia* .... *etu sumku uzhe dva goda.*

3. *Ona* .... *stakan s vodoj i uronila ego.*

4. *My* .... *gostej po gorodu.*

5. *Nash parokhod* .... *banany v Rossiiu uzhe desiat' let.*

6. *Kuda ty* .... *etu knigu?*

7. *On vsegda* .... *syna v shkoly na mashine.*

8. *On* .... *buket tsvetov domoj, dlia svoej zheny; segodnia u nikh iubilej.*

Exercise 14: Nonsense Sentences

These sentences don't make sense. Find out what's wrong with them and rewrite them using a different verb, so that the sentences make sense.

1. *Molodoj chelovek nesiot roial' po gorodu.*

   ....

2. *Zavtra ia nesu syna v Moskvu.*

   ....

3. *Mashina nesiot kartofel' i pomidory.*

   ....

4. *Natasha veziot chashku chaia po komnate.*

   ....

5. *Ty vsegda vozish' etu sumku?*

   ....

6. *Devochka veziot koshku na rukakh.*

   ....

7. *Korabl' nesiot tabak v Evropu.*

   ....

8. *My tri chasa nosili babushku po gorodu.*

   ....

Prefixed Motion Verbs

All the motion verbs discussed in the previous sections can be used with prefixes.

Table 9-9

Prefix	Its meaning	Example	Translation
pri-	to	*priletat'*	to arrive by plane
v-	in(to)	*vkhodit'*	to enter
pod-	up to	*podplyt'*	to approach by boat
do-	"reaching"	*doletet'*	to reach by plane
u-	from	*uezzhat'*	to leave by vehicle
vy-	out of	*vykhodit'*	to walk out of
ot-	away from	*otplyt'*	to move away from by boat
pere-	across	*pereletat'*	to fly across
pro-	through or by	*prokhodit'*	to walk through or to walk by
s-	down from	*skhodit'*	to walk down from

Exercise 15: Which Prefix?

Complete each sentence with the best verb in parenthesis. Remember to put the verbs in the appropriate grammatical form.

1. *My* .... *cherez dorogu. (perekhodit', vkhodit')*

2. *Poezd* .... *k Moskve. (pod"ezzhat', uezzhat')*

3. *Samoliot* .... *v vosem' chasov. (pereletat', priletat')*

4. *Zavtra Lena* .... *v Moskvu. (proezzhat', uezzhat')*

5. *Kater* .... *cherez reku. (pereplyt', doplyt')*

6. *Nash parokhod* .... *k Odesse. (podplyt', pereplyt')*

7. *Turisty* .... *v tserkov'. (dokhodit', vkhodit')*

8. *Avtobus* .... *ot ostanovki. (pod"ezzhat', ot"ezzhat')*

Exercise 16: Translating Phrases

Translate the following phrases into English, paying special attention to the motion verbs prefixes. The first phrase has been translated for you.

1. *pod"ezzhat' k gorodu*
   to approach the city by vehicle

2. *uletat' iz Moskvy*

   ....

3. *podplyt' k portu*

   ....

4. *perekhodit' cherez ploshchad'*

   ....

5. *proezzhat' mimo parka*

   ....

6. *prokhodit' cherez tunnel'*

....

7. *vyezzhat' iz goroda*

....

8. *vykhodit' iz komnaty*

....

Review

In this section, practice using different types of motion verbs. If you face difficulties with a particular type of motion verb, go back to the section devoted to this type and go over the exercises there.

Exercise 17: A Story about Dasha

Read the text. Then complete each sentence with an appropriate motion verb from the list. Remember to put the verbs in the correct grammatical form. You can use the same verb twice.

pereezzhat', vykhodit, vkhodit', perekhodit', priezzhat', ekhat', otkhodit', proezzhat', podkhodit', pod"ezzhat', prikhodit', idti

Dasha .... iz doma v deviat utra. Ona

.... na rabotu. Dasha .... cherez

dorogu, ... mimo tserkvi, i .... k

avtobusnoj ostanovke. Avtobus obychno .... v 9.15.

Dasha saditsia na avtobus i .... na rabotu. Avtobus

.... po glavnoj ulitse, ... mimo teatra, i .... reku po mostu. Kogda avtobus ....

k dashinoj ostanovke, Dasha .... iz avtobusa i

.... v svoj ofis. Dasha .... na rabotu

v 9.45. Ona .... v svoj ofis i srazu ....

k stolu svoej podrugi Natashi. Oni razgovarivaiut minut piatnadstat',

potom Dasha .... ot eio stola, i nachinaet rabotat'.

Exercise 18: What Kind of Motion?

TRACK 52

The sentences below are lacking motion verbs. Listen to the speaker and complete the sentences with motion verbs. Then identify them as either MF (motion on foot) or MV (motion by vehicle).

Example:
Speaker: *My idiom po gorodu.*
Your answer: *My idiom po gorodu. – MF*

1. My .... v Moskvu. ....

2. Devushka .... cherez dorogu. ....

3. V zoopark .... slona. ....

4. Ofitsiant .... kofe. ....

5. My .... na novuiu kvartiru. ....

6. Ia .... po parku. ....

7. Ona .... na dachu. ....

8. On .... na rabotu. ....

Part 10

Conditional, Subjunctive, Imperative

In this part, you will practice using different verbal moods: conditional, subjunctive, and imperative. This will provide you with the grammatical knowledge to give commands, make requests, discuss conditions, and talk about your wishes.

Conditional

When talking about an action that depends on a certain condition, use the conditional mood: *Esli zavtra pojdiot dozhd', my ostanemsia doma.* (If it rains tomorrow, we'll stay at home.)

In Russian, both parts of the sentences in the conditional mood have to be in real time. If you are talking about a condition that will take place in the future, you need to use the future tense in both parts of the sentence: *Esli ona budet doma, my budem rabotat'.* (If she is at home, we'll work.) Note that in English, the first part of the sentence is in the present tense. You have to remember to use real time when using the conditional mood in Russian.

Exercise 1: Writing Conditional Sentences

Combine the phrases to form a sentence in the conditional mood. The first sentence has been done for you.

1. *ty: dostat' bilety / my: pojti na prem'eru spektaklia*
   Esli ty dostanesh' bilety, my pojdiom na prem'eru spektaklia.

2. *zavtra solnechnyj den' / my: skhodit' na pliazh*

   ....

3. *zavtra khoroshij sneg / oni: pojti na lyzhnuiu progulku.*

   ....

4. *khoroshaia komanda: sobrat'sia / my: pojti v turpokhod*

   ....

5. *zavtra nastroenie / ia: spech' pirog*

   ....

6. *ty: prigotovit' uroki / ty: pojti guliat'*

    ....

7. *ty: khorosho sebia vesti / ia: podarit' tebe sobaku*

    ....

8. *vy: zanimat'sia sportom / vy: byt' zdorovym*

    ....

Exercise 2: Making Plans

TRACK 53

Listen to the speaker read the text. Then answer the questions.

1. *Chto ia budu delat', esli priedet Lena?*

    ....

2. *Chto ia budu delat', esli Lena ne priedet?*

    ....

3. *Chto ia budu delat', esli Leny ne budet doma?*

    ....

4. *Chto ia budu delat', esli Leny ne budet na rabote?*

    ....

5. *Chto ia budu delat', esli budet teplo?*

    ....

6. *Chto ia budu delat', esli budet zharko?*

....

7. *Chto ia budu delat', esli budet kholodno?*

....

8. *Chto ia budu delat', esli budet idti dozhd'?*

....

Subjunctive

When talking about hypothetical or unreal situations, you need to use the subjunctive mood. The Russian subjunctive mood is very easy to form: put both verbs in the past tense, and add the particle *by* to both parts of the sentences. For instance: *Esli by ia byl Nobelem, ia by ne izobriol dinamit.* (If I had been Nobel, I wouldn't have invented dynamite.)

Exercise 3: Writing Subjunctive Sentences

Combine the phrases to form a sentence in the subjunctive mood. The first sentence has been done for you.

1. *ia – kosmonavt / poletet' na Mars*
   Esli by ia byl kosmonavtom, ia by poletel na Mars.

2. *ia – millioner / kupit' ostrov v Karibskom more*

....

3. *ia – ptitsa / poletet' v tioplye kraia*

....

4. *u neio vozmozhnost'/ prijti*

....

5. *u menia vremia / izuchit' vse iazyki mira*

....

6. *u menia talant / stat' znamenitoj pevitsej*

....

7. *u nikh mashina / priekhat'*

....

8. *u nas iakhta / priglasit' vsekh druzej v gosti*

....

Exercise 4: Changing the Mood

The following sentences are in the conditional mood. Rewrite them in the subjunctive mood. The first sentence has been done for you.

1. *Esli on pozvonit, my emu rasskazhem.*
   Esli by on pozvonil, my by emu rasskazali.

2. *Esli Olga prijdiot, ia otdam ej knigu.*

....

3. *Esli prijdut klienty, ia pokazhu im kvartiru.*

....

4. *Esli turisty priedut, u turagenta budet rabota.*

....

5. *Esli u menia budet vremia, ia napishu tebe.*

....

6. *Esli u nikh budet zhelanie, oni tebe pomogut.*

....

7. *Esli ty vstretish' brata, vy pojdiote v kino.*

....

8. *Esli ia posmotriu etot fil'm, to ia tebe pozvoniu.*

....

Imperative

Use imperative mood to give commands or make requests. Remember to add *-te* at the end of the imperative if you are addressing a group of people or someone with whom you are on formal terms. For instance, when addressing a person with whom you are on familiar terms, you can say *chitaj* (Read!). However, when addressing a group of people or someone with whom you are on formal terms, you need to say *chitajte!*

Exercise 5: Forming Imperatives

Form imperative forms from the following verbs. Use the singular / informal imperative form.

1. *smotret'* ....

2. *igrat'* ....

3. *lovit'* ....

4. *derzhat'* ....

5. *pomnit'* ....

6. *bezhat'* ....

7. *nesti* ....

8. *varit'* ....

Exercise 6: Giving Commands

TRACK 54

Listen to the speaker read phrases with infinitives. Form imperatives from these infinitives, and write down the phrases with the imperatives. Form formal imperatives, e.g., *smotrite*.

Example:
Speaker: *slushat' radio*
Your answer: *Slushajte radio.*

1. ....

2. ....

3. ....

4. ....

5. ....

6. ....

7. ....

8. ....

Exercise 7: Making Requests

Complete each sentence with the imperative of the verb in parenthesis. Use the plural/formal imperative form.

1. .... *pal'to. (podat')*

2. .... *zakaz. (vziat')*

3. .... *privet. (peredat')*

4. .... *vperiod. (prokhodit')*

5. .... *dver'. (zakryt')*

6. .... *rabotat'. (nachinat')*

7. .... *strizhku. (sdelat')*

8. .... *pis'mo. (napisat')*

Review

In this section, practice using verbs in conditional, subjunctive, and imperative moods. If you face any difficulties, go back to the section devoted to the type of the mood you are having difficulties with and go over the exercises there.

Exercise 8: Reading Chekhov

These sentences are from the short story *Dama s sobachkoj* ("Lady With a Lapdog") by Anton Chekhov. Translate the sentences into English, paying special attention to the verbs in conditional, subjunctive, and imperative mood.

1. *- Perestan', moia khoroshaia, - govoril on.*

   ....

2. *Esli ona zdes' bez muzha i bez znakomykj ... to bylo by ne lishnee poznakomit'sia s nej.*

   ....

3. *Esli by ne sliozy na glazakh, to mozhno bylo by podumat', chto ona shutit ili igraet rol'.*

   ....

4. *Esli zhe poslat' zapisku, to ona, pozhaluj, popadiot v ruki muzhu.*

   ....

5. *Esli by Vy znali, s kakoj ocharovatel'noj zhenshchinoj ia poznakomilsia v Ialte!*

   ....

6. *Ver'te, ver'te mne, umoliaiu Vas...*

   ....

Exercise 9: A Story about Dasha

Read the text and complete the sentences with the verbs in parentheses. Remember to put the verbs in the appropriate grammatical form.

Odnazhdy, kogda Dasha guliala po parku, k nej podoshiol molodoj che-

lovek i skazal chto-to po-ital'ianski. "Esli by ia .... *(znat')*

ital'ianskij iazyk, to ia .... *(otvetit') by," podumala Dahsa.*

"Esli Vy .... *(govorit') po-russki, to my* ....

(moch') pogovorit'," skazala Dasha. Molodoj chelovek otvetil po-russki:

" .... *(skazat') mne, pozhalujsta, chto mozhno posmotret'*

v etom gorode?" Dasha podumala i otvetila: "Esli Vy ....

(liubit') prirodu, to .... *(idti) k moriu. Esli Vam*

.... *(nravit'sia) istoriia, to* .... *(pojti) v*

muzej. Esli Vy .... *(khotet') poznakomit'sia s mestnymi*

zhiteliami, to .... *(otpravliat'sia) v kafe. Esli by u menia*

.... *(byt') vremia, to ia* .... *(pojti) by s*

Vami."

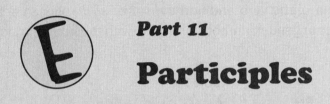

Part 11

Participles

Participles are derived from verbs. Adjectival participles modify nouns and adverbial participles modify verbs. Participles aren't very common in conversational Russian, but are widely used in formal writing. In this part, you will practice producing and using all the various types of participles.

Active Adjectival Participles

Active adjectival participles modify nouns. They are adjectives made from the verbs that describe the action of the subject in the sentence. The present active participle describes action carried out in the present. The past active participle describes action that was carried out in the past.

To form the present active participle, remove the final -t from the third person plural form of the verb and add the suffix -shch- plus an adjective ending that agrees in gender, number, and case with the noun it modifies.

Table 11-1

Present active participle endings			
Gender and number form	**Ending**	**Example**	**Translation**
Masculine sing·	-ij	tantsuiushchij	dancing
Feminine sing·	-aia	zhivushchaia	living
Neuter sing·	-ee	skripiashchee	creaking
Plural	-ie	begushchie	running

To form the active past participle, add the suffix -vsh- to the verbal stem, and then add an adjective ending depending on the gender and number of the noun the participle modifies.

Table 11-2

Past active participle endings			
Gender and number form	**Ending**	**Example**	**Translation**
Masculine sing·	-ij	tantsevavshij	one who had danced
Feminine sing·	-aia	zhivshaia	one who had lived
Neuter sing·	-ee	skripevshee	one that creacked
Plural	-ie	bezhavshie	one that ran

Exercise 1: Forming Active Present Participles

Use the verbs and nouns to form present active participles phrases. Remember to agree each participle with the gender and number of the noun. The first phrase has been done for you.

1. *govorit' / popugai*
   govoriashchie popugai

2. *sidet' / muzhchina*

   ....

3. *rabotat' / zhenshchina*

   ....

4. *idti / avtobus*

   ....

5. *goret' / kostior*

   ....

6. *pit' / zhivotnye*

   ....

7. *shumet' / more*

   ....

8. *igrat' / deti*

   ....

Exercise 2: Forming Active Past Participles

Use the verbs and nouns to form active past participles phrases. Remember to agree each participle with the gender and number of the noun. The first phrase has been done for you.

1. *zhit' / chelovek*
   zhivshij chelovek

2. *lezhat' / sobaka*

   ....

3. *guliat' / koshka*

   ....

4. *rabotat' / drug*

   ....

5. *pisat' / uchenitsa*

   ....

6. *spat' / turist*

   ....

7. *risovat' / studenty*

   ....

8. *letet' / ptitsa*

   ....

Passive Adjectival Participles

Passive adjectival participles modify nouns. They are produced from the verbs naming the action applied onto the noun. The present passive adjectival participles can be produced from imperfective verbs only. The past passive adjectival participles are produced from both perfective and imperfective verbs.

To form the present passive adjectival participles, add an adjective ending to the first person plural form of the verb. The participle agrees in gender and number with the noun it modifies.

Table 11-3

Present passive participle endings			
Gender and number form	**Ending**	**Example**	**Translation**
Masculine sing·	‑yj	*liubimyj*	one that is being loved
Feminine sing·	‑aia	*chitaemaia*	one that is being read
Neuter sing·	‑oe	*preziraemoe*	one that is being despised
Plural	‑ye	*gonimye*	ones that are being shunned

To form the past passive participle, add one of these suffixes— -n-, -nn-, -ion-, or -t- —to the verbal stem, and then add an adjective ending depending on the gender and number of the noun it modifies.

Table 11-4

Past passive participle endings			
Gender and number form	**Ending**	**Example**	**Translation**
Masculine sing·	⁻yj	*sdelannyj*	one that has been done
Feminine sing·	⁻aia	*s"edennaia*	one that has been eaten
Neuter sing·	⁻oe	*nevidannoe*	unique (literally: one that has not been seen)
Plural	⁻ye	*zapertye*	ones that have been locked

Exercise 3: Forming Present Passive Participles

Use the verbs and nouns to form present passive participle phrases. Remember that each participle has to agree with the noun in gender and in number. The first phrase has been done for you.

1. *opisyvat' / situatsiia*
   opisyvaemaia situatsiia

2. *trebovat' / summa*

   ....

3. *proizvodit' / tovar*

   ....

4. *chitat' / avtory*

   ....

5. *publikovat' / poet*

....

6. *terpet' / usloviia*

....

7. *proiznosit' / soglasnye*

....

8. *liubit' / skazka*

....

Exercise 4: Forming Past Passive Participles

Use the verbs and nouns to form past passive participle phrases. Remember that each participle has to agree with the noun in gender and in number. The first phrase has been done for you.

1. *proizvesti / vpechatlenie*
   proizvedionnoe vpechatlenie

2. *opisat' / pejzazh*

....

3. *ozabotit' / chelovek*

....

4. *narisovat' / luna*

....

5. *napisat' / stikhi*

....

6. *prigotovit' / uzhin*

....

7. *postelit' / postel'*

....

8. *ispech' / pirogi*

....

Adverbial Participles

Adverbial participles modify verbs. They are produced from the verbs naming the secondary action performed by the actor of the main verb of the sentence.

The present adverbial participle indicates an action performed simultaneously with the main action of the sentence. For example, *Ona ulyba-las', gliadia na menia* (She smiled while looking at me). To form the present adverbial participles, add *-ia* to the verbal stem: *rabotat'* (to work) – *rabotaia* (while working).

The past adverbial participle is formed by adding the suffix *-v-* to the verbal stem: *uvidet'* (to see) – *uvidev* (having seen).

Exercise 5: Forming Present Adverbial Participles

Use the verbs to form present adverbial participles. The first task has been done for you.

1. *idti*   *idia* ....

2. *rabotat'*   ....

3. *smotret'*   ....

4. *ulybat'sia*   ....

5. *risovat'*   ....

6. *delat'*   ....

7. *guliat'*   ....

8. *sidet'*   ....

Exercise 6: Forming Past Adverbial Participles

Use the verbs to form past adverbial participles. The first task has been done for you.

1. *uznat'*   *uznav* ....

2. *napisat'*   ....

3. *posmotret'*   ....

4. *uvidet'*   ....

5. *porvat'*   ....

6. *sdat'* ....

7. *postupit'* ....

8. *podarit'* ....

Review

In this section, practice using different types of participles. If you face diffi-culties with a particular type of participle, go back to the section devoted to this type, and go over the exercises there.

Exercise 7: Rewriting Sentences

Rewrite the sentences, replacing "*kotoryj*" clauses with participles. If the "*kotoryj*" clause is in the present tense, use a present active adjectival parti-ciple. If the "*kotoryj*" clause is in the past tense, use a past active adjectival participle. Remember to put the participles in the correct grammatical form. The first sentence has been done for you.

1. *Eto devushka, kotoraia zhiviot v nashem dome.*
   Eto devushka, zhivushchaia v nashem dome.

2. *Po ulitse idiot professor, kotoryj rabotaet v moiom universitete.*

   ....

3. *My razgovarivali s muzhchinoj, kotoryj prochital etot roman.*

   ....

4. *Na terrase sidel mal'chik, kotoryj napisal pis'mo.*

   ....

5. *Na stsene stoiala zhenshchina, kotoraia poiot romansy.*

....

6. *My vstretili devushku, kotoraia govorila po telefonu.*

....

7. *On smotrit serial, kotoryj idiot po televizoru.*

....

8. *U dveri stoial student, kotoryj sdal ekzamen.*

....

Exercise 8: Completing Sentences

Complete each sentence with a present passive adjectival participle or with a past passive adjectival participle using the verb in parenthesis. Remember to put each participle in the appropriate grammatical form.

1. *Eto* .... *(liubit') mnogimi kniga.* (present passive adjectival participle)

2. *Zhara v etom godu dovol'no* .... *(terpet').* (present passive adjectival participle)

3. *Ona sozhgla vse* .... *(poluchit') pis'ma.* (past passive adjectival participle)

4. *Vam udalos' dostignut'* .... *(zhelat') rezul'tata?* (present passive adjectival participle)

5. *V kamorke papy Karlo byl* .... *(narisovat') ochag.* (past passive adjectival participle)

6. *Nado priznavat'* .... *(sdelat') oshibki.* (past passive adjectival participle)

7. *Eto postupok,* .... *(karat') zakonom.* (present passive adjectival participle)

8. *On rasskazal militsii ob* .... *(uvidet') proisshestvii.* (past passive adjectival participle)

Exercise 9: Practicing Adverbial Participles

Complete each sentence with either a present adverbial participle or a past adverbial participles using the verb in parentheses.

1. *On pel,* .... *(shagat') po ulitse.* (present adverbial participle).

2. .... *(uvidet') druga, on ostanovil mashinu.* (past adverbial participle)

3. *Ona zadumalas',* .... *(chitat') knigu.* (present adverbial participle)

4. *On chital,* .... *(sidet') na skamejke.* (present adverbial participle)

5. .... *(ubrat') so stola, on liog spat'.* (past adverbial participle)

6. .... *(zakonchit') rabotu, Lena poshla domoj.* (past adverbial participle)

7. *On smotrel televizor,* .... *(lezhat') na divane.* (present adverbial participle)

8. .... *(uslyshat') novost', ona srazu priekhala.* (past adverbial participle)

Part 12

Prepositions and Conjunctions

Prepositions and conjunctions are the small words that always pose difficulties for students of foreign languages. Neither Russian prepositions nor Russian conjunctions translate literally into English. Prepositions and conjunctions have to be practiced in context because their choice is often connected to the choice of the verb and to the case of connected nouns.

Prepositions of Place

Prepositions of place help describe location of people and things. Each Russian preposition requires a specific case. Some prepositions can be used with more than one case. Such prepositions have slightly different meanings when used with different cases.

E.g., when one of the most frequently used Russian preposition *v* is used with the Prepositional case, it means "in" or "at." However, when it is used with the Accusative case, it means "into" or "to" (when the object is in motion). Compare the use of *v* in the following two sentences: *Ia zanimaius' v biblioteke.* (I am studying at the library.) *Ia idu v biblioteku.* (I am going to the library.) The same rule applies to the preposition *na* (on, onto, to).

Exercise 1: Where Is the Butterfly?

Imagine that you are trying to catch a butterfly that is flying around your desk. Your friend is observing your attempts, and giving you updates on where the butterfly is. Complete the sentences, using the appropriate prepositions and putting the word *stol* (desk) in the appropriate case.

1. *Babochka* .... (on the desk)

2. *Babochka* .... (under the desk)

3. *Babochka* .... (inside the desk)

4. *Babochka* .... (above the desk)

5. *Babochka* .... (by the desk)

6. *Babochka* .... (behind the desk)

7. *Babochka* .... (in front of the desk)

8. *Babochka letaet* .... (around the desk)

Exercise 2: Where Is It Located?

Translate each phrase, using the Russian noun in parenthesis. Remember to put the nouns in the appropriate case.

1. in the city *(gorod)* ....

2. next to the monument *(pamiatnik)* ....

3. above the bed *(krovat')* ....

4. under ground *(zemlia)* ....

5. across the street *(doroga)* ....

6. from Europe *(Evropa)* ....

7. behind the wall *(stena)* ....

8. in front of the theater *(teatr)* ....

Exercise 3: V or na?

Complete each sentence with the preposition *v* or *na*.

1. *Ona idiot* .... *rabotu.*

2. *My pojdiom* .... *stadion.*

3. *Gorod Novorossijsk nakhoditsia* .... *iuge Rossii.*

4. *Oni idut* .... *teatr.*

5. *Davaj poedem* .... *Parizh.*

6. *Ia khochu pojti* .... *ital'ianskij restoran.*

7. *Oni vstretilis'* .... *ulitse.*

8. *Ty poedesh'* .... *kino* ....
avtobuse ili .... *taksi?*

Exercise 4: Prepositional or Accusative?

Read the sentences with the prepositions *v* and *na*. Depending on whether the subject of the sentence is stationary or still in motion, complete the sentences with the nouns in either Prepositional or Accusative case.

1. *Moia doch' uchitsia v* .... *(shkola)*

2. *Ty provodish' slishkom mnogo vremeni na* ....
(rabota)

3. *Davaj poedem na* .... *(sever)*

4. *Lena ushla v* .... *(magazin)*

5. *My idiom v* .... *(park)*

6. *Turisty zhivut v* .... *(gostinitse)*

7. *Moj brat rabotaet v* .... *(ofis)*

8. *Davajte zajdiom v* .... *(komnata)*

Prepositions of Time

In English, expressions of time are sometimes used without prepositions: "this week," "last month." In Russian, however, expressions of time always include a preposition. Different units of time are put in different cases after prepositions.

Table 12-1

Use of time units with prepositions				
Time unit	Preposition	Case	Example	Translation
minute	*v*	Accusative	*v tu zhe minutu*	at the same very moment
hour	*v*	Accusative	*v piat' chasov*	at five o'clock
day of the week	*v*	Accusative	*v ponedel'nik*	on Monday
week	*na*	Prepositional	*na etoj nedele*	this week
month	*v*	Prepositional	*v ianvare*	in January
year	*v*	Prepositional	*v proshlom godu*	last year
century	*v*	Prepositional	*v dvadtsatom veke*	in the twentieth century

Exercise 5: When Did It Happen?

Translate each phrase, using the Russian noun in parenthesis. Remember to put each noun in the appropriate case.

1. before dinner *(obed)* ....

2. after the performance *(spektakl')* ....

    ....

3. from morning till evening *(utro, vecher)* ....

    ....

4. until Friday *(piatnitsa)* ....

5. a month ago *(mesiats)* ....

6. during the lecture *(lektsiia)* ....

....

7. in two years *(goda)* ....

....

8. after the wedding *(svad'ba)* ....

....

Exercise 6: Saying "When"

Complete the sentences, using the phrases given in parentheses.

1. .... *my khodili*

v pokhod. (last week)

2. ....

.... *v dver' postuchali.* (at the same very moment)

3. *Poet Pushkin rodilsia* ....

................................, *a pisat' nachal* ....

.... (18th century, 19th century)

4. *On pozvonil* .... (at

2:00)

5. .... *u nas budet piknik.* (on Wednes-

day)

6. *Liudi nachinaiut kupat'sia v Chiornom more* ....

.... (in June)

7. .... *my budem izu-chat' glagoly.* (next week)

8. .... *v Rossii otmechaiut Den' Pobedy.* (in May)

Other Prepositions

In this section, practice using miscellaneous Russian prepositions.

Exercise 7: Finding the Equivalent

Each of the following words and expressions can be translated into Russian by a preposition. Write down these prepositions.

1. without ....

2. for ....

3. except ....

4. during the reign of ....

5. opposed to ....

6. in the presence of ....

7. about (in the meaning of "concerning") ....

8. in support of ....

Exercise 8: Giving Details

Translate each phrase, using the Russian noun in parentheses. Remember to put each noun in the appropriate case.

1. except for math *(matematika)* ....

2. during the reign of socialism *(sotsializm)* ....

3. in support of peace *(mir)* ....

4. against the war *(vojna)* ....

5. in the presence of children *(deti)* ....

6. about love *(liubov')* ....

7. for Mother *(mat')* ....

8. without shame *(styd)* ....

Exercise 9: Completing Sentences

Use the phrases in parentheses to complete the sentences.

1. *On poekhal otdykhat' odin,* ....
   (without friends)

2. *Ona pozvonila materi* .... (in my presence)

3. *U menia* .... *est' podarok.* (for you)

4. *Ia* .... (against smoking)

5. *Ia liubliu vsekh russkikh pisatelej, ...*
   (except for Tolstoj).

6. *Davajte pogovorim ....* (about politics)

7. *Ia ....* (in support of equality)

8. *......................... , kazhdyj den' byl prazdnikom.*
   (for him)

Prepositional Phrases

While such words as *v, na, za,* or *dlia* are easily identified as prepositions, some longer constructions, known as prepositional phrases, are less obvious. Often, they are very similar to non-prepositional phrases from which they have been derived. Thus, the prepositional phrase *v techenie* (during) is very similar to the expressions *v techenii* (in the current).

Table 12-2

Most common Russian prepositional phrases	
Prepositional phrase	**Translation**
v techenie	during
nedaleko ot	near
nesmotria na	despite
v sled za	following
v vide	as (in a shape of, acting as)
v silu	because of
v sviazi s	because of, in connection to
v zakliuchenie	in conclusion
vo izbezhanie	in order to avoid
za iskliucheniem	except

Exercise 10: Completing Phrases

Complete each phrase with the word in parenthesis. Remember to put the noun in the appropriate case. Then translate the phrases.

1. *nesmotria na* .... *(dozhd')*

_____

2. *v zakliuchenie* .... *(seminar)*

_____

3. *v sviazi s* .... *(pogoda)*

_____

4. *vo izbezhanie* .... *(neschastnyj sluchaj)*

_____

5. *v silu* .... *(prikaz)*

_____

6. *v sled za* .... *(proisshestvie)*

_____

7. *nedaleko ot* .... *(teatr)*

_____

8. *nesmotria na* .... *(slaboe zdorov'e)*

_____

Exercise 11: Completing Sentences

Complete each sentence with one of the prepositional phrases from the list.

nesmotria na, v zakliuchenie, v sviazi s, vo izbezhanie, v techenie, za iskliucheniem, v sled za, nedaleko ot

1. *Moia kvartira nakhoditsia* .... *universiteta.*

2. .... *pozhara, ne kurite v posteli.*

3. .... *chasa on vstaval, sadilsia, i snova vstaval.*

4. .... *zharu, oni poshli v pokhod.*

5. .... *svoej rechi dokladchik poblagodaril slushateley za vnimanie.*

6. .... *vojnoj nachalsia golod.*

7. .... *Leny, vsem fil'm ponravilsia.*

8. .... *remontom, biblioteka zakryta.*

Coordinating Conjunctions

Conjunctions are small function words that connect various parts of a sentence. Coordinating conjunctions join two independent clauses.

Table 12-3

Most common Russian coordinating conjunctions	
Coordinating conjunction	**Translation**
i	and
a	but
no	but
i ... i	both ... and
ni ... ni	neither ... nor
to ... to	first ... then

Russian has two conjunctions that correspond to the English "but:" *a* and *no*. When two clauses of a sentence deal with analogous pieces of information, *a* is used: *Ona khotela pojti v pokhod, a poshla v biblioteku.* (She wanted to go hiking, but went to the library.) Both clauses deal with analogous pieces of information: an activity. The coordinating conjunction *no* is used when two clauses deal with non-analogous pieces of information: *Ona khotela pojti v pokhod, no poshiol dozhd'.* (She wanted to go hiking, but it started to rain.) Here, the first clause deals with an activity, but the second clause deals with the weather conditions. These pieces of information are non-analogous; that is why the conjunction *no* has to be used.

The coordinating conjunction *a* is sometimes translated into English as "and:" *Ona khotela pojti v pokhod, a on khotel pojti v kino.* (She wanted to go hiking, and he wanted to go to the movies.)

Exercise 12: Joining Clauses

Combine the two sentences into one, using coordinating conjunctions. Write down each new sentence.

1. *Lena rabotaet v teatre. Misha rabotaet v teatre.*

   ....

2. *Lena rabotaet v teatre. Misha rabotaet v ofise.*

   ....

3. *Lena rabotaet v teatre. Lena sobiraetsia uvol'niat'sia.*

   ....

4. *Lena ne rabotaet v teatre. Misha ne rabotaet v teatre.*

   ....

5. *Lena rabotala v teatre. Potom Lena rabotala v ofise. Potom Lena opiat' rabotala v teatre.*

   ....

6. *Lena rabotaet v teatre. Ona ne aktrisa.*

   ....

7. *Lena rabotaet v teatre. Misha ne rabotaet.*

   ....

8. *Lena rabotaet v teatre. Lena rabotaet v ofise.*

   ....

Exercise 13: Composing Sentences

Use appropriate coordinating conjunctions and the words given to write sentences.

1. *Olia, Andrej, ne govoriat, po-ital'ianski*

   ....

2. *Mama, papa, rabotaiut, v bol'nitse*

   ....

3. *Brat, uchitsia, v universitete, sestra, v shkole*

   ....

4. *Ia, prishiol, na kontsert, zabyl, bilet*

   ....

5. *Turisty, poekhali, v gostinitsu, gid, domoj*

   ....

6. *Mersedes, kadillak, khoroshie, mashiny*

   ....

7. *U nikh, net, faksa, kseroksa*

   ....

8. *On, igraet, na skripke, na pianino*

   ....

Exercise 14: Translating into Russian

Translate the sentences into Russian, using coordinating conjunctions.

1. Both Natasha and Dania work here.

   ....

2. Neither Vera, nor Boris knows the answer.

   ....

3. Mama is sleeping and papa is working.

   ....

4. Neither he nor she read this book.

   ....

5. Tourists came to the museum, but the museum was closed.

   ....

6. He's lived both in Moscow and in Saint Petersburg.

   ....

7. She's been neither to England nor to France.

   ....

8. She usually goes to London, but she likes Paris better.

   ....

Subordinating Conjunctions

Subordinating conjunctions connect two clauses, one of which is dependent on the other. Subordinate clauses include those of (a) causation: *Ia prishla, potomu chto ia poluchila tvoio pis'mo* (I came because I received your letter); (b) purpose: *Ia prishla, chtoby pogovorit'* (I came in order to talk); or (c) condition: *Ia pridu, esli ty pozvonish'* (I'll come if you call).

Table 12-4

Most common Russian subordinating conjunctions	
Subordinating conjunction	**Translation**
(dlia togo,) chtoby	(in order) to
potomu chto, tak kak	since, because
esli	if
poka	as long as
poka ne	until

Exercise 15: Joining Clauses

Complete each sentence by adding the information in parenthesis as a subordinate clause. Use subordinating conjunctions from Table 12-4. Translating the sentences will help you to choose the right subordinating conjunction.

1. *Masha priekhala v Moskvu. (sdelat' kar'eru)*

....

2. *Masha priekhala v Moskvu. (dolgo ob etom mechtala)*

....

3. *Masha priedet v Moskvu. (najdiot den'gi)*

....

4. *Masha ne priedet v Moskvu. (ne zakonchit institut)*

....

5. *Masha ne priedet v Moskvu. (ona ne mogla kupit' bilet)*

....

6. *Masha priedet v Moskvu. (najti svoego brata)*

....

Exercise 16: Matching Clauses

Complete each sentence with the appropriate subordinate clause from the list.

tak kak on ne zakonchil universitet
esli projdiot sobesedovanie
esli smogu kupit' billet
dlia togo, chtoby ob"iasnit' psikhologiiu liudej
chtoby letat' v kosmos
potomu chto on skazal: "Zemlia vertitsia!"

1. *Galileo Galileia sozhgli na kostre,*

....

2. *Liudi stroiat rakety,*

....

3. *Ia pojdu na kontsert,*

....

4. *Vasia ne mozhet najti rabotu,*

....

5. *Professor pokazal fil'm ob obez'ianakh*

....

6. *On poluchit rabotu,*

....

Review

In this section, review using all prepositions and conjunctions. If you encounter difficulties with a particular type of preposition or conjunction, go back to the section devoted to this type and go over the exercises there.

Exercise 17: A Story about Dasha

Read the text. Then complete it with the missing prepositions and conjunctions.

Dasha zhiviot .... *gorode Novorossijske,*

.... *ulitse Karamzina.* .... *neio doma*

chasto sobiraiutsia gosti, ... *pogovorit'* ....

muzyke .... *literatura. Dasha khorosho razbiraetsia*

.... *iskusstve,* .... *ona sama – khudozhnitsa.*

.... *Dasha,* .... *eio druz'ia chasto khodiat*

.... *vystavku* ....

kontserty. Oni by khodili ....

teatr, ... *Novorossijske net*

khoroshego teatra. Dasha dolzhna ezdit' ....

Moskvu, ... *skhodit'* .... *teatr.*

Exercise 18: Translating into Russian

Translate the sentences into Russian, paying special attention to prepositions and conjunctions.

1. Lena lives not far from the office.

   ....

2. He came home to have lunch.

   ....

3. I live in an apartment and my friend lives in a house.

   ....

4. I have seen both the sea and the ocean.

   ....

5. This is a present for you.

   ....

6. A picture was hanging above the couch.

   ....

7. Last week we worked in the garden.

....

8. In May we are going to Moscow.

....

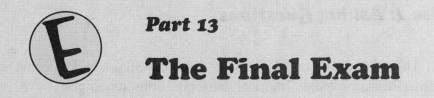

Part 13

The Final Exam

In this part, you will find out how comfortable you are with Russian overall. The exercises here require the use of all the grammatical material you have practiced throughout the book. See how well you can do without any external help. After checking your answers, you can go back and spend more time on the parts that seemed most troublesome. Good luck!

Basic Understanding

After working through this book, you understand a lot of Russian. Practice your understanding and basic conversational skills with the exercises in this section.

Exercise 1: Asking Questions

These are the common questions you may encounter in a conversation with a Russian speaker. Translate these questions into English.

1. *Kak Vas zovut?*

   ....

2. *Gde Vy zhiviote?*

   ....

3. *Otkuda Vy priekhali?*

   ....

4. *Skol'ko Vam let?*

   ....

5. *Gde Vy rabotaete?*

   ....

6. *Chem Vy interesuetes'?*

   ....

7. *Vy zdes' v pervyj raz?*

   ....

8. *Vam zdes' nravitsia?*

....

Exercise 2: Answering Questions

TRACK 55

Listen to the speaker read the questions and answer them. Practice answering the questions several times until the answers come naturally. Feel free to express yourself. The answers offered in the answer key provide just one possible variant.

Exercise 3: Reading the Text

Read the text. Then answer the questions.

V iiule Toni edet v Rossiiu. On ochen' rad, potomu chto on nikogda ne byl v Rossii. On zhil v Germanni i puteshestvoval v Italii, no nikogda ne byl v drugikh stranakh Evropy. Toni nemnogo volnuetsia, potomu chto on ne ochen' khorosho govorit po-russki. On izuchal russkij iazyk v universitete i u sebia doma, v Chicago. No u nego ne bylo dostatochno praktiki. V Rossii Toni mechtaet posmotret' Moskvu, Sankt Peterburg, i iug Rossii. On khochet poekhat' na Kavkaz, potomu chto on liubit gory i interesuetsia istoriej.

1. *Kogda Toni edet v Rossiiu?*

....

2. *Toni uzhe byl v Rossii?*

....

3. *Kakie strany Evropy poseshchal Toni?*

....

4. *Pochemu Toni volnuetsia?*

....

5. *Gde Toni izuchal russkij iazyk?*

....

6. *U Toni bylo dostatochno praktiki?*

....

7. *Kakie goroda Toni khochet posmotret' v Rossii?*

....

8. *Pochemu Toni khochet poekhat' na Kavkaz?*

....

Nouns and Adjectives

In this sections, test your knowledge of cases, declensions, and noun-adjective agreement.

Exercise 4: Completing Sentences

Complete each sentence with the "noun + adjective" phrase in parenthesis. Remember to put the noun in the correct case, and agree the adjective with the noun in gender, number, and case.

1. *My uvideli* .... *(bol'shaia ryba)*

2. *Lena sidit v parke s* .... *(liubimaia kniga)*

3. *U nego nikogda net* .... *(khoroshie otsenki)*

4. *Moia sem'ia zhiviot v* .... *(krasivyj dom)*

•

5. *Mal'chik poslal pis'mo* .... *(starshij brat)*

6. *Eto kabinet* .... *(glavnyj inzhener)*

7. *Ty liubish' smotret'* ....? *(starye fil'my)*

8. *My chasto razgovarivaem o* .... *(daliokie strany)*

Exercise 5: Talking about an Apartment

TRACK 56

Listen to the speaker read the text. Then answer the questions below. You may need to listen to the text several times. In your answers, remember to put the nouns in the correct case, and agree the adjectives with the nouns in gender, number, and case.

1. *Chto ishchut Vika i Kirill?*

....

2. *Kakuiu kvartiru khochet Vika?*

....

3. *Kakie okna i potolki khochet Vika?*

....

4. *Kakuiu kvartiru ishchet Kirill?*

....

5. *Kakie steny khochet Vika?*

....

6. *Kakie tsveta predpochitaet Kirill?*

    ....

7. *Kakuiu kukhniu khochet Kirill?*

    ....

8. *Vozle kakogo sada khochet najti kvartiru Vika?*

    ....

Exercise 6: Describing Appearance

TRACK 57

Read the text describing the appearance of two sisters. Then listen to the speaker ask you questions, and write down the answers.

Marina i Natasha – siostry, no oni sovsem ne pokhozhi drug na druga. U Mariny dlinnye chiornye volosy. U Natashi korotkie svetlye volosy. U Mariny karie glaza. Natashiny glaza – golubye. Natasha zanimaetsia gimnastikoj, i u neio sportivnaia figura. Marina liubit smotret' televizor, i u eio figura ne ochen' sportivnaia. Natasha liubit nosit' serye svitera i briuki. Marina obychno nosit krasnye plat'ia i iubki.

Example:
Speaker: *U Natashi krasivaia ulybka.*
Question: *Kakaia u Natashi ulybka?*
Your answer: *U Natashi krasivaia ulybka.*

1. ....

2. ....

3. ....

4. ....

5. ....

6. ....

7. ....

8. ....

Verbs and Adverbs

In this sections, test your ability to use various types of Russian verbs in different tenses, aspects, and moods.

Exercise 7: Which Verb?

Choose the best verbal form from to complete each sentence.

1. *Direktor* .... *magazin kazhdyj den' v deviat' chasov vechera. (zakroet, zakryvaet, zakryvaetsia)*

2. *Ia* .... *na rabotu peshkom kazhdyj den'. (ezzhu, khozhu, prishiol)*

3. *Oni* .... *na vecherinke v proshlom godu. (poznakomiat-sia, poznakomili, poznakomilis')*

4. *On* .... *v komandirovku na samoliote. (poletit, poedet, pojdiot)*

5. *Moia sestra* .... *v biblioteke. (rabotaiu, rabotaem, rabotaet)*

6. *Zavtra my* .... *v Moskvu. (pojdiom, poedem, poekhali)*

7. *Vy* .... *segodnia prijti? (mogu, mozhete, mogut)*

8. *Ia ochen'* .... *morozhennoe. (liubliu, liubite, liubiat)*

Exercise 8: Listening to Chekhov

TRACK 58

Listen to the speaker read sentences from the short story *Dama s sobach-koj* ("Lady With a Lapdog") by Anton Chekhov. Answer the questions about each sentence.

1. *Chto oni delali kazhdyj polden'?*

   ....

2. *Chto oni delali v Oreande?*

   ....

3. *Chto oni delali kazhdyj vecher?*

   ....

4. *Chto ona budet delat'?*

   ....

5. *Kogda na naberezhnoj ne bylo ni dushi?*

   ....

6. *Chem pakhlo u neio v komnate?*

   ....

7. *Chto ona skazala?*

   ....

8. *Chto sluchilos' po sluchaiu volneniia na more?*

   ....

Exercise 9: Dasha's Schedule

TRACK 59

Listen to the speaker tell us about Dasha's schedule. Then fill out the blanks below with the information about Dasha's activities. The first task has been done for you.

1. 7:00 A.M.: **Dasha prosypaetsia.**

2. 7:30 A.M.: ....

3. 8:00 A.M.: ....

4. 8:30 A.M.: ....

5. 9:00 A.M.: ....

6. 9:30 A.M.: ....

7. 9:45 A.M.: ....

8. 10:30 A.M.: ....

Exercise 10: How Is It Done?

Translate these sentences into English, paying special attention to verbs and adverbs.

1. *On prishiol rano.*

....

2. *Ona risuet luchshe vsekh.*

....

3. *Moj brat begaet ochen' bystro.*

....

4. *Oni zhivut zdes' uzhe davno.*

    ....

5. *Ty dolgo budesh' guliat' v parke?*

    ....

6. *On shiol po ulitse i gromko pel.*

    ....

7. *Ona mozhet prekrasno govorit' po-russki.*

    ....

8. *Ia plokho vozhu mashinu.*

    ....

Pronouns, Prepositions, and Conjunctions

Sometimes, the little words are the hardest ones to master. In this section, test your knowledge of pronouns, prepositions, and conjunctions.

Exercise 11: No Names Mentioned

Rewrite the sentences, replacing the underlined words with pronouns. Remember to put each pronoun in the appropriate case.

1. <u>Lena</u> *rabotaet v teatre.*

    ....

2. <u>Dima</u> *pozvonil* <u>babushke</u>.

    ....

3. *Vecherinka budet u <u>Denisa</u> doma.*

....

4. *Eto <u>mamino</u> plat'e.*

....

5. *<u>Kolia i Misha</u> vsegda dumaiut o <u>sestre</u>.*

....

6. *<u>Moi drug i ia</u> pojdiom segodnia v kino.*

....

7. *<u>Koshka</u> lezhit na podokonnike.*

....

8. *<u>Sobaku</u> zovut Zhuchka.*

....

Exercise 12: What, Who, and Why?

TRACK 60

Listen to the speaker read sentences. Ask questions to each sentence beginning with the offered interrogative pronouns. The first question has been written for you.

1. *Chto **liubit Olia**?*

2. *Gde ?* ....

3. *Pochemu ?* ....

4. *Kogda ?* ....

5. *Kuda ?* ....

6. *Kto ?* ....

7. *Otkuda ?* ....

8. *Zachem ?* ....

Exercise 13: Little Words

Complete each sentence with the best choice in parenthesis.

1. *My idiom* .... *kino. (na, za, v)*

2. *Ona znaet* .... *anglijskij,* .... *nemetskij iazyk. (i...i, ni...ni, to...to)*

3. *Tebe nuzhno pojti* .... *doktoru. (k, s, u)*

4. *Oni dolgo guliali* .... *moria. (nad, u, pod)*

5. *Chto ty znaesh'* .... *etom dele? (o, ob, a)*

6. *Ia khotel pozvonit',* .... *ne smog. (no, otkuda, zachem)*

7. *Natasha priekhala* .... *Moskvy. (s, v, iz)*

8. *On vsegda delaet zariadku* .... *zavtrakom. (pered, pod, iz-za)*

Transliteration Used in
The Everything® Russian Practice Book

Russian	Latin
А а	a
Б б	b
В в	v
Г г	g
Д д	d
Е е	e
Ё ё	io
Ж ж	zh
З з	z
И и	i
Й й	j
К к	k
Л л	l
М м	m
Н н	n
О о	o
П п	p

Russian	Latin
Р р	r
С с	s
Т т	t
У у	u
Ф ф	f
Х х	kh
Ц ц	ts
Ч ч	ch
Ш ш	sh
Щ щ	shch
Ъ ъ	"
Ы ы	y
Ь ь	'
Э э	e
Ю ю	iu
Я я	ia

Appendix B

Verb Tables

delat' (to do)

Regular e-verb

Person	Present	Past	Future
ia	delaiu	delal/delala	budu delat'
ty	delaesh'	delal/delala	budesh' delat'
on/ona/ono	delaet	delal/delala/delalo	budet delat'
my	delaem	delali	budem delat'
vy	delaete	delali	budete delat'
oni	delaiut	delali	budut delat'

govorit' (to talk)

Regular i-verb.

Person	Present	Past	Future
ia	govoriu	govoril/govorila	budu govorit'
ty	govorish'	govoril/govorila	budesh' govorit'
on/ona/ono	govorit	govoril/govorila/ govorilo	budet govorit'
my	govorim	govorili	budem govorit'
vy	govorite	govorili	budete govorit'
oni	govoriat	govorili	budut govorit'

liubit' (to love/like)

Verb with an inserted -l-.

Person	Present	Past	Future
ia	liubliu	liubil/liubila	budu liubit'
ty	liubish'	liubil/liubila	budesh' liubit'
on/ona/ono	liubit	liubil/liubila/liubilo	budet liubit'
my	liubim	liubili	budem liubit'
vy	liubite	liubili	budete liubit'
oni	liubiat	liubili	budut liubit'

videt' (to see)

Verb with consonant mutation.

Person	Present	Past	Future
ia	vizhu	videl/videla	budu videt'
ty	vidish'	videl/videla	budesh' videt'
on/ona/ono	vidit	videl/videla/videlo	budet videt'
my	vidim	videli	budem videt'
vy	vidite	videli	budete videt'
oni	vidiat	videli	budut videt'

davat' (to give)

-ava- type verb

Person	Present	Past	Future
ia	daiu	daval/davala	budu davat'
ty	daiosh'	daval/davala	budesh' davat'
on/ona/ono	daiot	daval/davala/davalo	budet davat'
my	daiom	davali	budem davat'
vy	daiote	davali	budete davat'
oni	daiut	davali	budut davat'

trebovat' (to demand)

-ova- type verb

Person	Present	Past	Future
ia	trebuiu	treboval/trebovala	budu trebovat'
ty	trebuesh'	treboval/trebovala	budesh' trebovat'
on/ona/ono	trebuet	treboval/trebovala/ trebovalo	budet trebovat'
my	trebuem	trebovali	budem trebovat'
vy	trebuete	trebovali	budete trebovat'
oni	trebuiut	trebovali	budut trebovat'

byt' (to be)

Irregular verb

Person	Present	Past	Future
ia	none	byl/byla	budu
ty	none	byl/byla	budesh'
on/ona/ono	none	byl/byla/bylo	budet
my	none	byli	budem
vy	none	byli	budete
oni	none	byli	budut

ekhat' (to go to vehicle)

Irregular verb

Person	Present	Past	Future
ia	edu	ekhal/ekhala	budu ekhat'
ty	edesh'	ekhal/ekhala	budesh' ekhat'
on/ona/ono	edet	ekhal/ekhala/ekhalo	budet ekhat'
my	edem	ekhali	budem ekhat'
vy	edete	ekhali	budete ekhat'
oni	edut	ekhali	budut ekhat'

est' (to eat)

Irregular verb

Person	Present	Past	Future
ia	em	el/ela	budu est'
ty	esh'	el/ela	budesh' est'
on/ona/ono	est	el/ela/elo	budet est'
my	edim	eli	budem est'
vy	edite	eli	budete est'
oni	ediat	eli	budut est'

idti (to go by foot)

Irregular verb

Person	Present	Past	Future
ia	idu	shiol/shla	budu idti
ty	idiosh'	shiol/shla	budesh' idti
on/ona/ono	idiot	shiol/shla/shlo	budet idti
my	idiom	shli	budem idti
vy	idiote	shli	budete idti
oni	idut	shli	budut idti

iskat' (to look for)

Irregular verb

Person	Present	Past	Future
ia	ishchu	iskal/iskala	budu iskat'
ty	ishchesh'	iskal/iskala	budesh' iskat'
on/ona/ono	ishchet	iskal/iskala/iskalo	budet iskat'
my	ishchem	iskali	budem iskat'
vy	ishchete	iskali	budete iskat'
oni	ishchut	iskali	budut iskat'

khotet' (to want)

Irregular verb

Person	Present	past	Future
ia	khochu	khotel/khotela	budu khotet'
ty	khochesh'	khotel/khotela	budesh' khotet'
on/ona/ono	khochet	khotel/khotela/khotelo	budet khotet'
my	khotim	khoteli	budem khotet'
vy	khotite	khoteli	budete khotet'
oni	khotiat	khoteli	budut khotet'

moch' (to be able to)

Irregular verb

Person	Present	Past	Future
ia	mogu	mog/mogla	none
ty	mozhesh'	mog/mogla	none
on/ona/ono	mozhet	mog/mogla/moglo	none
my	mozhem	mogli	none
vy	mozhete	mogli	none
oni	mogut	mogli	none

myt' (to wash)

Irregular verb

Person	Present	Past	Future
ia	moiu	myl/myla	budu myt'
ty	moesh'	myl/myla	budesh' myt'
on/ona/ono	moet	myl/myla/mylo	budet myt'
my	moem	myli	budem myt'
vy	moete	myli	budete myt'
oni	moiut	myli	budut myt'

pisat' (to write)

Irregular verb

Person	Present	Past	Future
ia	pishu	pisal/pisala	budu pisat'
ty	pishesh'	pisal/pisala	budesh' pisat'
on/ona/ono	pishet	pisal/pisala/pisalo	budet pisat'
my	pishem	pisali	budem pisat'
vy	pishete	pisali	budete pisat'
oni	pishut	pisali	budut pisat'

pit' (to drink)

Irregular verb

Person	Present	Past	Future
ia	p'iu	pil/pila	budu pit'
ty	p'iosh'	pil/pila	budesh' pit'
on/ona/ono	p'iot	pil/pila/pilo	budet pit'
my	p'iom	pili	budem pit'
vy	p'iote	pili	budete pit'
oni	p'iut	pili	budut pit'

zhit' (to live)

Irregular verb

Person	Present	Past	Future
ia	zhivu	zhil/zhila	budu zhit'
ty	zhiviosh'	zhil/zhila	budesh' zhit'
on/ona/ono	zhiviot	zhil/zhila/zhilo	budet zhit'
my	zhiviom	zhili	budem zhit'
vy	zhiviote	zhili	budete zhit'
oni	zhivut	zhili	budut zhit'

Appendix C

Russian-to-English Glossary

A

Russian	English
adres	address
aeroport	airport
Amerika	America
amerikanets	American
aprel'	April
arkhitektor	architect
avgust	August
avtobus	bus

B

Russian	English
babushka	grandmother
bank	bank
belyj	white
bilet	ticket
bol'nitsa	hospital
bol'she	more
bol'shoj	big
bol'shoj	large
bolen	ill
brat	brother
brat'	take
bumaga	paper
byt'	be

C

Russian	English
chashka	cup
chastnyj	private
chasy	clock
chek	check
chemodan	suitcase
chiornyj	black
chto	what
chto-to	something

D

Russian	English
daleko	far
davat'	give
dedushka	grandfather
dekabr'	December
delat'	do
delat'	make
den'	day
den'gi	money
derzhat'	hold
desert	dessert
deshiovyj	cheap
devochka	girl
diadia	uncle
dlinnyj	long
do skorogo	See you later·
do svidaniia	Good-bye·
do zavtra	See you tomorrow·
dobroe utro	Good morning·
dobryj vecher	Good evening·
doch'	daughter

Russian	English
dolzhen	have to
dom	home
dom	house
doroga	road
dorogoj	dear
dorogoj	expensive
dostat'	get
dozhd'	rain
drug	friend
drugoj	different
dumat'	think
dver'	door
dvorets	palace
dzhinsy	jeans

E	
Russian	**English**
eda	food
est'	eat

F	
Russian	**English**
fevral'	February
firma	firm
frukt	fruit
futbol	soccer

G	
Russian	**English**
galstuk	tie
gazeta	newspaper
gde	where
glavnyj	main
glaz	eye

Russian	English
god	year
golodnyj	hungry
golos	voice
gora	mountain
gorod	city
gost'	guest
gostinitsa	hotel
gruppa	group

I	
Russian	**English**
ia	I
ianvar'	January
idti	go
iiul'	July
iiun'	June
imet'	have
imia	name
indeks	zip code
inostrannyj	foreign
interes	interest
iskat'	look for
ispol'zovat'	use
iubka	skirt
iug	south
iurist	lawyer
iz	from

K	
Russian	**English**
kak	how
kanadets	Canadian
kassa	cash register
kazat'sia	seem

khleb	bread
kholodnyj	cold
khoroshij	good
khorosho	well
khotet'	want
khudozhnik	artist
kino	movie theater
klubnika	strawberry
kniga	book
kofe	coffee
kogda	when
koleno	knee
komnata	room
kompaniia	company
konets	end
korichnevyj	brown
kosheliok	wallet
kostium	suit
kotoryj	which
krasivyj	beautiful
krasnyj	red
kreditnaia kartochka	credit card
krovat'	bed
kto	who
kupal'nik	bathing suit
kurtka	jacket
kvartira	apartment

liubit'	love
liudi	people

M

Russian	English
magazine	shop
maj	May
mal'chik	boy
malen'kij	small
mart	March
mashina	car
mat'	mother
medsestra	nurse
men'she	less
mesiats	month
mestnyj	local
mesto	seat
metro	subway
miaso	meat
militsiia	police
milyj	nice
minuta	minute
mir	world
moch'	can
moj	my
molodoj	young
moloko	milk
more	sea
morozhennoe	ice cream
mozhno	May
muzh	husband
my	we

L

Russian	English
legko	easy
lekarstvo	medicine
liod	ice
litso	face

N

Russian	English
nakhodit'	find
nalichnye	cash
nalog	tax
nastoiashchij	real
nedelia	week
nesti	carry
nikogda	never
no	but
noch'	night
noiabr'	November
nomer	number
nos	nose
nosh	knife
nosit'	wear
novyj	new

O

Russian	English
obed	lunch
obrazovanie	education
obshchestvennyj	public
ofis	office
ofitsiant	waiter
okno	window
oktiabr'	October
on	he
oni	they
otdel	department
otets	father
otpusk	vacation
ovoshchi	vegetables
ozero	lake

P

Russian	English
p'esa	play
pal'to	coat
passport	passport
pis'mo	letter
pit'	drink
pivo	beer
plashch	raincoat
plat'e	dress
platit'	pay
plavat'	swim
plecho	shoulder
pliazh	beach
plokhoj	bad
ploshchad'	square
pochemu	why
pod	under
podarok	gift
poezd	train
poiavliat'sia	appear
poka	see you
pokazyvat'	show
pokupat'	buy
polozhit'	put
pomogat'	help
povorachivat'	turn
pozdno	late
pozhalujsta	please
pozhalujsta	You're welcome
predpochitat'	prefer
predstavliat'	introduce
pribyvat'	arrive
priglashenie	invitation

Russian	English
prikhodit'	come
prinosit'	bring
privet	Hi!
problema	problem
prodavat'	sell
puteshestvovat'	travel

R	
Russian	**English**
rabota	job
rabotat'	work
rano	early
rasprodazha	sale
rasskazat'	tell
razgovarivat'	talk
razreshat'	allow
rebionok	child
ris	rice
rubashka	shirt
ruka	arm
ruka	hand
ryba	fish
rynok	market

S	
Russian	**English**
sad	garden
sakhar	sugar
salat	salad
samoliot	airplane
sdacha	change
segodnia	today
sejchas	now
sekretar'	secretary

Russian	English
sem'ia	family
sentiabr'	September
seryj	gray
sestra	sister
sever	north
shapka	hat
sheia	neck
shkola	school
shtat	state
sidet'	sit
sinij	blue
skazat'	say
skol'ko	how many/how much
skuchnyj	boring
sladkij	sweet
slishkom	too (excessively)
slovo	word
smeiat'sia	laugh
smotret'	look
smotret'	watch
sneg	snow
snimat'	rent
sobor	cathedral
sobytie	event
sol'	salt
solntse	sun
suvenir	souvenir
spasibo	thank you
spat'	sleep
spokojnoj nochi	Good night
sprashivat'	ask
stakan	glass
starat'sia	try
staryj	old

Russian	English
stat'	become
stoiat	stand
strana	country
sumka	bag
syn	son
syr	cheese

T

Russian	English
takzhe	also
tamozhnia	customs
tarelka	plate
teatr	theater
telefon	phone
telefon	telephone
teper'	now
terapevt	physician
tiomnyj	dark
tioplyj	warm
tip	type
tol'ko	only
tselyj	whole
tsena	price
tserkov'	church
tsvetok	flower
tufli	shoes
ty	you (sing., inform.)

U

Russian	English
uchitel'	teacher
ukhodit'	leave
ulitsa	street
universitet	university

Russian	English
ustalyj	tired
utro	morning
uzhin	dinner

V

Russian	English
vazhnyj	important
vchera	yesterday
vecherinka	party
vek	century
velosiped	bicycle
verit'	believe
veshch'	thing
vid	view
videt'	see
vino	wine
viza	visa
vkhod	entrance
vkhodit'	enter
voda	water
vokzal	station
volosy	hair
vopros	question
vostok	east
vozrast	age
vrach	doctor
vremia	tme
vse	everybody
vsio	everything
vstrecha	meeting
vy	you (pl., form.)
vykhod	exit
vysokij	high
vysokij	tall

Z

Russian	English
zaiavlenie	application
zakanchivat'	finish
zakon	law
zakuska	appetizer
zapad	west
zavtra	tomorrow
zavtrak	breakfast
zdanie	building
zdes'	here
zdorov'e	health
zdravstvujte	hello

Russian	English
zelionyj	green
zharko	hot
zhdat'	wait
zhena	wife
zhenshchina	woman
zhioltyj	yellow
zhit'	live
znachenie	meaning
znachit'	mean
znat'	know
zubnoj vrach	dentist
zvonit'	call

English-to-Russian Glossary

A

English	Russian
address	adres
age	vozrast
airplane	samoliot
airport	aeroport
allow	razreshat'
also	takzhe
America	Amerika
American	amerikanets/amerikanka
apartment	kvartira
appear	poiavliat'sia
appetizer	zakuska
application	zaiavlenie
April	aprel'
architect	arkhitektor
arm	ruka
arrive	pribyvat'
artist	khudozhnik
ask	sprashivat'
August	avgust
avenue	bul'var

B

English	Russian
bad	plokhoj
bag	sumka
bank	bank
bathing suit	kupal'nik
be	byt'

beach	pliazh
beautiful	krasivyj
become	stat'
bed	krovat'
beer	pivo
believe	verit'
bicycle	velosiped
big	bol'shoj
black	chiornyj
blue	sinij
book	kniga
boring	skuchnyj
bottle	butylka
boy	mal'chik
bread	khleb
breakfast	zavtrak
bring	prinosit'
brother	brat
brown	korichnevyj
building	zdanie
bus	avtobus
but	no
buy	pokupat'

C

English	Russian
call	zvonit'
can	moch'
Canadian	kanadets/kanadka
car	mashina

carry	nesti
cash register	kassa
cash	nalichnye
cathedral	sobor
century	vek
change	sdacha
cheap	deshiovyj
check	chek
cheese	syr
child	rebionok
church	tserkov'
city	gorod
clock	chasy
coat	pal'to
coffee	kofe
cold	kholodnyj
come	prikhodit'
company	kompaniia
country	strana
credit card	kreditnaia kartochka
cup	chashka
customs	tamozhnia

D	
English	**Russian**
dark	tiomnyj
daughter	doch'
day	den'
dear	dorogoj
December	dekabr'
dentist	zubnoj vrach
department	otdel
dessert	desert
different	drugoj

dinner	uzhin
do	delat'
doctor	vrach
door	dver'
dress	plat'e
drink	pit'

E	
English	**Russian**
early	rano
east	vostok
easy	legko
eat	est'
education	obrazovanie
end	konets
engineer	inzhener
enter	vkhodit'
entrance	vkhod
event	sobytie
everybody	vse
everything	vsio
exit	vykhod
expensive	dorogoj
eye	glaz

F	
English	**Russian**
face	litso
family	sem'ia
far	daleko
father	otets
February	fevral'
find	nakhodit'
finish	zakanchivat'

firm	firma
fish	ryba
flower	tsvetok
food	eda
friend	drug
from	iz
fruit	frukt

G

English	Russian
garden	sad
get	dostat'
gift	podarok
girl	devochka
give	davat'
glass	stakan
go	idti/yekhat'
Good evening·	dobryj vecher
Good morning·	dobroe utro
Good night·	spokojnoj nochi
good	khoroshij
good·bye	do svidaniia
grandfather	dedushka
grandmother	babushka
gray	seryj
green	zelionyj
guest	gost'

H

English	Russian
hair	volosy
hand	ruka
hat	shapka
have to	dolzhen

have	imet'
he	on
hello	zdravstvujte
help	pomogat'
here	zdes'/tut
Hi!	privet
high	vysokij
hold	derzhat'
home	dom
hospital	bol'nitsa
hot	zharko
hotel	gostinitsa
house	dom
how many	skol'ko
how much	skol'ko
how	kak
hungry	golodnyj
husband	muzh

I

English	Russian
I	ia
ice cream	morozhennoe
ice	liod
ill	bolen
important	vazhnyj
interest	interes
introduce	predstavliat'
invitation	priglashenie

J

English	Russian
jacket	kurtka
January	ianvar'

English	Russian
jeans	dzhinsy
job	rabota
July	iiul'
June	iiun'

K

English	Russian
knee	koleno
knife	nozh
know	znat'

L

English	Russian
lake	ozero
large	bol'shoj
late	pozdno
laugh	smeiat'sia
law	zakon
leave	ukhodit'
less	men'she
letter	pis'mo
live	zhit'
local	mestnyj
long	dlinnyj
look for	iskat'
look	smotret'
love	liubit'
lunch	obed

M

English	Russian
main	glavnyj
make	delat'
March	mart

English	Russian
market	rynok
May	maj
may	mozhno
mean	znachit'
meaning	znachenie
meat	miaso
medicine	lekarstvo
meeting	vstrecha
milk	moloko
minute	minuta
money	den'gi
month	mesiats
more	bol'she
morning	utro
mother	mat'
mountain	gora
movie theater	kino
my	moj

N

English	Russian
name	imia
neck	sheia
never	nikogda
new	novyj
newspaper	gazeta
nice	milyj
night	noch'
north	sever
nose	nos
November	noiabr'
now	sejchas/teper'
number	nomer
nurse	medsestra

O

English	Russian
October	oktiabr'
office	ofis
old	staryj
only	tol'ko

P

English	Russian
palace	dvorets
paper	bumaga
party	vecherinka
passport	pasport
pay	platit'
people	liudi
phone	telefon
physician	terapevt
plate	tarelka
play	p'esa
please	pozhalujsta
police	militsiia
prefer	predpochitat'
price	tsena
private	chastnyj
put	polozhit'

Q

question	vopros

R

English	Russian
rain	dozhd'
raincoat	plashch
real	nastoiashchij
red	krasnyj
rent	snimat'
rice	ris
road	doroga
room	komnata

S

English	Russian
salad	salat
sale	rasprodazha
sales assistant	prodavets/ prodavshchitsa
salt	sol'
say	skazat'
school	shkola
sea	more
seat	mesto
secretary	sekretar'
See you later	do skorogo
See you tomorrow	do zavtra
See you	poka
see	videt'
seem	kazat'sia
sell	prodavat'
September	sentiabr'
shirt	rubashka
shoes	tufli
shop	magazin
shoulder	plecho
show	pokazyvat'
sister	sestra
sit	sidet'
skirt	iubka
sleep	spat'

English	Russian
small	malen'kij
snow	sneg
soccer	futbol
something	chto-to
son	syn
south	iug
souvenir	suvenir
square	ploshchad'
stand	stoiat
state	shtat
station	vokzal
strawberry	klubnika
street	ulitsa
subway	metro
sugar	sakhar
suit	kostium
suitcase	chemodan
sun	solntse
sweet	sladkij
swim	plavat'

T	
English	**Russian**
take	brat'
talk	razgovarivat'
tall	vysokij
tax	nalog
teacher	uchitel'
telephone	telefon
tell	rasskazat'
thank you	spasibo
theater	teatr
they	oni
thing	veshch'

English	Russian
think	dumat'
ticket	bilet
tie	galstuk
time	vremia
tired	ustalyj
today	segodnia
tomorrow	zavtra
too (excessively)	slishkom
train	poezd
travel	puteshestvovat'
try	starat'sia
turn	povorachivat'
type	tip

U	
English	**Russian**
uncle	diadia
under	pod
university	universitet
use	ispol'zovat'

V	
English	**Russian**
vacation	otpusk
vegetables	ovoshchi
view	vid
visa	viza
voice	golos

W	
English	**Russian**
wait	zhdat'
waiter	ofitsiant
want	khotet'

English	Russian
warm	tioplyj
watch	smotret'
water	voda
we	my
wear	nosit'
week	nedelia
well	khorosho
west	zapad
what	chto
when	kogda
where	gde
which	kotoryj
white	belyj
who	kto
whole	tselyj
why	pochemu
wife	zhena
window	okno
wine	vino

English	Russian
woman	zhenshchina
word	slovo
work	rabotat'
world	mir

Y

English	Russian
year	god
yellow	zhioltyj
yesterday	vchera
you (pl. form.)	vy
you (sing. inform.)	ty
You're welcome.	pozhalujsta
young	molodoj

Z

English	Russian
zip code	indeks

Appendix E

Answer Key

Check your answers to the exercises and trace your progress using this handy answer key.

Part 1

Exercise 1: Recognizing Masculine Nouns

1. *okno, komnata, <u>stol</u>*
2. *<u>medvied'</u>, lisa, zmeia*
3. *<u>tramvaj</u>, ulitsa, taksi*
4. *devochka, <u>mal'chik</u>, devushka*
5. *<u>komp'iuter</u>, kniga, ruchka*
6. *svoboda, <u>mir</u>, druzhba*
7. *more, reka, <u>okean</u>*
8. *gitara, <u>baraban</u>, pianino*
9. *<u>dvorets</u>, statuia, Kreml'*
10. *vystavka, <u>muzej</u>, gallereia*

Exercise 2: Writing Down Masculine Nouns

1. *stol*
2. *gorod*
3. *vopros*
4. *chajnik*
5. *divan*
6. *samoliot*
7. *chemodan*
8. *den'*
9. *chas*
10. *muzej*

Exercise 3: What's the Gender?

1. rain, M (Masculine)
2. daughter, F (Feminine)
3. teacher, M
4. moose, M
5. night, F
6. square, F
7. salt, F
8. mother, F
9. nail, M
10. cliché, F

Exercise 4: She or He?

1. *uchitel'nitsa*
2. *podruga*
3. *stiuardessa*
4. *uchenitsa*
5. *ofitsiantka*
6. *studentka*
7. *bol'naia*
8. *aktrisa*
9. *pisatel'nitsa*
10. *pevitsa*

Exercise 5: Where's the Neuter Noun?

1. *Otkrojte, pozhalujsta, <u>okno</u>!*
2. *K etomu syru <u>vino</u> podhodit bol'she, chem <u>pivo</u>.*
3. *<u>Pis'mo</u> ot syna prishlo cherez mesiats.*
4. *My sideli v <u>kafe</u> i pili kofe.*
5. *Bol'she vsego na svete ya liubliu <u>more</u>, <u>solntse</u> i <u>leto</u>.*
6. *Na ulitse kholodno; naden' <u>pal'to</u>.*
7. *Vse russkie devushki iz khoroshikh semej igrali na <u>pia-nino</u> i govorili na neskol'kikh inostrannykh iazykakh.*
8. *Nakonets on reshilsia priglasit' Lenu v <u>kino</u>.*
9. *Eto <u>zdanie</u> postroeno v stile <u>barokko</u>.*
10. *Ona voshla v kontsertnyj zal i zaniala svoio <u>mesto</u>.*

Exercise 6: Which Gender?

1. *dolgoe* **vremia,** N (Neuter)
2. *moi* **diadia,** F
3. *dorogoj* **papa,** F
4. *sinee* **plamia,** N
5. *liubimyj* **dedushka,** F
6. *vashe* **imia,** N
7. *vysokij* **muzhchina,** F
8. *beloe* **znamia,** N
9. *dnevnoe* **vremia,** N
10. *neznakomaia* **zhenshchina,** F

Exercise 7: Animate or Inanimate?

1. *lisa,* A (Animate)
2. *professor,* A
3. *televizor,* I (Inanimate)
4. *chelovek,* A
5. *medved',* A
6. *mal'chik,* A
7. *mashina,* I
8. *uchitel'nitsa,* A
9. *gorod,* I
10. *prokhozhij,* A

Exercise 8: Trivial Pursuit

1. *Tchaikovsky*
2. *Gagarin*
3. *Rim*
4. *Vatikan*
5. *Tolstoj*
6. *Everest*
7. *Indiia*
8. *Bajkal*
9. *Avstraliia*
10. *Konstantinopol'*

Exercise 9: Completing Phrases

1. *stolitsa Rossii* — **Moskva**
2. *poet i pisatel'* **Pushkin**
3. *avtor baleta "Romeo i Dzhul'etta"* —*kompozitor* **Prokof'ev**

4. *kosmicheskaia stantsiia "***Mir***"*
5. *drevnij moskovskij* **Kreml'**
6. *samaia dlinnaia reka Evropy* **Volga**
7. *avtor romana "Lolita"* — *Vladimir* **Nabokov**
8. *planeta* **Zemlia**

Exercise 10: Telling the Gender

1. *ozero,* N
2. *sol',* F
3. *strana,* F
4. *papa,* F
5. *khudozhnik,* M
6. *den',* M
7. *pesnia,* F
8. *gostinitsa,* F
9. *noch',* F
10. *muzej,* M

Exercise 11: What Kind of Noun?

1. A, nP (not Proper), M
2. A, nP, F
3. I, nP, F
4. A, nP, F
5. I, nP, M
6. I, nP, M
7. I, P, M
8. I, P, F
9. A, nP, F
10. A, nP, F

Part 2

Exercise 1: Finding the Noun in Nominative

1. *Molodoj* <u>muzhchina</u> *voshiol v pod'ezd.*
2. <u>Motsart</u> *rodilsia v 18 veke.*
3. *Eta* <u>devushka</u> *prekrasno poiot.*
4. *Moia* <u>babushka</u> *prozhila do sta let.*
5. <u>Moskva</u> *rastiot kazhdyj den'.*
6. *V etot den' emu pozvonila ego* <u>mat'</u>.

7. *"Lunnuiu sonatu" napisal* <u>Betkhoven</u>.

8. *Eto* <u>leto</u> *zapomnilos' mne nadolgo.*

9. *Nastupil tioplyj* <u>vecher</u>.

10. *Poshiol* <u>dozhd'</u>.

8. *Liudi so vsego Sovetskogo Soiuza priezzh-ali otdykhat' na Chiornoe* <u>more</u>. **Moria**

9. *Davaj poedem domoj na* <u>metro</u>. Doesn't change.

10. <u>Biuro</u> *zakryto na pereryv.* Doesn't change.

Exercise 2: Completing Sentences

1. **Kniga** *upala so stola.*

2. *Na nego laiala bol'shaia* **sobaka**.

3. **Professor** *opiat' opozdal na lektsiiu.*

4. *Eta* **ruchka** *pishet sinimi chernilami.*

5. **Zapakh** *dukhov raznosilsia po vsej kvartire.*

6. **Mashina** *neozhidanno ostanovilas'.*

7. *Ko mne prishli* **gosti**.

8. **Pravda** *govorit za sebia.*

9. *Molodoe* **pokolenie** *vybiraet rok muzyku.*

10. *Opiat' idiot* **sneg**.

Exercise 5: Plural or Singular?

1. *avtomobili* – **avtomobil'**

2. *derevnia* — **derevni**

3. *rubli* — **rubl'**

4. *televizory* — **televizor**

5. *zhizn'* — **zhizni**

6. *samoliot* — **samolioty**

7. *okna* — **okno**

8. *zdanie* – **zdaniia**

9. *muzei* — **muzej**

10. *roial'* — **roiali**

Exercise 3: Making It Plural

1. *stol* — **stoly**

2. *kvartira* — **kvartiry**

3. *mashina* — **mashiny**

4. *ploshchad'* — **ploshchadi**

5. *kukhnia* — **kukhni**

6. *ten'* — **teni**

7. *vokzal* — **vokzaly**

8. *tiotia* — **tioti**

9. *geroj* — **geroi**

10. *tsar'* – **tsari**

Exercise 6: Forming Irregular Plurals

1. *syn* — **synov'ia**

2. *den'* — **dni**

3. *drug* — **druz'ia**

4. *stul* — **stul'ia**

5. *brat* — **brat'ia**

6. *uchitel'* — **uchitelia**

7. *mat'* — **materi**

8. *vremia* — **vremena**

9. *pasport* — **pasporta**

10. *direktor* — **direktora**

Exercise 4: Changing the Neuter Noun

1. *Nochnoe* <u>pole</u> *v lunnom svete bylo neobychajno krasivo.* **polia**

2. *Zdes' zharko, snimajte* <u>pal'to</u>. Doesn't change.

3. *V dome gorelo tol'ko odno* <u>okno</u>. **okna**

4. <u>Ozero</u> *Bajkal – samoe glubokoe* <u>oze-ro</u> *v mire.* **oziora** (irregular plural)

5. *Oni liubili sidet' v* <u>kafe</u> *na naberezhnoj.* Doesn't change.

6. *V vozraste shesti let ona uzhe igra-la na* <u>pianino</u>. Doesn't change.

7. *Za obedom oni obychno p'iut moldavskoe* <u>vino</u>. **vina**

Exercise 7: Putting Nouns in the Accusative

1. *Ia slyshu krasivuiu* **muzyku**.
   I hear beautiful music.

2. *My sideli i smotreli na* **gorod**.
   We were sitting and looking at the city.

3. *Davajte priglasim na den' rozhdeniia* **Oliu**.
   Let's invite Olia to the birthday party.

4. *On vstal, chtoby zakryt'* **okno**.
   He got up to close the window.

5. *Vy znaete etogo* **cheloveka**?
   Do you know this person?

6. *Ty uzhe videl Krasnuiu* **ploshchad'**?

Have you seen Red Square yet?

7. *Kak zovut tvoego* **uchitelia**?
   What is you teacher's name?

8. *Etot malysh ochen' liubit svoiu* **babushku**.
   This baby loves his Grandma very much.

9. *Pozovite vashu* **sobaku**.
   Call your dog.

10. *Bol'she vsekh kurortov mira ia liubliu Chiornoe* **more**.)
    More than all the resorts of the world, I love the Black Sea.

Exercise 8: Completing Sentences

1. *Etu* **zhenshchinu** *zovut Tat'iana Petrovna.* **(zhenshchina)**
2. *Moj otets sam sdelal etot* **stol**. **(stol)**
3. *Ty segodnia uzhe kormil svoiu* **koshku**? **(koshka)**
4. *Ia vchera prochitala zamechatel'nuiu* **knigu**. **(kniga)**
5. *Chto vy budete est',* **sup** *ili borshch?* **(sup)**
6. *Vy ne videli zdes' malen'kogo* **mal'chika**? **(mal'chik)**
7. *Na ulitse ona vstretila svoiu* **doch'**. **(doch')**
8. *Terpet' ne mogu* **dozhd'**. **(dozhd')**
9. *Studenty vnimatel'no slushali* **professora**. **(professor)**
10. *Ty kogda-nibud' videl* **ozero** *Bajkal?* **(ozero)**

Exercise 9: Putting Nouns in Accusative Plural

1. *doroga* — **dorogi**
2. *voditel'* — **voditelej**
3. *geroj* — **geroev**
4. *pis'mo* – **pis'ma**
5. *stol* — **stoly**
6. *ulitsa* — **ulitsy**
7. *uchitel'nitsa* – **uchitel'nits**
8. *professor* — **professorov**
9. *pasport* — **pasporta**
10. *noch'* – **nochi**

Exercise 10: Completing Sentences

1. *On mnogo chital russkikh* **pisatelej**.
   He read a lot of Russian authors.

2. *Na etoj vystavke mozhno vstretit' izvestnykh* **khudozhnits**.
   One can meet famous women painters at this exhibition.

3. *My prishli v zoopark, chtoby uvidet' belykh* **medvedej**.
   We came to the zoo to see the white bears.

4. *On znal vsekh* **direktorov** *v gorode*.
   He knew all the managers in the city.

5. *Ona stoiala u vkhoda v kinoteatr i zhdala svoikh* **podrug**.
   She was standing by the movie theater entrance waiting for her girlfriends.

6. *Ty chasto naveshchaesh svoikh* **tiot'**?
   Do you visit your aunts often?

7. *V romane "Miortvye dushi" Gogol' opisyvaet obyknoven-nykh* **obyvatelej**.
   In his novel *Dead Souls*, Gogol describes ordinary philistines.

8. *Ia ochen' liubliu* **sobak**.
   I love dogs very much.

9. *On rabotal na pochte i lichno znal mnogikh* **pochtal'onov**.
   He worked at the post office and knew many mail carriers personally.

10. *Mnogie prikhodiat v kino, tol'ko chtoby posmotret' na liu-bimykh* **aktris**.
    Many people come to the movies only to see their favorite actresses.

Exercise 11: Dative Endings

1. *moloko* – **moloku**
2. *roza* – **roze**
3. *devochka* – **devochke**
4. *avtobus* – **avtobusu**
5. *avtomobil'* – **avtomobiliu**
6. *simfoniia* – **simfonii**
7. *noch'* – **nochi**
8. *volia* – **vole**
9. *more* – **moriu**
10. *mat'* – **materi**

Exercise 12: Telling the case

1. *Mat' dala <u>synu</u> yabloko.* D
2. *Professor dal <u>studentu</u> zadanie.* D
3. *<u>Mariia</u> daiot uroki muzyki.* N
4. *Mne vchera pozvonil moj <u>sosed</u>.* N
5. *Ya chasto zvoniu <u>podruge</u>.* D
6. *<u>Muzyka</u> pomogaet Lene rasslabit'sia.* N
7. *My dali etoj <u>pesne</u> smeshnoe nazvanie.* D
8. *Dajte kusok torta <u>Mashe</u>.* D
9. *<u>More</u> daiot cheloveku zariad bodrosti.* N
10. *Etot mal'chik pomogaet svoej <u>babushke</u>.* D

Exercise 13: Completing Sentences

1. *Ty uzhe dal **koshke** moloko?*
2. *Misha rasskazal **drugu** smeshuiu istoriiu.*
3. *Eta **devochka** ochen' liubit chitat'.*
4. *Pozvoni, pozhalujsta, **sosedu**!*
5. *Ya pokazala **puteshestvenniku** dorogu.*
6. *Eta **aktrisa** igraet v teatre i kino.*
7. ***Poet** napisal eto stikhotvorenie v rannej iunosti.*
8. *Misha dal **sestre** kliuchi.*
9. *Pervogo sentiabria deti prinosiat tsvety **uchiteliu**.*
10. *Militsioner pomog **turistu** najti Bol'shoj teatr.*

Exercise 14: Dative Plural Nouns

1. *Na 8 marta muzhchiny dariat **zhenshchinam** tsvety.*
2. *Ekskursovod rasskazal **turistam** legendu.*
3. *Pozvonite **roditeliam**!*
4. *Prezident vruchil **geroiam** medali.*
5. *Khoroshaia muzyka pomogaet **fil'mam** stat' znamenitymi.*
6. *Konstitutsiia daiot **liudiam** pravo na svobodu slova.*
7. *Stiuardessa prinesla **passazhiram** vodu.*
8. *Publika dolgo aplodirovala **aktioram**.*
9. *On vsegda daval ulichnym **muzykantam** den'gi.*
10. *Uchitel' pokazal **detiam** novyj fil'm.*

Exercise 15: Answering Questions

1. *V Rossii priniato govorit' devushkam kom-plimenty.* Or *Devushkam.*
2. *V Rossii redko dariat muzhchinam tsvety.* Or *Muzhchinam.*
3. *Vnuki dolzhny pomogat' dedushkam i babushkam.* Or *Dedushkam i babushkam.*
4. *Mat' dala detiam konfety.* Or *Detiam.*
5. *Kassir daiot pokupateliam sdachu.* Or *Pokupateliam.*
6. *Oleniam dlia zdorov'ia daiut sol'.* Or *Oleniam.*
7. *Ia daiu svoim koshkam moloko.* Or *Koshkam.*
8. *Ekskursovod pokazal turistam starinnyj zamok.* Or *Turistam.*
9. *Voditel' pomog passazhiram vyjti na ostanovke.* Or *Passazhiram.*
10. *Uchitelia chasto zvoniat roditeliam.* Or *Roditeliam.*

Exercise 16: Putting Nouns in Prepositional

1. *stadion – **stadione***
2. *pochta – **pochte***
3. *ploshchad' – **ploshchadi***
4. *dom – **dome***
5. *zdanie – **zdanii***
6. *pole – **pole***
7. *avtobus – **avtobuse***
8. *konservatoriia – **konservatorii***
9. *okno – **okne***
10. *vishnia – **vishne***

Exercise 17: A Working Family

1. *Mama rabotaet v universitete.*
2. *Papa rabotaet v banke.*
3. *Babushka rabotaet v gostinitse.*
4. *Dedushka rabotaet v magazine.*
5. *Tiotia rabotaet v laboratorii.*
6. *Diadia rabotaet v ofise.*
7. *Sestra rabotaet v teatre.*
8. *Brat rabotaet na zavode.*

Exercise 18: Natural Wonders

1. *Niagarskij vodopad nakhoditsia v **Amerike**.*
2. *Zhirafy zhivut v **Afrike**.*
3. *Kity zhivut v **okeane**.*
4. *Kenguru zhivut v **Avstralii**.*
5. *Pingviny zhivut v **Antarktike**.*
6. *Ozero Bajkal nakhoditsia v **Rossii**.*
7. *Gory Al'py nakhodiatsia v **Evrope**.*
8. *Everest nakhoditsia v **Azii**.*

Exercise 19: Making It Prepositional Plural

1. *stol; na stolakh*
2. *mesto; na mestakh*
3. *les; v lesakh*
4. *dacha; na dachakh*
5. *svad'ba; na svad'bakh*
6. *avtobus; v avtobusakh*
7. *metro; na metro*
8. *ulitsa; na ulitsakh*
9. *gorod; v gorodakh*
10. *gazeta; v gazetakh*

Exercise 20: Where Does This Happen?

1. *V futbol igraiut **na stadionakh**.*
2. *Vystavki khudozhnikov prokhodiat **v muzeiakh**.*
3. *Doma stroiatsia **v gorodakh**.*
4. *Parakhody plavaiut **v okeanakh**.*
5. *Spektakli staviat **v teatrakh**.*
6. *Liudi rabotaiut **v ofisakh**.*
7. *Studenty uchatsia **v universitetakh**.*
8. *Fermery vyrashchivaiut ovoshchi **na fermakh**.*
9. *Liudi chitaiut knigi **v bibliotekakh**.*
10. *Vse liubiat otdykhat' **na ostrovakh**.*

Exercise 21: Describing Supplies

1. *kilogram sakhara*
2. *bokal vina*
3. *tarelka supa*
4. *stakan moloka*
5. *lozhka soli*
6. *butylka soka*
7. *polkilo miasa*
8. *litr benzina*
9. *kilogram masla*
10. *korobka pechen'ia*

Exercise 22: Urban Landscape

1. *Zdes' net goroda.*
2. *Zdes' net ozera.*
3. *Zdes' net restorana.*
4. *Zdes' net moria.*
5. *Zdes' net banka.*
6. *Zdes' net klumby.*
7. *Zdes' net gallerei.*
8. *Zdes' net pruda.*
9. *Zdes' net ulitsy.*
10. *Zdes' net muzeia.*

Exercise 23: Whose Is This?

1. *miach futbolista*
2. *gitara muzykanta*
3. *kniga professora*
4. *mashina voditelia*
5. *komp'iuter programmista*
6. *samoliot pilota*
7. *pistolet militsionera*
8. *molotok stroitelia*

Exercise 24: Who's the Author?

1. *"Rekviem" Amadeia Motsarta*
2. *"Lunnaia sonata" Liudviga Van Betkhovena*
3. *roman "Tom Sojer" Marka Tvejna*
4. *"Dialogi" Sokrata*
5. *roman "Proshchaj, oruzhie" Ernesta Khemingueia*
6. *roman "Velikij Getsbi" Skota Fitszheral'da*
7. *philosophiia Seneki*
8. *p'esa "Chajka" Antona Chekhova*
9. *roman "Evgenij Onegin" Aleksandra Pushkina*
10. *kartina "Chiornyj kvadrat" Kazemira Malevicha*

Exercise 25: A Happy Bunch

1. *gruppa studentov*
2. *mnogo oshibok* (inserted *o* because of consonant cluster)
3. *buket roz*
4. *neskol'ko turistov*
5. *korobka konfet*
6. *mnogo druzej*
7. *korobka krekerov*
8. *buket tiul'panov*
9. *neskol'ko zdanij*
10. *gruppa pisatelej*

Exercise 26: Contradicting the Speaker

1. *V biblioteke **net knig.***
2. *Na ulitse **net avtobusov.***
3. *V metro **net liudej.***
4. *V universitete **net studentov.***
5. *V shkole **net detej.***
6. *V muzee **net turistov.***
7. *V ofise **net komp'iuterov.***
8. *V restorane **net stolov.***
9. *V kvartire **net komnat.***
10. *V okeane **net parokhodov.***

Exercise 27: How Is It Done?

1. *Ia pishu **ruchkoj.***
2. *Misha edet v Moskvu **poezdom.***
3. *Sup ediat **lozhkoj.***
4. *On uletel v Parizh **samoliotom** "Aeroflota."*
5. *Ia em makarony **vilkoj.***
6. *Olia rezhet kolbasu **nozhom.***
7. *Zhenshchina pokazyvaet na zdanie **rukoj.***
8. *Petia ezdit na rabotu **avtobusom.***

Exercise 28: Paraphrasing

1. ***Mama s papoj** poekhali v Moskvu.*
2. ***Babushka s dedushkoj** poshli v teatr.*
3. ***Sestra s bratom** risuiut.*
4. ***Lena s eio podrugoj** poshli v shkolu.*
5. ***Oleg s ego drugom** igraiut v futbol.*
6. ***Sasha s Mishej** poshli na progulku.*
7. ***Deti s uchitelem** voshli v shkolu.*
8. ***Turisty s gidom** zashli v muzej.*

Exercise 29: Reading the Story

*Kogda Dashe bylo 10 let, ona interesovalas' **baletom**. Kak vse russkie devochki, ona khotela byt' **balerinoj**. A eio brat Seriozha, kak vse russkie mal'chiki, khotel stat' **kosmonavtom**. Proshlo 10 let, i Dasha stala **inzhenerom**. Ona rabotaet na bol'shom zavode i ochen' gorditsia svoej **professiej**. A Seriozha nachal zanimat'sia **iskusstvom**. On stal **khudozhnikom**, i chasto pishet kartiny na temu baleta.*

Exercise 30: Putting It in Instrumentals

1. *Pro takikh govoriat: "On stoit na zemle obeimi **nogami**."*
2. *Roditeli vsegda gorditsia svoimi **det'mi**.*
3. *Futbolisty chasto otbivaiut miach **golovami**.*
4. *Renuar pisal **kraskami**.*
5. *On derzhal sumku obeimi **rukami**.*
6. *Byvshie druz'ya stali **vragami**.*
7. *On vstal na travu **botinkami**.* (fleeting *o*)
8. *On svobodno vladeet tremia inostrannymi **iazykami**.*

Exercise 31: Which Case?

1. *Ivan kupil doroguiu **kartinu Renuara**.*
   Ivan bought an expensive painting by Renoir.
2. *Mama stoiala na **kukhne** i meshala **borshch** dereviannoj **lozhkoj**.*
   Mom was standing in the kitchen and stirring the borshch with a wooden spoon.
3. *Za vremia turpoezdki gruppa **turistov** videla **Moskvu, Vladimir, i reku Volgu**.*
   During their trip a group of tourists saw Moscow, Vladimir, and the river Volga.
4. *Dedushka sidel na **divane** i chital **gazetu**.*
   Grandfather was sitting on the coach and reading a newspaper.
5. *V **zooparke** deti videli **medvedia, lisu, i slona**.*
   In the zoo the children saw a bear, a fox, and an elephant.
6. *Biznesmen podpisal **kontrakt** i otoslal ego **partnioru**.*

The businessman signed the contract and sent it to his partner.

7. *Nina s **Nadej** guliali v **parke.***
   Nina and Nadia were taking a walk in the park.
8. *Vadim pozvonil **kollege** i poprosil prislat' **kontrakt.***
   Vadim called his colleague and asked him to send him a contract.

Exercise 32: A Story about Dasha

1. *Etu **devushku** zovut Dasha.*
2. *Dasha zhiviot v **gorode** Novorossijske.*
3. *Dasha zhiviot ne v **dome**, a v bol'shoj **kvartire.***
4. *Dasha liubit svoiu **sobaku.***
5. *Dasha uchitsia v **universitete.***
6. *Dasha khochet stat' **professorom.***
7. *Dasha liubit chitat' **rasskazy Chekhova.***
8. *Lena – podruga **Dashi.*** (spelling rule)
9. *Lena zhiviot v **Moskve.***
10. *Dasha pishet pis'ma **Lene.***

Exercise 33: Translating into Russian

1. *Ia pishu pis'mo babushke.*
2. *Andrej s Olej zhivut v Moskve.*
3. *Ia liubliu teatr, muzyku i knigi.*
4. *Moj brat khotel stat' uchitelem.*
5. *Professor pomogaet studentam perevodit' rasskaz.*
6. *Ia chasto zvoniu drugu.*
7. *Dasha poslala Lene knigu stikhov Pushkina.*
8. *Dasha s Lenoj edut avtobusom.* [or *na avtobuse*]

Part 3

Exercise 1: How to Address?

1. *ty*
2. *vy*
3. *vy*
4. *ty*
5. *vy*
6. *ty*
7. *vy*
8. *ty*

Exercise 2: Rewriting Sentences

1. ***On** rabotaet v redaktsii.*
2. ***Oni** zhivut v Moskve.*
3. ***Ono** nazyvaetsia "Skazka."*
4. ***My** sobiraemsia poiti v kino.*
5. ***Ona** igraet na skripke.*
6. ***Vy** vchera byli v parke?*
7. ***Ono** zakryvaetsia v chas nochi.*
8. ***Oni** ochen' sladkie.*

Exercise 3: Completing the Sentences

1. ***On** poshiol domoj.*
2. ***Ona** pozvonila pozdno.*
3. ***Ono** prigotovleno iz ryby.*
4. ***Oni** pribyli v gostinitsu.*
5. ***My** pojdiom v kino.*
6. ***Vy** budete na vecherinke?*
7. ***Oni** uekhali v otpusk.*
8. ***Ona** rabotaet na pochte.*

Exercise 4: Rewriting Sentences

1. *Olia vstretila **ego.***
2. *Ia nikogda ne videla **eio.***
3. *Vy chitali **eio?***
4. *Ia chasto naveshchaiu **ikh.***
5. ***Nas** priglasili v gosti.*
6. *Ia ne videla vchera **vas.***
7. ***Ikh** nazyvali "peredvizhnikami."*
8. ***Ego** zovut Vasilij Petrov.*

Exercise 5: Choosing the Correct Case

1. ***Ona** idiot v kino.*
   She is going to the movies.
2. *Ty videl **eio** po televizoru?*
   Have you seen her on TV?
3. *Vy znaete **ego?***

Do you know him?

4. **Oni** rabotaiut s moim muzhem.
   They work with my husband.

5. **Nas** nazyvaiut luchshimi druz'iami.
   They call us best friends.

6. **Vy** segodnia prekrasno vygliadite.
   You look great today.

7. Ia vstretila **ego** na ulitse.
   I met him on the street.

8. **Ikh** davno nikto ne videl.
   No one has seen them for a long time.

Exercise 6: Completing Sentences

1. Misha liubit **ego.**
2. Lena uvidela **ego.**
3. Turisty smotriat **ego.**
4. Ia prinesu **eio.**
5. Khoziajka prigotovila **ikh.**
6. Militsioner ostanovil **ego.**
7. Vy videli vchera **eio?**
8. **Ego** prigotovil novyj povar.

Exercise 7: Rewriting Sentences

1. Natasha pozvonila **ej.**
2. Olia podarila **emu** knigu.
3. **Vam** prihsla posylka.
4. **Emu** chasto zvonili devushki.
5. **Im** prinosiat gazety kazhdyj den'.
6. **Nam** podarili sobaku.
7. **Ej** 20 let.
8. Napishite pis'mo **ej.** [Napishi ej pis'mo.]

Exercise 8: Choosing the Correct Case

1. My prishli k **nej.**
   We came to visit her.
2. **Ty** liubish' chitat'?
   Do you like to read?
3. **Tebe** nravitsia eta kniga?
   Do you like this book?
4. My chasto khodim k **nej** v gosti.
   We often go to visit her.

5. Peredajte **mne**, pozhalujsta, sol'.
   Pass me the salt, please!
6. **Oni** zhivut v tsentre goroda.
   They live downtown.
7. K **nim** priekhali gosti iz Sibiri.
   They have visitors from Siberia.
8. **Nam** nravitsia zdes' zhit'.
   We like living here.

Exercise 9: Completing Sentences

1. Vera pozvonila **ej.**
2. Podari etu knigu **emu.**
3. **Nam** eta muzyka ne nravitsia.
4. Mal'chik pomogaet **ej.**
5. **Vam**, navernoe, kholodno.
6. Nadia pokazala **im** gorod.
7. Rasskazhi **im** novosti.
8. Pokazhi **emu** dorogu.

Exercise 10: Rewriting Sentences

1. Kniga lezhit na **niom.**
2. My liubim otdykhat' na **niom.**
3. Druz'ia sideli v kafe i razgovarivali o **nej.**
4. Moj kosheliok v **nej.**
5. Na vystavke oni razgovarivali o **nikh.**
6. Ia chasto dumala o **nas.**
7. Na **nej** bylo krasnoe plat'e.
8. V **niom** zhivut liudi raznykh natsional'nostej.

Exercise 11: Choosing the Correct Case

1. **On** zanimaetsia muzykoj.
   He studies music.
2. Lena vsegda dumaet o **nikh.**
   Lena always thinks about them.
3. Vam rasskazyvali chto-nibud' o **nas**?
   Have you been told anything about us?
4. Davajte pogovorim o **nej.**
   Let's talk about her.
5. Na **niom** opasno ezdit'.
   It's dangerous to ride it.
6. **My** igraem na pianino.

We play/are playing the piano.

7. *O **vas** khodiat legendy.*
   You are a legendary figure. (Literally: There are legends circulating about you.)

8. ***Ona** tantsuet v Bol'shom teatre.*
   She dances for the Bolshoy theater.

Exercise 12: Choosing the Correct Pronoun

1. *V **niom** malo smysla.*
2. *Nam nado pogovorit' o **nej**.*
3. *Na **niom** davno nikto ne igraet.*
4. *On podumal o **nikh**.*
5. *Etot pisatel' napisal vse svoi rasskazy o **nej**.*
6. *V **niom** zhivut moi znakomye.*
7. *Na **nikh** rastiot vinograd.*
8. *My vchera razgovarivali o **vas**.*

Exercise 13: Rewriting Sentences

1. *Deti proveli leto u **neio**.*
2. ***Eio** segodnia net.*
3. *U nas sovsem net **ego**.*
4. *Turisty ostanovilis' okolo **nego**.*
5. *Davajte vstretimsia u **nego** doma.*
6. *V etikh lesakh net **ikh**.*
7. *Eto mashina **ego**.*
8. *Eto gazon **ikh**.*

Exercise 14: Choosing the Correct Case

1. *U **nikh** vsegda khoroshee nastroenie.*
   They are always in a good mood.
2. ***Ia** skoro poedu vo Frantsiiu.*
   I will soon go to France.
3. ***Ego** nikogda net doma.*
   He is never home.
4. ***Nas** ne bylo na etoj vecherinke.*
   We weren't at that party.
5. *U **vas** est' bilety?*
   Do you have tickets?
6. ***My** liubim puteshestvovat'.*
   We love to travel.
7. *Okolo **neio** vsegda vrashchaiutsia liudi.*

She is always surrounded by people. (Literally: People are always rotating around her.)

8. *U **nego** prekrasnye sposobnosti.*
   He is very gifted. (Literally: He has wonderful abilities.)

Exercise 15: Phone Conversations

1. *Eio net.*
2. *Ego net.*
3. *Ego net.*
4. *Eio net.*
5. *Ikh net.*
6. *Ikh net.*
7. *Eio net.*
8. *Ikh net.*

Exercise 16: Rewriting Sentences

1. *Lena ochen' zainteresovalas' **im**.*
2. *Vy chasto vidites' s **nimi**?*
3. *Moia dochka druzhit s **nej**.*
4. *Gid zajmiotsia **imi**.*
5. *Ty risuesh' **im**?*
6. *Prikhodite v gosti s **nim**.*
7. *Ia chasto razgovarivaiu s **nimi** po telefonu.*
8. *On uvlioksia **ej**.*

Exercise 17: Choosing the Correct Case

1. *Masha razgovarivala s **nej** po telefonu.*
   Masha talked to her on the phone.
2. ***My** razgovarivali ochen' gromko.*
   We talked very loudly.
3. *Kogda on byl molodym, devushki chasto **im** uvlekalis'.*
   When he was young, young women were often infatuated with him.
4. *Vy pojdiote s **nami** v teatr?*
   Will you go to the theater with us?
5. ***On** igraet v futbol.*
   He plays soccer.
6. *Vasia igraet s **nim** v shakhmaty.*
   Vasia plays chess with him.
7. ***Ona** uvlekaetsia iskusstvom.*
   She is interested in art.
8. *On uvlekaetsia **ej**.*
   He is interested in her.

Exercise 18: Completing Sentences

1. *Ia pogovoriu s **nim**.*
2. *Ia idu v kino s **nej**.*
3. *Vadim liubit sporit' s **nimi**.*
4. *My khotim vstretit'sia s **vami**.*
5. *My chasto razgovarivaem s **nimi**.*
6. *Moj brat edet v otpusk s **nej**.*
7. *On vsegda prikhodit s **nim**.*
8. *Viktor khochet pogovorit' s **nami**.*

Exercise 19: Using Reflexive Pronouns

2. They bought a present for themselves.
3. She saw herself in the mirror.
5. She congratulated herself.
8. They took a dog along.

Exercise 20: Completing Sentences

1. *Ona kupila **sebe** mashinu.*
2. *Volodia vzial s **soboj** syna.*
3. *On liubil smotret' **sebia** po televizoru.*
4. *Oni prigotovili **sebe** uzhin.*
5. *On nazyval **sebia** velikim kompozitorom.*
6. *Ulitka nosit svoj domik na **sebe**.*
7. *Ona vsegda nakhodila v **sebe** mnogo nedostatkov.*
8. *Vy mozhete gordit'sya **soboj**.*

Exercise 21: Translating Sentences

1. *On gorditsia soboj.*
2. *Ona sdelala sebe podarok.*
3. *Sobaka uvidela sebia v zerkale.*
4. *Oni kupili sebe dom.*
5. *Ty mozhesh' sebia slyshat'?*
6. *Ia kupil sebe tsvety.*
7. *Oni uvideli sebia po televizoru.*
8. *On schital sebia schastlivym.*

Exercise 22: Declining *etotz*.

1. Nominative: *etot*
2. Accusative: *etot* (inanimate), *etogo* (animate)
3. Dative: *etomu*
4. Prepositional: *etom*
5. Genitive: *etogo*
6. Instrumental: *etim*

Exercise 23: Declining *ta*

1. Nominative: *ta*
2. Accusative: *tu*
3. Dative: *toj*
4. Prepositional: *toj*
5. Genitive: *toj*
6. Instrumental: *toj*

Exercise 24: Declining *takie*

1. Nominative: *takie*
2. Accusative: *takie* (inanimate); *takikh* (animate)
3. Dative: *takim*
4. Prepositional: *takikh*
5. Genitive: *takikh*
6. Instrumental: *takimi*

Exercise 25: Translating Phrases

1. *etot dom*
2. *ta zhenshchina*
3. *eti pis'ma*
4. *takaia kniga*
5. *takoj krasivyj den'*
6. *te liudi*
7. *takie tseny*
8. *eta gostinitsa*

Exercise 26: Completing Sentences

1. *Ia nikogda ne videla **takogo** dozhdia.*
2. *Vy znaete **etogo** cheloveka?*
3. *Moia mashina von **ta**, belaia.*
4. ***Takie** dni luchshe provodit' na svezhem vozdukhe.*
5. ***Ta** kvartira byla luchshe, chem novaia.*
6. *V **takuiu** pogodu ia liubliu chitat'.*
7. ***Eti** frukty ochen' vkusnye.*
8. ***Etimi** kraskami trudno risovat'.*

Exercise 27: Completing Sentences

1. *Eto* **moia** *mashina.*
2. *Ia ne pomniu* **Vashe** *imia.*
3. *Gde zhivut* **tvoi** *roditeli?*
4. **Nash** *dom stoit u moria.*
5. *V etom dome zhiviot* **ego** *sestra.*
6. **Eio** *kniga stala ochen' populiarnoj.*
7. **Ikh** *kvartira na vtorom etazhe.*
8. **Eio** *deti khodiat v shkolu.*

Exercise 28: Completing Sentences

1. *Ia liubliu* **moj gorod.**
2. *Ia guliaiu s* **moej sobakoj.**
3. *Kak proshiol* **Vash otpusk?**
4. *Vy znaete* **ego sestru?**
5. *My poedem na* **eio mashine.**
6. *Eto* **ikh deti.**
7. *U menia net* **tvoego nomera.**
8. *My kupili tsvety* **nashemy uchiteliu.**

Exercise 29: Completing Sentences

1. *Eto* **ego** *mashina.*
2. *Eto* **ikh** *dacha.*
3. *Eto* **eio** *kniga.*
4. *Eto* **eio** *pal'to.*
5. *Eto* **nashi** *diski.*
6. *Eto* **vashi** *podarki.*
7. *Eto* **ego** *dom.*
8. *Eto* **eio** *tarelka.*

Exercise 30: Completing Sentences

1. *Ona sela v* **svoiu** *mashinu.*
2. *On chasto razgovarival so* **svoimi** *roditeliami.*
3. *Oni zanimalis'* **svoimi** *delami.*
4. *Lena zapisala* **svoj** *nomer telefona.*
5. *More imeet* **svoj** *nepovtorimyj zapakh.*
6. *Turisty dostali* **svoi** *fotoapparaty.*
7. *Moj drug uekhal na* **svoiu** *dachu.*
8. *Nadia sidela na* **svoej** *liubimoj skamejke.*

Exercise 31: Who Has What?

1. *U Leny est' sobaka. Natasha guliaet s* **eio** *sobakoj.*
2. *U Vadima est' mashina. Vadim edet na* **svoej** *mashine.*
3. *U moikh roditelej est' dacha. Moi roditeli uekhali na* **svoiu** *dachu.*
4. *U moikh sosedej est' dzhakuzi. Ia sizhu v* **ikh** *dzhakuzi.*
5. *U Nadi est' samoliot. Nadia letaet na* **svoiom** *samoliote.*
6. *U Very est' mototsikl. Vera ezdit na* **svoiom** *mototsikle.*
7. *U Oli est' televizor. Natasha smotrit* **eio** *televizor.*
8. *U Ivana est' koshka. Andrei kormit* **ego** *koshku.*

Exercise 32: Changing the Pronouns

1. *dozhd'* – **Kakoj? Chej?**
2. *strana* – **Kakaia? Ch'ia?**
3. *stol* – **Kakoj? Chej?**
4. *ploshchad'* – **Kakaia? Ch'ia?**
5. *druz'ia* – **Kakie? Ch'i?**
6. *telefon* – **Kakoj? Chej?**
7. *veshchi* – **Kakie? Ch'i?**
8. *plat'e* – **Kakoe? Ch'io?**

Exercise 33: Asking Questions

1. *Kakoe okno?*
2. *Ch'ia rabota?*
3. *Kakoj sobor?*
4. *Ch'io pis'mo?*
5. *Kakie podarki?*
6. *Ch'i deti?*
7. *Ch'i knigi?*
8. *Ch'io imia?*

Exercise 34: Who or What?

1. *Komu my podarili podarok?*
2. *Kogo ia uvidela?*
3. *Kem gordiatsia roditeli?*
4. *Chto risuet mal'shik?*
5. *Chego ona boitsia?*
6. *Komu ia pozvonil?*
7. *Chem oni risuiut?*
8. *S kem ona poshla v pokhod?*

Exercise 35: Asking Questions

1. *Kto rabotaet v shkole?*
2. *Chto stoialo v komnate?*
3. *Kto ran'she zhil v Moskve?*
4. *Chto prodaiotsia na rynke?*
5. *Kto pishet romany?*
6. *Kto liubit moloko?*
7. *Kto priekhal iz Kanady?*
8. *Chto stoit pered domom?*

Exercise 36: Something or Someone

1. *Na stole lezhalo **chto-to**.*
2. *V komnate zhdal **kto-to**.*
3. *K vrachu prishiol **kto-to**.*
4. ***Kto-to** prislal sestre podarok.*
5. ***Kto-to** pozvonil mne po telefonu.*
6. ***Kto-to** napisal knigu.*
7. ***Chto-to** stoialo u doma.*
8. ***Chto-to** viselo na veshalke.*

Exercise 37: Something Indefinite

1. *Ya videla **kogo-to**.*
2. *My videli **chto-to**.*
3. *Gid rasskazyvaet legendu **komu-to**.*
4. *Ya chasto pishu pis'ma **komu-to**.*
5. *Vadim dumaet o **chiom-to**.*
6. *Kolia dumaet o **kom-to**.*
7. *Ania interesuetsa **chem-to**.*
8. *Ania khochet stat' **kem-to**.*

Exercise 38: Specific or Unspecific?

1. *Eto **kakaia-to** kniga.*
2. *On uvidel **kakoe-to** zdanie.*
3. *Vy chitaete **kakie-nibud'** romany?*
4. *Pozvonite **ch'im-to** roditeliam.*
5. *Vy znaete **chej-nibud'** adres?*
6. *Ona liubit **kakuiu-nibud'** muzyku?*
7. *U vas est' **chej-nibud'** telefon?*
8. *Na stole stoiala **kakaia-to** chashka.*

Exercise 39: Producing Negative Pronouns

1. *nikto* – nobody
2. *nikakoj* – none (literally: no kind)
3. *nichej* – nobody's
4. *nichego* – nothing
5. *nikakaja* – none (literally: no kind)
6. *nich'i* – nobody's
7. *nikakie* – none (literally: no kind)
8. *nich'io* – nobody's

Exercise 40: Being Negative

1. *Nikto ne napisal pis'mo.*
2. *Eto nichej telefon.*
3. *Nikto ne napisal knigu.*
4. *Na stole nichego ne lezhit.*
5. *Mne ne nraviatsia nikakie sobaki.*
6. *Nikto ne zashiol v gostinitsu.*
7. *Nichego ne prishlo po pochte.*
8. *On ne liubit nikakie pesni.*

Exercise 41: Declining *kotoryj*

1. *Vot devushka, **kotoraia** zhiviot v moiom pod'ezde.*
2. *Vot dom, v **kotorom** ya zhivu.*
3. *Eto liudi, s **kotorymi** my vmeste rabotaem.*
4. *Vot to kafe, v **kotorom** my vstretilis'.*
5. *Eto sportsmen, **kotoryj** vyigral sorevnovanie.*
6. *Vot kniga, **kotoruiu** ia napisal.*
7. *Eto vrach, **kotoromu** ty dolzhen pozvonit'.*
8. *Eto mashina, **kotoruiu** vodit moj drug.*

Exercise 42: Making Complex Sentences

1. *Po ulitse shiol molodoj chelovek, kotoryj rabotaet v banke.*
2. *Na stsenu vyshla aktrisa, kotoraia igrala v fil'me "S liogkim parom."*
3. *V dver' postuchala sosedka, kotoraia zhiviot naprotiv.*
4. *Mne pozvonil drug, kotoryj zhiviot v Parizhe.*
5. *Ia napisala knigu, kotoraia stala izvestnoj.*
6. *Lena poteriala sumku, kotoruiu ej podarila eio mama.*
7. *My nashli khoroshee kafe, v kotorom podaiut otlichnyj chaj s travami.*
8. *Moj drug napisal roman, kotoryj sdelal ego bogatym.*

Exercise 43: A Story about Dasha

1. *Dasha zhiviot s **nej**.*
2. ***Ona** rabotaet v muzee.*
3. ***On** zakryvaetsia rano.*
4. *Posle raboty Dasha vstrechaet **eio**.*
5. ***Oni** idut v kino ili v kafe.*
6. *V kafe Dasha i Olia vstrechaiutsia s **nimi**.*
7. *Oni razgovarivaiut o **nej**.*
8. *Druz'ia ochen' liubiat **eio**.*

Exercise 44: Reading Chekhov

1. And later he met her in the city garden and in the park …
2. He wasn't even forty, but he already had a twelve-year-old daughter …
3. There was something attractive in his appearance …
4. But after each new meeting with an interesting woman, this experience somehow slipped from his memory.
5. Her expression, her stride … told him that she is from decent society … that she is bored here.
6. She did not answer. (Literally: She answered nothing)
7. Gurov cut a piece for himself and started to eat unhurriedly.
8. And now I've become a vulgar, bad woman, whom anyone can despise.

Exercise 45: Translating into Russian

1. *Kakuiu iubku ty nadenesh'?*
2. *Eio roditeli gordiatsia ej.*

3. *My s nim vmeste uchilis' v shkole.*
4. *Emu sorok chetyre.*
5. *Ch'i eto deti?*
6. *Prinesi knigu, kotoruiu tebe dala tvoia sestra.*
7. *Ona pozvonila svoej sestre.*
8. *Oni kupili sebe podarok.*

Part 4

Exercise 1: Changing the Adjective

1. *goluboj* – **golubaia, goluboe, golubye**
2. *sil'nyj* – **sil'naia, sil'noe, sil'nye**
3. *pravyj* – **pravaia, pravoe, pravye**
4. *vesiolyj* – **vesiolaia, vesioloe, vesiolye**
5. *goriachij* – **goriachaia, goriachee, goriachie**
6. *poslednij* – **posledniaia, poslednee, poslednie**
7. *ryzhij* – **ryzhaia, ryzhee, ryzhie**
8. *smeshnoj* – **smeshnaia, smeshnoe, smeshnye**

Exercise 2: Agreeing Adjectives with Nouns

1. ***khoroshaia** kniga*
2. ***molodoj** chelovek*
3. ***bol'shoe** okno*
4. ***khudoj** muzhchina*
5. ***chistyj** gorod*
6. ***sinee** plat'e*
7. ***vysokaia** devushka*
8. ***tsentral'naia** ploshchad'*
9. ***korotkij** den'*
10. ***letniaia** noch'*

Exercise 3: Geography

1. *Chiornoe more*
2. *Beloe more*
3. *Krasnoe more*
4. *Zhioltoe more*
5. *Krasnaia ploshchad'*
6. *Tikhij okean*
7. *Baltijskoe more*

8. *Miortvoe more*
9. *Mramornoe more*
10. *Kitajskaia stena*

Exercise 4: Recognizing Plural Adjectives

1. **tioplye** *zimy;* **tioplyj**
2. **malen'kie** *deti;* **malen'kij**
3. **krasnye** *avtobusy;* **krasnyj**
4. **glavnye** *ulitsy;* **glavnyj**
5. **krasivye** *tsvety;* **krasivyj**
6. **belye** *nochi;* **belyj**
7. **dorogie** *podarki;* **dorogoj**
8. **dlinnye** *pis'ma;* **dlinnyj**
9. **golubye** *glaza;* **goluboj**
10. **vesiolye** *pesni;* **vesiolyj**

Exercise 5: Completing Sentences

1. *Ya vstretil* **umnogo** *cheloveka.*
2. *Daj pochitat'* **interesnuiu** *knigu!*
3. *Ia uvidel na ulitse* **starogo** *druga.*
4. *Nadia liubit slushat'* **klassicheskuiu** *muzyku.*
5. *Ona napisala muzhu* **dlinnoe** *pis'mo.*
6. *Naden' svoio* **liubimoe** *plat'e.*
7. *My pojmali* **bol'shuiu** *rybu.*
8. *Oni kupili* **novyj** *stol.*
9. *Vy kogda-nibud' videli* **afrikanskogo** *slona?*
10. *On chitaet* **tolstyj** *zhurnal.*

Exercise 6: Answering Questions

1. *krasnaia; krasnyj*
2. *malen'kij; malen'kij*
3. *kholodnaia; kholodnyj*
4. *krasivoe; krasivyj*
5. *tioplyj; tioplyj*
6. *belye; belyj*
7. *spelye; spelyj*
8. *vkusnyj; vkusnyj*
9. *smeshnye; smeshnoj*
10. *bol'shoj; bol'shoj*

Exercise 7: Changing Phrases

1. *beluiu majku*
2. *vkusnyj obed*
3. *zhioltyj tiul'pan*
4. *amerikanskogo turista*
5. *Krasnuiu ploshchad'*
6. *dereviannyj stol*
7. *vysokuiu temperaturu*
8. *iuzhnoe more*
9. *polnuiu lunu*
10. *gornoe ozero*

Exercise 8: Putting It in Dative

1. *molodoj uchitel' –* **molodomu uchiteliu**
2. *bol'shoj sad –* **bol'shomu sadu**
3. *starinnyj dvorets –* **starinnomu dvortsu**
4. *drevniaia tserkov' –* **drevnej tserkvi**
5. *glavnyj prospect –* **glavnomu prospektu**
6. *sinee plat'e –* **sinemu plat'iu**
7. *dorogaia gostinitsa –* **dorogoj gostinitse**
8. *starshij brat–* **starshemu bratu**
9. *tioploe more–* **tioplomu moriu**
10. *zolotoe kol'tso –* **zolotomu kol'tsu**

Exercise 9: Completing Sentences

1. *Professor chitaet lektsiiu* **novym** *studentam.*
2. *Gid pokazyvaet dvorets* **amerikanskim** *turistam.*
3. *Sasha zvonit* **liubimomu** *bratu.*
4. *Misha dal edu* **chiornoj** *sobake.*
5. *Babushka rasskazala* **malen'komu** *vnuku skazku.*
6. *Zhurnal "Zdorov'e" pomogaet* **molodym** *roditeliam.*
7. *Eta gazeta daiot* **novym** *chitateliam skidku.*
8. *John prislal otkrytku svoemu* **russkomu** *drugu.*

Exercise 10: Telling Where

1. *Pitstsu mozhno zakazat' v* **ital'ianskom** *restorane.*
2. *Boston nakhoditsia na* **vostochnom** *poberezh'e SShA.*
3. *V* **russkikh** *sem'yakh chasto gotoviat borshch.*
4. *My chasto otdykhaem na* **tropicheskikh** *ostrovakh.*
5. *Gavajskie ostrova raspolozheny v* **Tikhom** *okeane.*

6. *Turisty liubiat byvat' v **drevnem** Kremle.*
7. *Gorod Odessa nakhoditsia na **Chiornom** more.*
8. *Roman Khemingueia "Proshchaj, oruzhie" rasskazyvaet o Pervoj **mirovoj** vojne.*

Exercise 11: Describing Locations

1. *malen'kij gorod – v malen'kom gorode*
2. *chistoe ozero – v chistom ozere*
3. *svetlaia komnata – v svetloj komnate*
4. *bol'shoj stadion – na bol'shom stadione*
5. *iuzhnaia strana – v iuzhnoj strane*
6. *severnyj ostrov – na severnom ostrove*
7. *glavnaia ulitsa – na glavnoj ulitse*
8. *tioploe more – v tioplom more*
9. *shirokij prospekt – na shirokom prospekte*
10. *tsentral'naia ploshchad' – tsentral'noj ploshchadi*

Exercise 12: Is There or Not?

1. *V Moskve **net vysokikh gor**.*
2. *V Kalifornii **net belykh medvedej**.*
3. *V Rossii **net bol'shikh krokodilov**.*
4. *V Tekhase **net shirokikh rek**.*
5. *V Los Andzhelese **net drevnikh soborov**.*
6. *Na ekvatore **net kholodnykh mesiatsev**.*
7. *V Venetsii **net krasivykh neboskriobov**.*
8. *V Moskve **net vodnykh kanalov**.*

Exercise 13: Making It Genitive

1. *muzyka **izvestnogo kompozitora***
   a well-known composer's music
2. *kartina **znamenitogo khudozhnika***
   a famous painter's painting
3. *pesni **ital'ianskikh ispolnitelej***
   music by Italian performers
4. *doma **molodykh iuristov***
   houses of young lawyers
5. *ulitsy **novykh gorodov***
   streets of new cities
6. *geroi **liubimykh knig***
   characters of favorite books
7. *rubashka **starshego brata***
   an elder brother's shirt
8. *telefon **miloj devushki***
   the phone number of a nice young woman

Exercise 14: Completing Sentences

1. *Vadim stanet **bol'shim** nachal'nikom.*
2. *Nadia poshla v kino s **liubimymi** podrugami.*
3. *Olia khotela stat' **opernoj** pevitsej.*
4. *Etot khudozhnik pishet kartiny **maslianymi** kraskami.*
5. *Turisty osmotreli gorod s **otlichnym** ekskursovodom.*
6. *Vika zanimaetsia **khudozhestvennoj** gimnastikoj.*
7. *Okhotnik pobedil l'va **golymi** rukami.*
8. *Anna interesuetsia **russkoj** literaturoj.*

Exercise 15: Answering Questions

1. *Devochka risuet sinim karandashom.*
2. *Mal'chik pishet chiornoj ruchkoj.*
3. *Khudozhnik risuet yarkimi kraskami.*
4. *Tom zanimaetsia amerikanskim futbolom.*
5. *Sveta interesuetsia klassicheskoj muzykoj.*
6. *Nadia sidit v parke s liubimoj knigoj.*
7. *Devushka ukrashaet komnatu belymi tsvetami.*
8. *Alla interesuetsia evropejskoj istoriej.*

Exercise 16: Paraphrasing

2. *Stol svoboden.*
3. *Gorod krasiv.*
4. *Klimat surov.*
5. *Devushka pechal'na.*

Exercise 17: Using Short Adjectives

1. *Biblioteka zakryta.*
2. *Mesta zaniaty.*
3. *Ty segodnia svoboden? Or Vy segodnia svobodny?*
4. *Magazin otkryt.*
5. *On segodnia bolen.*
6. *Anna zaniata.*
7. *Eto kupe svobodno.*
8. *Vse okna zakryty.*

Exercise 18: Whose Is This?

1. *Valia – **Valin***
2. *Misha – **Mishin***
3. *Sergej – **Sergeev***
4. *Seriozha – **Seriozhin***
5. *Masha – **Mashin***
6. *Oleg – **Olegov***
7. *Irina – **Irinin***
8. *Liosha – **Lioshin***

Exercise 19: Paraphrasing the Possessives

1. *kniga Vadima – vadimova kniga*
2. *dom Nadi – **nadin dom***
3. *zhurnal papy – **papin zhurnal***
4. *plat'e mamy – **mamino plat'e***
5. *ochki dedushki – **dedushkiny ochki***
6. *telefon Oli - **olin telefon***
7. *adres Sashi – **sashin adres***
8. *vaza babushka – **babushkina vaza***

Exercise 20: Forming Comparatives

1. *svetlyj – **svetlee***
2. *krasivyj – **krasivee***
3. *novyj – **novee***
4. *milyj – **milee***
5. *dostupnyj – **dostupnee***
6. *nezhnyj – **nezhnee***
7. *vesiolyj – **veselee***
8. *staryj – **staree***

Exercise 21: Paraphrasing Comparatives

2. *Imejl bystree pis'ma.*
3. *Leto teplee zimy.*
4. *Galstuk temnee kostiuma.*
5. *Grusha vkusnee iabloka.*
6. *Avtobus medlennee metro.*
7. *Plat'e krasivee briuk.*
8. *Ania smelee Borisa.*

Exercise 22: Forming Superlatives

2. *umnejshij – **samyj umnyj***
3. *dobrejshij – **samyj dobryj***
4. *schastlivejshij – **samyj schastlivyj***
5. *novejshij – **samyj novyj***
6. *chistejshij – **samyj chistyj***
7. *milejshij – **samyj milyj***
8. *strojnejshij – **samyj strojnyj***

Exercise 23: Translating Phrases

1. *samyj umnyj rebionok*
2. *samyj dorogoj podarok*
3. *samaia populiarnaia pesnia*
4. *samaia staraia traditsiia*
5. *samyj opytnyj uchitel'*
6. *samyj vkusnyj tort*
7. *samoe tioploe pal'to*
8. *samaia bystraia mashina*

Exercise 24: What Is Better?

1. *Leto **luchshe** zimy.*
2. *Kvartira **dorozhe** mashiny.*
3. *Okean **dal'she** moria.*
4. *Baraban **gromche** skripki.*
5. *Konfety **deshevle** pechen'ia.*
6. *Golos Mishi **khuzhe,** chem golos Very.*
7. *Reka Volga **koroche,** chem reka Nil.*
8. *Sobaka **men'she,** chem slon.*

Exercise 25: Answering Questions

2. *Mersedes dorozhe Volgi.*
3. *Solntse bol'she luny.*
4. *Fevral' koroche yanvaria.*
5. *Piramidy starshe Kremlia.*
6. *Everest vyshe Olimpa.*
7. *V Maiami zharche, chem v Moskve.*
8. *Luna blizhe solntsa.*

Exercise 26: Completing Sentences

1. *My zhiviom na **prekrasnoj** planete s **zelionymi** lesami i **golubymi** oziorami.*
   We live on a wonderful planet with green forests and blue lakes.
2. *Uchitel' vruchil priz **samomu talantlivomu** ucheniku.*
   The teacher gave the price to the most talented student.
3. *Olia liubim nosit' **krasnuiu** rubashku i **sinie** briuki.*
   She likes to wear a red shirt and blue pants.
4. *Gruppa **russkikh** turistov posetila **drevnie** khramy **solnechnoj** Ispanii.*
   A group of tourists visited the ancient churches of sunny Spain.
5. *Oni vstretilis' v **samom romantichnom** gorode v mire – Parizhe.*
   They met in the most romantic city in the world – Paris.
6. *Ania chasto pishet **dlinnye** pis'ma **amerikanskoj** podruge.*
   Ania often writes long letters to her American friend.
7. *Ia liubliu kupat'sia v **chistoj** vode **gornykh** ozior.*
   I like to bathe in the clean water of mountain lakes.
8. *Vera segodnia **bol'na**, a apteka **zakryta**.*
   Vera is feeling sick today, and the pharmacy is closed.

Exercise 27: A Story about Dasha

1. *Dasha zhiviot v **tioplom** klimate.*
2. *Zimoj Dasha nosit **beluiu** kurtku.*
3. ***Dashin** liubimyj sviter – **goluboj**.*
4. *V **zharkie** mesiatsy Dasha nosit **letnie** plat'ia.*
5. *Dasha guliaet v **samom bol'shom** parke.*
6. *Dasha chitaet v parke, esli ona ne ochen' **zaniata**.*
7. *V parke Dasha chitaet **liubimye** knigi.*
8. *Eto knigi **russkikh** pisatelej.*

Part 5

Exercise 1: Forming Adverbs

1. *vkusnyj – **vkusno***
2. *kholodnyj – **kholodno***
3. *medlennyj – **medlenno***
4. *gratsioznyj – **gratsiozno***
5. *effektivnyj – **effektivno***

6. *umelyj – **umelo***
7. *khoroshij – **khorosho***
8. *vesiolyj – **veselo***

Exercise 2: Writing Adverbs

1. *khorosho*
2. *bystro*
3. *redko*
4. *plokho*
5. *chasto*
6. *medlenno*
7. *otlichno*
8. *prekrasno*

Exercise 3: Making a Comparison

1. *Olen' begaet bystree, chem cherepakha.*
2. *Del'fin plavaet gratsioznee, chem sobaka.*
3. *Chelovek govorit luchshe, chem obez'iana.*
4. *Velosiped ezdit medlennee, chem mashina.*
5. *Povar gotovit vkusnee, chem mama.* (or *Mama gotovit vkusnee, chem povar.*)
6. *Ptitsy poiut gromche, chem ryby.*
7. *Futbolist igraet agressivnee, chem shakhmatist.*
8. *Obez'iana dvigaetsia energichnee, chem koala.*

Exercise 4: Doing It the Best

1. *Moia sestra risuet **luchshe vsego**.*
2. *Kolia igraet v futbol **energichnee vsekh**.*
3. *Isidora Dunkan tantsevala **krasivee vsekh**.*
4. *Ia govoriu po-anglijski **bystree vsego**.*
5. *My znaem etogo uchitelia **khuzhe vsekh**.*
6. *Karuzo poiot **gromche vsekh**.*
7. *Natasha liubit morozhennoe **bol'she vsego**.*
8. *Kostia opiat' el **men'she vsekh**.*

Exercise 5: Where Did It Happen?

1. *vverkhu*
2. *blizko*
3. *sleva*
4. *szadi*
5. *vnutri*
6. *tam*

Exercise 6: Where or Where to?

1. *Gde Vy rabotaete?*
2. *Idi siuda.*
3. *Zdes' ia zhivu.*
4. *Kuda ty edesh' v otpusk?*
5. *Ia ne liubliu tuda khodit'.*
6. *Tam nakhoditsia biblioteka.*
7. *Kuda idiot etot avtobus?*
8. *Zavtra siuda priedet populiarnaia rok-gruppa.*

Exercise 7: Giving Details about Time

1. *On rabotal v shkole 55 let. On rabotal v shkole dolgo.*
2. *V poslednij raz ia byla v Parizhe v 1979 godu. V poslednij raz ia byla v Parizhe davno.*
3. *Vchera ia nachala novuiu knigu. Ia nedavno* (or *uzhe*) *nachala novuiu knigu.*
4. *Cherez 10 minut Lena ujdiot s raboty. Lena eshchio na rabote.*
5. *V 2000 godu mne bylo 20 let. Togda mne bylo 20 let.*
6. *On uezzhaet zavtra. Kogda on uezzhaet?*
7. *Vchera ia vstretil starogo druga. Nedavno ia vstretil starogo druga.*
8. *Oni sideli v restorane 4 chasa. Oni dolgo sideli v restorane.*

Exercise 8: A Story about Dasha

1. *Dasha prekrasno risuet.*
2. *Dasha pishet kartiny redko.*
3. *Dasha zakanchivaet kartiny bystro.*
4. *Dasha podpisyvaet svoi kartiny vnizu sprava.*
5. *Dasha eshchio* (or *poka*) *ne prodala ni odnoj svoej kartiny.*
6. *Dasha nadeetsya prodat' svoi kartiny skoro i dorogo.*

Exercise 9: Reading Chekhov

1. They married him early, . . .
2. She read a lot, . . .
3. He started to cheat on her a long time ago; he cheated often, . . .
4. It seemed to him that the bitter experiences sufficiently taught him . . .
5. In the company of men, he was bored . . .
6. He beckoned the spitz-dog blandly . . .
7. Time goes fast . . .

8. It's only customary to say that it's boring here.

Exercise 10: Translating into Russian

1. *On prishiol rano.*
2. *Ona eshchio ne pozvonila.*
3. *Lena pishet krasivo.*
4. *On znaet matematiku khuzhe, chem ego brat.*
5. *Kuda on idiot?*
6. *On dolgo spal.*
7. *Vy ochen' khorosho govorite po-russki.*
8. *Ona risuet luchshe vsekh v svoiom klasse.*

Part 6

Exercise 1: Recognizing Numerals

1. *8*
2. *12*
3. *90*
4. *4*
5. *25*
6. *10*
7. *50*
8. *100*
9. *2*
10. *18*
11. *80*
12. *43*
13. *15*
14. *7*
15. *11*

Exercise 2: One or Two?

1. *2 – dve devushki*
2. *2 – dva okna*
3. *1 – odno slovo*
4. *1 – odin restoran*
5. *2 – dva stula*
6. *1 – odin dom*
7. *2 – dve koshki*
8. *1 – odna sobaka*
9. *2 – dve mashiny*
10. *1 – odna iubka*

Exercise 3: Planning a Party

1. *sorok buterbrodov*
2. *piatnadtsat' arbuzov*
3. *sorok chetyre iabloka*
4. *dvenadtsat' tarelok*
5. *dvadtsat' dva stakana*
6. *tridtsat' odin banan*
7. *tridtsat' tri apel'sina*
8. *tridtsat' piat' mandarinov*

Exercise 4: Age and Time

1. *Lene dvadtsat' piat' let.*
2. *Ia zhdal chetyre chasa.*
3. *Ia zdes' zhivu dva goda.*
4. *Moemu synu tri mesiatsa.*
5. *Moemu bratu odin god.*
6. *On spal vosem' chasov.*
7. *Fil'm idiot sorok dve minuty.*
8. *Podozhdi piat' minut.*

Exercise 5: Recognizing Numerals

1. *piatyj*
2. *desiatyj*
3. *piatnadtsatys*
4. *pervyj*
5. *chetviortys*
6. *vtoraj*
7. *dvadtsatyj*
8. *sotyj*
9. *dvadtsat' shestoj*
10. *odinadtsatyj*

Exercise 6: Days and Months

1. *Ianvar' – **pervyj** mesiats goda.*
2. *Piatnitsa – **piatyj** den' nedeli.*
3. *Mart – **tretij** mesiats goda.*
4. *Iiul' – **sed'moj** mesiats goda.*
5. *Voskresen'e – **sed'moj** den' nedeli.*
6. *Dekabr' – **dvenadtsatyj** mesiats goda.*
7. *Oktiabr' – **desiatyj** mesiats goda.*
8. *Sreda – **tretij** den' nedeli.*
9. *Maj – **piatyj** mesiats goda.*
10. *Subbota – **shestoj** den' nedeli.*

Exercise 7. Completing Sentences

1. *Moiu **pervuiu** sobaku zvali Kutia.*
2. *Ikh **chetviortyj** syn stal diplomatom.*
3. *Oni kupili sebe **vtoruiu** kvartiru.*
4. *Ia ochen' liubliu **sorok pervuiu** simfoniiu Motsarta.*
5. *Eto moj **desiatyj** visit v Moskvu.*
6. *Segodnia na obed **tret'e** bliudo – shokoladnyj tort.*
7. *On chasto slushal **piatuiu** simfoniiu Chajkovskogo.*
8. *Eta zhenshchina – **odinnadtsataia** zhena izvestnogo pisatelia.*

Exercise 8: How Many?

1. ***Dvoe** sidiat v stolovoj.*
2. ***Troe** prishli v kino.*
3. ***Chetvero** priekhali na Kavkaz.*
4. ***Dvoe** poselilis' v gostinitse.*
5. ***Chetvero** ostanovilis' u nas doma.*
6. ***Troe** priekhala na kurort.*
7. ***Dvoe** sideli v parke.*
8. ***Dvoe** otdykhali v Italii.*

Exercise 9: A Story about Dasha

1. *U Dashi est' **odna** sobaka i **dve** koshki.*
2. *Eto Dashina **pervaia** sobaka.*
3. *Dashinu **pervuiu** koshku zvali Pushinka.*
4. *Pushinka prozhila **dvadtsat' chetyre** goda.*
5. *Dasha otmechala den' rozhdeniia svoej koshki **desiatogo** maia.*
6. *U Dashi takzhe bylo **chetyrnadtsat'** rybok i **tri** khomiachka.*

Exercise 10: Making up Phrases

1. *tri mushketiora*
2. *chetyre vremeni goda*
3. *chetyre storony sveta*
4. *dvenadtsat' mesiatsev*
5. *dvadtsat' chetyre chasa*
6. *sem' dnej nedeli*

Exercise 11: Translating from Russian

1. He has two sons and two daughters.
2. He finished tenth grade.
3. Where is bus number eight going?
4. I'll buy one box of chocolates and one bag of coffee.
5. Two people were sitting in the room.
6. I called four times and he called five times.
7. We have two hundred forty-three employees in our office.
8. He won the first prize in the competition.

Part 7

Exercise 1: Finding Infinitives

1. *On brosil* <u>*kurit'*</u>*.*
2. *Turisty probovali* <u>*govorit'*</u> *po-russki.*
3. *My liubim* <u>*smotret'*</u> *fil'my.*
4. *Edinstvennoe, chto emu nado – eto* <u>*begat'*</u> *po ulitse.*
5. *Moi brat'ia uekhali* <u>*lovit'*</u> *rybu.*
6. *Pomogi mne, pozhalujsta,* <u>*nesti*</u> *sumku.*
7. *A vy dumaete,* <u>*rastit'*</u> *detej legko?*
8. *Emu pora* <u>*vesti*</u> *dochku v detskij sad.*

Exercise 2: Recognizing Infinitives

1. *smotret'*
2. *videt'*
3. *zakryvat'sia*
4. *zakryvat'*
5. *zhit'*
6. *uchit'sia*
7. *bezhat'*
8. *verit'*
9. *spat'*
10. *est'*

Exercise 3: Writing Infinitives

1. *igrat'*; to play
2. *idti*; to go
3. *risovat'*; to draw
4. *zhit'*; to live
5. *otdykhat'*; to rest
6. *zvonit'*; to call (on the telephone)
7. *ostavat'sia*; to stay
8. *uchit'sia*; to study

Exercise 4: Conjugating -e Verbs

1. *oni kashliaiut*
2. *my imeem*
3. *vy sprashivaete*
4. *ia slyshaiu*
5. *ona igraet*
6. *my znaem*
7. *ty letaesh'*
8. *oni vyshivaiut*

Exercise 5: Matching the Parts

1. *Moia sestra otlichno **znaet** astronomiiu.*
2. *Moi druz'ia **znaiut** khoroshij restoranchik.*
3. *Ia **znaiu** pravdu.*
4. *Moj drug **znaet** persidskij iazyk.*
5. *Ty **znaesh'** etu devushku?*
6. *Vy ne **znaete**, kotoryj chas?*
7. *My **znaem** drug druga.*
8. *Ital'iantsy **znaiut**, kak naslazhdat'sia zhizn'iu.*

Exercise 6: Completing Sentences

1. *Lena prekrasno **igraet** na gitare.*
2. *Vy **znaete** ital'ianskij iazyk?*
3. *Ia **rabotaiu** nad knigoj.*
4. *Oni **pokupaiut** novuiu kvartiru.*
5. *My vsegda **otvechaem** na voprosy.*
6. *V nashe vremia deti redko **chitaiut** knigi.*
7. *Ty khorosho **ponimaesh'** matematiku?*
8. *Moi roditeli chasto **guliaiut** v parke.*

Exercise 7: Conjugating -*i* Verbs

1. *oni variat*
2. *my gotovim*
3. *vy govorite*
4. *ia stroiu*
5. *ona stoit*
6. *my slyshim*
7. *ty lezhish'*
8. *oni smotriat*

Exercise 8: Matching the Parts

1. *Moj drug prekrasno **govorit** po-ispanski.*
2. *My chasto **govorim** po telefonu.*
3. *S kem ty **govorish'**?*
4. *Vy ochen' krasivo **govorite**.*
5. *Moi roditeli ne **govoriat** po-russki.*
6. *Ia chasto **govoriu** vo sne.*
7. *Moia sestra vsegda **govorit** gromko.*
8. *Turisty **govoriat**, chto im ponravilos'.*

Exercise 9: Completing Sentences

1. *Ty chasto **smotrish'** televizor?*
2. *Kogda on obychno **zvonit**?*
3. *Ia **slyshu** priiatnuiu muzyku.*
4. *Skol'ko **stoit** eto pal'to?*
5. *Segodnia vy **gotovite** obed?*
6. *Na etoj nedele oni **variat** varen'e.*
7. *Turisty **lezhat** na pliazhe.*
8. *Ia uzhe davno ne **kuriu**.*

Exercise 10: Conjugating Verbs with an Inserted Consonant -*l*-

1. *ia kupliu*
2. *my kopim*
3. *vy terpite*
4. *ia kormliu*
5. *ona toropit*
6. *my lovim*
7. *ia rubliu*
8. *oni liubiat*

Exercise 11: Completing Sentences

1. *Dlia podniatiia dukha on **rubit** drova.*
2. *Po voskresen'iam ia **lovliu** rybu.*
3. *Dver' sil'no **skripit**.*
4. *Mal'chik **kopit** den'gi na velosiped.*
5. *Ia **liubliu** puteshestvovat'.*
6. *Na etoj nedele ia **kupliu** sebe iakhtu.*
7. *Oni davno uzhe **terpiat**.*
8. *Chestno, ia ne **lukavliu**.*

Exercise 12: Conjugating Verbs with Consonant Mutation

1. *ia sizhu*
2. *my kosim*
3. *vy katite*
4. *ia vozhu*
5. *ona brodit*
6. *my krutim*
7. *ia krashu*
8. *oni chistiat*

Exercise 13: Matching the Parts

1. *On vsegda **sidit** v pervom riadu.*
2. *Gde ty obychno **sidish'** na lektsii?*
3. *Ia **sizhu** v parke i chitaiu knigu.*
4. *My **sidim** na divane i smotrim televizor.*
5. *Moi druz'ia **sidiat** v restorane.*
6. *Vy **sidite** na moiom meste.*

Exercise 14: Completing Sentences

1. *Ia **proshu** vas priekhat' k nam v gosti.*
2. *On idiot po ulitse i **svistit**.*
3. *Oni **voziat** tovary iz Turtsii.*
4. *Ia uzhe dva chasa **brozhu** po gorodu.*
5. *Tom Sojer **krasit** zabor ves' den'.*
6. *Gde vy obychno **sidite** na kontserte?*
7. *Mal'chik **chistit** zuby.*
8. *Ia obychno **noshu** dzhinsy i sviter.*

Exercise 15: Conjugating *-ava-* and *-ova-* Type Verbs

1. *my puteshestvuem*
2. *vy daiote*
3. *oni sovetuiut*
4. *ia uznaiu*
5. *ona trebuet*
6. *my riskuem*
7. *ty vstaiosh'*
8. *oni rekomenduiut*

Exercise 16: Matching the Parts

1. *Vy vsegda udachno **uznaiote** dorogu.*
2. *Moia sobaka **uznaiot** moi shagi.*
3. *Ty menia ne **uznaiosh'**?*
4. *My vsio **uznaiom** poslednimi.*
5. *Ia vas ne **uznaiu**.*
6. *Moi druz'ia **uznaiut** vremia.*

Exercise 17: Completing Sentences

1. *On slishkom chasto **riskuet**.*
2. *Gde Vy obychno **puteshestvuete**?*
3. *Kak ty **ispol'zuesh'** etot pribor?*
4. *Oni **trebuiut** povyshennogo vnimaniia.*
5. *Ia **sovetuiu** ne prodolzhat' igru.*
6. *Po ponedel'nikam my **tantsuem** sving.*
7. *Vy **rekomenduete** etot kurort?*
8. *Ia **vstaiu** ochen' pozdno.*

Exercise 18: Conjugating Irregular Verbs

2. *vy mozhete*
3. *oni pishut*
4. *ia ishchu*
5. *ona plachet*
6. *my moem*
7. *ty p'iosh'*
8. *oni ediat*

Exercise 19: Matching the Parts

1. *My vsegda **edim** v 5 chasov.*
2. *Ia ne **em** klubniku.*
3. *Turisty **ediat** v restorane.*
4. *Vy **edite** rybu?*
5. *Ona ne **est** uzhe dva dnia.*
6. *Chto **est** eto zhivotnoe?*

Exercise 20: Completing Sentences

1. *Vse liudi **ishchut** nastoiashchuiu liubov'.*
2. *My vsegda **moem** ruki pered edoj.*
3. *V Rossii govoriat, chto mal'chiki ne **plachut**.*
4. *Chto Vy **pishete**?*
5. *Ia bol'she ne **mogu** zdes' rabotat'.*
6. *Chto ty **khochesh'**: morozhennoe ili konfety?*
7. *Moj brat ne **p'iot** kofe.*
8. *Chto ty obychno **esh'** na zavtrak?*

Exercise 21: Being Negative

1. *Ia nichego ne znaiu.*
2. *My nichego ne nashli.*
3. *On nikogda ne zvonit.*
4. *Vy zdes' ne zhiviote?*
5. *Ia ne liubliu chitat' nikakie knigi.*
6. *On ni o chiom ne dumaet.*
7. *Ona nichego ne pishet.*
8. *My nikogda ne rabotaem.*

Exercise 22: Using Past Tense

1. *on liubil*
2. *vy khoteli*
3. *oni znali*
4. *ona pomnila*
5. *ono shumelo*
6. *my imeli*
7. *ona tantsevala*
8. *on terpel*

Exercise 23: Matching the Parts

1. A more **zhilo** svoej zagadochnoj zhizn'iu.
2. Ona ran'she **zhila** v tom dome.
3. My togda **zhili** v Moskve.
4. Vy tozhe ran'she **zhili** u moria?
5. Do 17 let Ivan **zhil** s roditeliami.
6. S nimi **zhila** simpatichnaia koshka.
7. Etot starik **zhil** odin.
8. Ona **zhila** v samom krasivom gorode mira.

Exercise 24: Completing Sentences

1. My dolgo **guliali** po parku.
2. Ona **pisala** emu pis'ma kazhdyj den'.
3. Deti **risovali** v al'bome.
4. Ozero **sverkalo** vdali.
5. Pochtal'on **postuchal** v dver'.
6. Drug **pozvonil** mne po telefonu.
7. Lena **vstretila** podrugu na ulitse.
8. Mal'chik **igral** na skripke.

Exercise 25: Listening

1. Ia chasto **letal** v Parizh.
2. Olia ochen' **liubila** shokolad.
3. My **igrali** v tennis.
4. Oni **govorili** po-russki.
5. Professor i ego zhena **uezzhali** v London.
6. Vy zdes' **zhili**?
7. Molodoj muzhchina **perekhodil** ulitsu.
8. Samoliot **pribyl** v sem' chasov.

Exercise 26: Using Compound Future Tense

1. Ia budu rabotat'
2. Vy budete zhdat'.
3. Oni budut uchit'.
4. Ona budet spat'.
5. Vy budete zhit.'
6. My budem smotret'.
7. Ona budet tantsevat'.
8. Oni budut pet'.

Exercise 27: Matching the Parts

1. Ia **budu zhdat'** na perone.
2. Moi druz'ia **budut zhdat'** nas v kafe.
3. Skol'ko Vy **budete zhdat'**?
4. Ty **budesh' zhdat'** ili pojdiosh' domoj?
5. Ona skazala, chto **budet zhdat'** do utra.
6. My **budem zhdat'** vas v gosti.
7. Moj brat **budet zhdat'** tam svoiu devushku.
8. On **budet zhdat'** pis'ma.

Exercise 28: Completing Sentences

1. Ia **budu prepodavat'** v universitete.
2. Ona **budet rabotat'** aktrisoj.
3. My **budem otdykhat'** na Kavkaze.
4. Chto vy **budete delat'** posle kontserta?)
5. Turisty **budut obedat'** v etom restorane.
6. Papa **budet gotovit'** uzhin.
7. Mama **budet vystupat'** na konferentsii.
8. Koshka ne **budet spat'** na divane.

Exercise 29: Listening

1. My **budem khodit'** v kino.
2. Lena **budet igrat'** na pianino.
3. Moi roditeli **budut otdykhat'** na dache.
4. Vy **budete govorit'** po-russki?
5. Ty **budesh' znat'** etogo cheloveka.
6. Ia **budu delat'** zariadku kazhdyj den'.
7. Magazin **budet zakryvat'sia** v vosem' chasov.
8. My **budem vstrechat'sia** kazhdoe voskresen'e.

Exercise 30: Finding Perfective Pairs

1. smotret'– **posmotret'**
2. slushat'– **poslushat'**
3. delat'– **sdelat'**
4. videt'– **uvidet'**
5. pokupat' – **kupit'**
6. prodavat'– **prodat'**
7. uznavat'– **uznat'**
8. risovat' – **narisovat'**

Exercise 31: Finding Imperfective Pairs

1. *priekhat'* – ***ekhat'***
2. *skazat'* – ***govorit'***
3. *napisat'* – ***pisat'***
4. *vyjti* – ***vykhodit'***
5. *dat'* – ***davat'***
6. *vziat'* – ***brat'***
7. *zakonchit'* – ***zakanchivat'***
8. *otkryt'* – ***otkryvat'***

Exercise 32: Listening

1. *Natasha **prochitaet** knigu.*
   Natasha will read the book.
2. *Rabochie **zakonchat** zdanie.*
   Workers will finish this building.
3. *Anna **kupit** plat'e.*
   Anna will buy the/a dress.
4. *My **napishem** dissertatsiiu.*
   We will write the/a dissertation.
5. *Mal'chik **narisuet** dom.*
   The boy will draw a house.
6. *Vy **pojdiote** v gosti?*
   Will you go to visit?
7. *Voditel' **uznaet** eto pravilo.*
   The driver will learn this rule.
8. *Papa **prigotovit** obed.*
   Papa will cook lunch.

Exercise 33: A Story about Dasha

*Dasha **guliaet** po parku. Ona **sobiraet** osennie list'ia. Dasha **ishchet** samyj krasivyh osennij listok. "Ia tak **liubliu** osen'," - **dumaet** Dasha. Osen'iu list'ia **meniaiut** tsvet. Deti **nachinaiut** khodit' v shkolu. Ptitsy **puteshestvuiut** na iug. "Zhal', chto ia ne **mogu** poekhat' na iug", - **vzdykhaet** Dasha. Ona tozhe **khochet** puteshestvo-vat'. "Koga ia **polechu** v tioplye strany?" - **govorit** Dasha. "Vmesto etogo, ia **sizhu** v skuchnom ofise." No Dasha uzhe **ezdila** v otpusk v etom godu. Teper' ona **budet rabo-tat'** do sleduiushchego goda.*

Exercise 34: Reading Chekhov

1. How you scared me!
2. She looked at him and went pale …
3. Anna Sergeevna and he loved each other …
4. His head was already turning grey …
5. At each step, he nodded his head, and… constantly bowed.
6. Probably it was the husband, whom she then, in Ialta … called a servant.
7. All the time while the audience was entering and tak-ing their places, Gurov avidly searched with his eyes.
8. What will I do during the night now?

Exercise 35: Completing Sentences

1. *Lena vchera **podarila** mne podarok.*
2. *Ia vsegda **pokupaiu** tut kofe.*
3. *Zavtra nashi druz'ia **budut rabotat'**.*
4. *On stoial i zhdal, poka ona **pisala**.*
5. *On nikogda nichego **ne zamechaet**.*
6. *Ran'she ona **tantsevala** v Bol'shom teatre.*
7. *Vy uzhe vsio **znaete**?*
8. *Gde ty **nashla** etot zamechatel'nyj sharf?*

Exercise 36: Conjugating Verbs

1. *Ia vam **sovetuiu** tuda ne idti.*
2. *Chto vy **daiote** sobake na obed?*
3. *Kazhdoe utro ia **glazhu** svoiu rubashku.*
4. *Ia chasto **lovliu** sebia na mysli, chto mne ochen' povezlo.*
5. *Oni chasto **pishut** drug drugu pis'ma.*
6. *Vy **mozhete** pozvonit' zavtra?*
7. *My **liubim** svoj gorod.*
8. *Ona **nosit** modnuiu odezhdu.*

Part 8

Exercise 1: Conjugating Reflexive Verbs

1. On chasto **ulybaetsia**.
2. Ona **dobivaetsia** vsego, chego khochet.
3. Oni nikogda ne **rasstaiutsia**.
4. Ia **ublekaius'** figurnym kataniem.
5. My **voskhishchaemsia** vashej knigoj.
6. Ty **uchish'sia** v shkole ili v institute?
7. Vy vsegda tut **liubuetes'** zakatom?
8. Moj diadia **kupaetsia** v Chiornom more kruglyj god.

Exercise 2: Scrambled Sentences

1. Moj drug stesniaetsia zajti v gosti.
2. Na fotografiiakh ia vsegda ulybaius'.
3. Vy skoro ubedites' v moej pravote.
4. My prosypaemsia rano.
5. Moi roditeli zanimaiutsia biznesom.
6. Ty chasto kataesh'sia na loshadi?

Exercise 3: Completing Sentences

1. Devochka **umyvaet** kotionka.
2. Etot molodoj chelovek **odevaetsia** ochen' modno.
3. Mat' **kupaet** rebionka.
4. Parikmakher **pichiosyvaet** klienta.
5. Ia **umyvaius'** kholodnoj vodoj.
6. Babushka **odevaet** vnuka.
7. Lena **prichiosyvaetsia** pered zerkalom.
8. Gosti **razdevaiutsia** v prikhozhej.

Exercise 4: Producing Reflexive Verbs

1. nazyvat' – to name
   nazyvat'sia – to be called
2. zakanchivat' – to end [something]
   zakanchivat'sia – to end
3. stroit' – to build
   stroit'sia – to be built
4. nachinat' – to begin [something]
   nachinat'sia – to begin
5. otkryvat' – to open [something]

otkryvat'sia – to open
6. otrazhat' – to reflect
   otrazhat'sia – to be reflected

Exercise 5: Active or Passive?

1. Apteka **otkryvaetsia** v shest utra.
2. Lena **otkryvaet** okno.
3. Etot muzej **nazyvaetsia** Ermitazh.
4. Liudi **nazyvaiut** Sankt Peterburg "Piter."
5. Professor **nachinaet** lektsiiu.
6. Fil'm **nachinaetsia** v vosem' chasov.
7. Moia rabota **zakanchivaetsia** v piat' chasov.
8. Pisatel' **zakanchivaet** knigu.

Exercise 6: Paraphrasing Sentences

1. Restoran zakryvaetsia.
2. Doklad nachinaetsia.
3. Glaza otkryvaiutsia.
4. Stat'ia zakanchivaetsia.
5. Otel' nazyvaetsia "Mecha."
6. Zdanie stroitsia uzhe desiat' let.
7. Kafe otkroetsia zavtra.
8. Banka kofe zakanchivaetsia.

Exercise 7: Is It Mutual?

1. Kazhdyj den' ia **vstrechaiu** etogo cheloveka na ulitse.
2. Druz'ia **vstrechaiutsia** v kafe kazhduiu subbotu.
3. Lena **poznakomila** menia s Mishej.
4. My **poznakomilis'** na vecherinke.
5. Mat' **tseluet** syna v lob.
6. Vliublionnye **tseluiutsia** v metro.
7. Ia **uvidela** Vaniu na pliazhe.
8. Oni nakonets-to **uvidelis'** posle dolgoj razluki.

Exercise 8: Paraphrasing Sentences

1. Lena **poznakomilas'** s Mishej.
2. Nina i Ivan **vstretilis'** u teatra.
3. Druz'ia **videlis'** na proshloj nedele.
4. Gosti **poznakomilis'**.
5. Olia i eio muzh **vstretilis'** v 2005.

Exercise 9: Completing Sentences

1. *Chto **sluchilos'**?*
2. *Moj syn **stanovitsia** vzroslym.*
3. *Mne **kazhetsia**, chto Vy ne pravy.*
4. *Moskvichi **gordiatsia** svoim gorodom.*
5. *Tebe **nravitsia** eto bliudo?*
6. *Ia zametila, chto Vy vsegda **ulybaetes'**.*
7. *On **boitsia** vysoty i sobak.*
8. *Oni liubiat **smeiat'sia**.*

Exercise 10: Our Family's Tastes

1. *Mame **nravitsia** chitat'.*
2. *Pape **nravitsia** smotret' televizor.*
3. *Babushke **nravitsia** gotovit'.*
4. *Dedushke **nravitsia** sport.*
5. *Bratu **nravitsia** muzyka.*
6. *Sestre **nravitsia** makarony.*
7. *Nam vsem **nravitsia** guliat' v parke.*
8. *Mne **nravitsia** moia sem'ia.*

Exercise 11: A Story about Dasha

*Dasha **prosypaetsia** v vosem' utra. Ona vstaiot, **umyvaetsia**, i **sobiraetsia** na rabotu. Dasha rabotaet v ofise, kotoryj **nazyvaetsia** "Mechta." Ofis **otkryvaetsia** v desiat' utra, no dashina rabota **nachinaetsia** ran'she. Tselyj den' dver' v dashin cabinet ne **zakryvaetsia**. Dasha **ulybaetsia** klientam i **smeiotsia** ikh shutkam. Dashe **nravitsia** eio rabota. Ona **gorditsia** tem, chto klienty eio liubiat. Kogda ofis **zakryvaetsia** v shest' chasov, Dasha idiot v kafe. Tam ona **vstrechaetsia** s druz'iami.*

Exercise 12: Completing the Sentences

1. *Gosti **kupaiutsia** v bassejne.*
2. *My **vstrechaemsia** v kafe.*
3. *Dedushka **odevaet** vnuka.*
4. *Biblioteka **zakryvaetsia** v 8 vechera.*
5. *Uchitel' **nachinaet** urok.*
6. *Turisty **poznakomilis'** vo vremia poezdki.*
7. *Devushka **otkryvaet** okno.*
8. *Podruga **predstavliaet** menia izvestnomu pisateliu.*

Part 9

Exercise 1: Using the Verb *idti*

1. *Ia **idu** na rabotu.*
2. *Ia videla devushku, kotoraia **shla** po beregu moria.*
3. *Kuda vy **idiote**?*
4. *Segodnia my **idiom** v kino.*
5. *Vo skol'ko vy vchera **shli** na rabotu?*
6. *Lena **idiot** v teatr.*
7. *Moi druz'ia **idut** na more.*
8. *Moj brat kupil apel'siny, kogda **shiol** domoj.*

Exercise 2: Using the Verb *prijti*

1. *On **prishiol** vchera pozdno vecherom.*
2. *Zavtra my **pridiom** k vam v gosti.*
3. *V proshloe voskresen'e Lena **prishla** domoj rano.*
4. *On **pridiot** v shest' chasov.*
5. *A kogda vy **pridiote**?*
6. *Ia segodnia ne **pridu** na rabotu.*
7. *Vchera vrach ne **prishiol**.*
8. *Moi druz'ia **pridut** v kafe s opozdaniem.*

Exercise 3: Using the Verb *ekhat'*

1. *My **edem** na mashine.*
2. *Vchera my **ekhali** na avtobuse.*
3. *Misha **edet** v Moskvu.*
4. *Kuda vy **edete** v otpusk?*
5. *Ty tozhe **edesh'** na Kavkaz?*
6. *Moi roditeli **edut** vo Frantsiiu.*
7. *Zavtra ia **edu** v komandirovku.*
8. *Kogda vy **edete** domoj?*

Exercise 4: By Foot or by Vehicle?

1. *Misha **edet** na dachu.*
2. *Lena **idiot** na rabotu peshkom.*
3. *Mo **idiom** po parku.*
4. *Moz druz'ia **edut** otdykhat' na iug.*
5. *Segodnia vecherom ia **idu** v teatr.*
6. *Sejchas oni **edut** na metro.*
7. *My **idiom** v kino.*
8. *Ty vsio eshchio **edesh'** na poezde?*

Exercise 5: Nonsense Sentences

1. *Vika edet v Moskvu.*
2. *Natasha idiot peshkom.*
3. *My edem na mashine.*
4. *Moj drug edet v Chicago.*
5. *Vy edete v otpusk na poezde ili na mashine?*
6. *Ia poedu na taksi.*

Exercise 6: Using the Verb *khodit'*

1. *Moia doch' **khodit** v shkolu.*
2. *My **khodim** k nim v gosti kazhdyj den'.*
3. *Kuda Vy vchera **khodili**?*
4. *Ia **khozhu** na balet.*
5. *Turisty **khodili** po muzeiu tri chasa.*
6. *Moemu synu chetyrnadsat' mesiatsev; on uzhe **khodit**.*
7. *Ty **khodil** vchera na lektsiiu?*
8. *Lena **khodit** po magazinam tselyj den'.*

Exercise 7: Using the Verb *ezdit'*

1. *Moj brat **ezdit** v Moskvy raz v mesiats.*
2. *Ia liubliu **ezdit'** na poezde.*
3. *Kuda **ezdila** Lena v proshlom mesiatse?*
4. *Letom my **ezdim** na dachu.*
5. *Zimoj oni **ezdiat** katat'sia na lyzhakh.*
6. *Ty chasto **ezdish'** na Kavkaz?*
7. *Vy uzhe **ezdili** v otpusk v etom godu?*
8. *Studenty obychno **ezdiat** na metro.*

Exercise 8: Completing Sentences

1. *Lena **khodit** v magazin.*
2. *Ia **khozhu** domoj.*
3. *Turisty **khodiat** v pokhod.*
4. *Vy **khodite** na vecherinki?*
5. *My **khodim** v gosti.*
6. *Ty **khodish'** na rabotu.*
7. *Anna **khodila** v biblioteku.*
8. *Oni **khodili** na kontsert.*

Exercise 9: *Idti* or *khodit'*?

1. *My **khodim** na progulku kazhdyj den'.*
2. *Ia videla Ivana; on **shiol** na rabotu.*
3. *My **khodim** na futbol raz v mesiats.*
4. *Kuda ty sejchas **idiosh'**?*
5. *Ia **khodil** v etu shkolu tri goda.*
6. *On nervno **khodit** po kvartire.*
7. *Vy **idiote** peshkom ili edete na mashine?*
8. *Oni dolgo **khodili** po parku.*

Exercise 10: *Ekhat'* or *ezdit'*?

1. *Kuda Vy sejchas **edete**?*
2. *Moi druz'ia skoro **edut** v otpusk.*
3. *Ona **ezdila** v London v proshlom godu.*
4. *Ia vstretila ego, kogda on **ekhal** v Moskvu.*
5. *Ona liubit **ezdit'** po gorodu na mashine.*
6. *My vstretilis' v poezde; my oba **ekhali** v Budapesht.*
7. *My vsegda **ezdim** na metro.*
8. *Na rabotu ia **ezzhu** na avtobuse.*

Exercise 11: By Ground, Air, or Water? (Unidirectional)

1. *Vy v pervyj raz **plyviote** po Volge?*
2. *On zavtra **letit** v Moskvu rejsom Aeroflota.*
3. *My poznakomilis', kogda **plyli** na katere cherez bukhtu.*
4. *Ty **edesh'** na poezde ili **letish'** na samoliote?*
5. *Etot parokhod **plyviot** v Turtsiiu.*
6. *Kuda **edet** etot avtobus?*
7. *Moia babushka v pervyj raz **letela** na samoliote, kogda ej bylo sem'desiat let.*
8. *Etot samoliot **letit** v London.*

Exercise 12: Ground, Air, or Water? (Multidirectional)

1. *Etot parokhod **khodit** po Missisipi.*
2. *On ne liubit **ezdit'** na metro.*
3. *Dasha vsegda **letaet** v komandirovku na samoliote.*
4. *Kater "Kometa" **khodit** iz Novorossijska v Odessu kazhdye dva chasa.*
5. *Etot kruiznyj lajner **khodit** na Bagamskie ostrova.*
6. *Kuda ty obychno **ezdish'** v otpusk?*
7. *Ia vsegda **ezzhu** na avtobuse.*
8. *Vy chasto **letaete** na samoliote?*

Exercise 13: Moving Things

1. *Sestra **veziot** mne podarok iz Moskvy.*
2. *Ia **noshu** etu sumku uzhe dva goda.*
3. *Ona **nesla** stakan s vodoj i uronila ego.*
4. *My **vozili** gostej po gorodu.*
5. *Nash parokhod **vozit** banany v Rossiiu uzhe desiat' let.*
6. *Kuda ty **nesiosh'** etu knigu?*
7. *On vsegda **vozit** syna v shkoly na mashine.*
8. *On **nesiot** buket tsvetov domoj, dlia svoej zheny; segodnia u nikh iubilej.*

Exercise 14: Nonsense Sentences

1. *Molodoj chelovek **veziot** roial' po gorodu.*
2. *Zavtra ia **vezu** syna v Moskvu.*
3. *Mashina **veziot** kartofel' i pomidory.*
4. *Natasha **nesiot** chashku chaia po komnate.*
5. *Ty vsegda **nosish'** etu sumku?*
6. *Devochka **nesiot** koshku na rukakh.*
7. *Korabl' **veziot** tabak v Evropu.*
8. *My tri chasa **vozili** babushku po gorodu.*

Exercise 15: Which Prefix?

1. *My **perekhodim** cherez dorogu.*
2. *Poezd **pod"ezzhaet** k Moskve.*
3. *Samoliot **priletaet** v vosem' chasov.*
4. *Zavtra Lena **uezzhaet** v Moskvu.*
5. *Kater **pereplyvaet** cherez reku.*
6. *Nash parokhod **podplyl** k Odesse.*
7. *Turisty **vkhodiat** v tserkov'.*
8. *Avtobus **ot"ezzhaet** ot ostanovki.*

Exercise 16: Translating Phrases

2. to leave Moscow by plane
3. to approach a port by water
4. to walk across the square
5. to pass by a park in a vehicle
6. to walk through a tunnel
7. to leave the city by a vehicle
8. to walk out of the room

Exercise 17: A Story about Dasha

*Dasha **vykhodit** iz doma v deviat' utra. Ona **idiot** na rabotu. Dasha **perekhodit** cherez dorogu, **prokhodit** mimo tserkvi, i **podkhodit** k avtobusnoj ostanovke. Avtobus obychno **priezzhaet** v 9.15. Dasha saditsia na avtobus i **edet** na rabotu. Avtobus **edet** po glavnoj ulitse, **proezzhaet** mimo teatra, i **pereezzhaet** reku po mostu. Kogda avtobus **pod"ezzhaet** k dashinoj ostanovke, Dasha **vykhodit** iz avtobusa i **vkhodit** v svoj ofis. Dasha **prikhodit** na rabotu v 9.45. Ona **vkhodit** v svoj ofis i srazu **podkhodit** k stolu svoej podrugi Natashi. Oni razgovarivaiut minut piatnadtsat', potom Dasha **otkhodit** ot eio stola, i nachinaet rabotat'.*

Exercise 18. What Kind of Motion?

1. *My **edem** v Moskvu.*	MV
2. *Devushka **perekhodit** cherez dorogu.*	MF
3. *V zoopark **privezli** slona.*	MV
4. *Ofitsiant **prinios** kofe.*	MF
5. *My **pereekhali** na novuiu kvartiru.*	MV
6. *Ia **idu** po parku.*	MF
7. *Ona **uekhala** na dachu.* MV	
8. *On **ushiol** na rabotu.*	MF

Part 10

Exercise 1: Writing Conditional Sentences

2. *Esli zavtra budet solnechnyj den', to my skhodim na pliazh.*
3. *Esli zavtra budet khoroshij sneg, to oni pojdut na lyzhnuiu progulku.*
4. *Esli soberiotsia khoroshaia komanda, my pojdiom v turpokhod.*
5. *Esli zavtra budet nastroenie, to ia speku pirog.*
6. *Esli ty prigotovish' uroki, to ty pojdiosh' guliat'.*
7. *Esli ty budesh' khorosho sebia vesti, to ia podariu tebe sobaku.*
8. *Esli vy budete zanimat'sia sportom, to vy bydete zdorovym.*

Exercise 2: Making Plans

1. *Esli priedet Lena, to ia pojdu k nej v gosti.*
2. *Esli Lena ne priedet, to ia ej pozvoniu.*
3. *Esli Leny ne budet doma, to ia pozvoniu ej na rabotu.*
4. *Esli Leny ne budet na rabote, to ia napishu ej imejl.*
5. *Esli budet teplo, to ia pojdu v pokhod.*
6. *Esli budet zharko, to ia pojdu na pliazh.*
7. *Esli budet kholodno, to ia pojdu v kino.*
8. *Esli budet idti dozhd', to ia ostanus' doma.*

Exercise 3: Writing Subjunctive Sentences

1. *Esli by ia byl kosmonavtom, ia by poletel na Mars.*
2. *Esli by ia byl millionerom, ia kupil by ostrov v Karibskom more.*
3. *Esli by ia byl ptitsej, ia by poletel v tioplye kraia.*
4. *Esli by u neio byla vozmozhnost', ona by prishla.*
5. *Esli by u menia bylo vremia, to ia by izuchila' vse iazyki mira.*
6. *Esli by u menia byl talant, to ia sta-la by znamenitoj pevitsej.*
7. *Esli by u nikh byla mashina, oni by priekhali.*
8. *Esli by u nas byla iakhta, my by pri-glasili vsekh druzej v gosti.*

Exercise 4: Changing the Mood

1. *Esli by on pozvonil, my by emu rasskazali.*
2. *Esli by Olga prishla, ia otdala by ej knigu.*
3. *Esli by klienty prishli, ia by pokazala im kvartiru.*
4. *Esli by turisty priekhali, u turagenta byla by rabota.*
5. *Esli by u menia bylo vremia, ia by napisala tebe.*
6. *Esli by u nikh bylo zhelanie, oni by tebe pomogli.*
7. *Esli by ty vstretila brata, to vy poshli by v kino.*
8. *Esli by ia posmotrela etot fil'm, to ia by tebe pozvonila.*

Exercise 5: Forming Imperatives

1. *smotret'–* **smotri**
2. *igrat –'* **igraj**
3. *lovit'–* **lovi**
4. *derzhat'–* **derzhi**
5. *pomnit' –* **pomni**
6. *bezhat' –* **begi**

7. *nesti –* **nesi**
8. *varit' –* **vari**

Exercise 6: Giving Commands

1. *Chitajte tekst.*
2. *Govorite po-russki.*
3. *Idite domoj.*
4. *Peredajte sol'.*
5. *Prinesite knigu.*
6. *Pokazhite gorod.*
7. *Rasskazhite istoriiu.*
8. *Pejte moloko.*

Exercise 7: Making Requests

1. **Podajte** *pal'to.*
2. **Voz'mite** *zakaz.*
3. **Peredajte** *privet.*
4. **Prokhodite** *vperiod.*
5. **Zakrojte** *dver'.*
6. **Nachinajte** *rabotat'.*
7. **Sdelajte** *strizhku.*
8. **Napishite** *pis'mo.*

Exercise 8: Reading Chekhov

1. Stop it, my dear one, he was saying.
2. If she is here without her husband and without any acquaintances…it wouldn't be a bad idea to get acquainted with her.
3. If not for the tears in her eyes, one would think that she was joking or playing a role.
4. If one is to send a note, then it will probably get into the husband's hands.
5. If you only knew what a charming woman I met in Yalta!
6. Believe me, believe me, I'm begging you…

Exercise 9: A Story about Dasha

Odnazhdy, kogda Dasha guliala po parku, k nej podoshi-ol molodoj chelovek i skazal chto-to po-ital'ianski. "Esli by ia **znala** *ital'ianskij iazyk, to ia* **otvetila** *by," podumala*

*Dahsa. "Esli Vy **govorite** po-russki, to my **mozhem** pogovorit'," skazala Dasha. Molodoj chelovek otvetil po-russki: "**Skazhite** mne, pozhalujsta, chto mozhno posmotret' v etom gorode?" Dasha podumala i otvetila: "Esli Vy **liubite** prirodu, to **idite** k moriu. Esli Vam **nravitsia** istoriia, to **pojdite** v muzej. Esli Vy **khotite** poznakomit'sia s mestnymi zhiteliami, to **otpravliajtes'** v kafe. Esli by u menia **bylo** vremia, to ia **poshla** by s Vami."*

Part 11

Exercise 1: Forming Active Present Participles

1. *govoriashchie popugai*
2. *sidiashchij muzhchina*
3. *rabotaiushchaia zhenshchina*
4. *idushchij avtobus*
5. *goriashchij kostior*
6. *p'iushchee zhivotnoe*
7. *shumiashchee more*
8. *igraiushchie deti*

Exercise 2: Forming Active Past Participles

1. *zhivshij chelovek*
2. *lezhavshaia sobaka*
3. *guliavshaia koshka*
4. *rabotavshij drug*
5. *pisavshaia uchenitsa*
6. *spavshij turist*
7. *risovavshie studenty*
8. *letevshaia ptitsa*

Exercise 3: Forming Present Passive Participles

1. *opisyvaemaia situatsiia*
2. *trebuemaia summa*
3. *proizvodimyj tovar*
4. *chitaemye avtory*
5. *publikuemyj poet*
6. *terpimye usloviia*
7. *proiznosimye soglasnye*
8. *liubimaia skazka*

Exercise 4: Forming Past Passive Participles

1. *proizvedionnoe vpechatlenie*
2. *opisanyj pejzazh*
3. *ozabochennyj chelovek*
4. *narisovannaia luna*
5. *napisannye stikhi*
6. *prigotovlennyj uzhin*
7. *postelennaia postel'*
8. *ispechionnye pirogi*

Exercise 5: Forming Present Adverbial Participles

1. *idti – **idia***
2. *rabotat' – **rabotaia***
3. *smotret' – **smotria***
4. *ulybat'sia – **ulybaias'***
5. *risovat'– **risuia***
6. *delat' – **delaia***
7. *guliat' – **guliaia***
8. *sidet' – **sidia***

Exercise 6: Forming Past Adverbial Participles

1. *uznat' – **uznav***
2. *napisat'– **napisav***
3. *posmotret' – **posmotrev***
4. *uvidet'– **uvidev***
5. *porvat'– **porvav***
6. *sdat' – **sdav***
7. *postupit' – **postupiv***
8. *podarit'– **podariv***

Exercise 7: Rewriting Sentences

1. *Eto devushka, zhivushchaia v nashem dome.*
2. *Po ulitse idiot professor, rabotaiushchij v moiom universitete.*
3. *My razgovarivali s muzhchinoj, prochitavshim etot roman.*
4. *Na terrase sidel mal'chik, napisavshij pis'mo.*
5. *Na stsene stoiala zhenshchina, poiushchaia romansy.*
6. *My vstretili devushku, govorivshuiu po telefonu.*
7. *On smotrit serial, idushchij po televizoru.*
8. *U dveri stoial student, sdavshij ekzamen.*

Exercise 8: Completing Sentences

1. *Eto* **liubimaia** *mnogimi kniga.*
2. *Zhara v etom godu dovol'no* **terpimaia**.
3. *Ona sozhgla vse* **poluchennye** *pis'ma.*
4. *Vam udalos' dostignut'* **zhelaemogo** *rezul'tata?*
5. *V kamorke papy Karlo byl* **narisovannyj** *ochag.*
6. *Nado priznavat'* **sdelannye** *oshibki.*
7. *Eto postupok,* **karaemyj** *zakonom.*
8. *On rasskazal militsii ob* **uvidennom** *proisshestvii.*

Exercise 9: Practicing Adverbial Participles

1. *On pel,* **shagaia** *po ulitse.*
2. **Uvidev** *druga, on ostanovil mashinu.*
3. *Ona zadumalas',* **chitaia** *knigu.*
4. *On chital,* **sidia** *na skamejke.*
5. **Ubrav** *so stola, on liog spat'.*
6. **Zakonchiv** *rabotu, Lena poshla domoj.*
7. *On smotrel televizor,* **liozha** *na divane.*
8. **Uslyshav** *novost', ona srazu priekhala.*

Part 12

Exercise 1: Where Is the Butterfly?

1. *Babochka* **na stole.**
2. *Babochka* **pod stolom.**
3. *Babochka* **v stole.**
4. *Babochka* **nad stolom.**
5. *Babochka* **u stola (okolo stola).**
6. *Babochka* **za stolom.**
7. *Babochka* **pered stolom.**
8. *Babochka letaet* **vokrug stola.**

Exercise 2: Where Is It Located?

1. in the city – *v gorode*
2. next to the monument – *u pamiatnika (okolo pamiatnika)*
3. above the bed – *nad krovat'iu*
4. under ground – *pod zemlioj*
5. across the street – *cherez dorogu*
6. from Europe – *iz Evropy*

7. behind the wall – *za stenoj*
8. in front of the theater– *pered teatrom*

Exercise 3: *V* or *na*?

1. *Ona idiot* **na** *rabotu.*
2. *My pojdiom* **na** *stadion.*
3. *Gorod Novorossijsk nakhoditsia* **na** *iuge Rossii.*
4. *Oni idut* **v** *teatr.*
5. *davaj poedem* **v** *Parizh.*
6. *Ia khochu pojti* **v** *ital'ianskij restoran.*
7. *Oni vstretilis'* **na** *ulitse*
8. *Ty poedesh'* **v** *kino* **na** *avtobuse ili* **na** *taksi?*

Exercise 4: Prepositional or Accusative?

1. *Moia doch' uchitsia v* **shkole.**
2. *Ty provodish' slishkom mnogo vremeni na* **rabote.**
3. *Davaj poedem na* **sever.**
4. *Lena ushla v* **magazin.**
5. *My idiom v* **park.**
6. *Turisty zhivut v* **gostinitse.**
7. *Moj brat rabotaet v* **ofise.**
8. *Davajte zajdiom v* **komnatu.**

Exercise 5: When Did It Happen?

1. before dinner – *pered obedom*
2. after the performance – *posle spektaklia*
3. from morning till evening – *s utra do vechera*
4. until Friday – *do piatnitsy*
5. a month ago – *mesiats nazad*
6. during the lecture – *vo vremia lektsii*
7. in two years – *cherez dva goda*
8. after the wedding – *posle svad'by*

Exercise 6: Saying "When"

1. *Na proshloj nedele my khodili v pokhod.*
2. *V tu zhe minutu v dver' postuchali.*
3. *Poet Pushkin rodilsia v* **18-om veke,**
   a pisat' nachal v **19-om veke.**
4. *On pozvonil v* **dva chasa.**

5. *V sredu* u nas budet piknik.

6. Liudi nachinaiut kupat'sia v Chiornom more *v iiune.*

7. *Na sleduiushchej nedele* my budem izuchat' glagoly.

8. *V mae* v Rossii otmechaiut Den' Pobedy.

Exercise 7: Finding the Equivalent

1. without – *bez*

2. for – *dlia*

3. except – *krome*

4. during the reign of – *pri*

5. opposed to – *protiv*

6. in the presence of – *pri*

7. about (in the meaning of "concerning") – *o*

8. in support of – *za*

Exercise 8: Giving Details

1. except for math– *krome matematiki*

2. during the reign of socialism– *pri sotsializme*

3. in support of peace– *za mir*

4. against the war – *protiv vojny*

5. in the presence of children – *pri detiakh*

6. about love– *o liubvi*

7. for Mother – *dlia materi*

8. without shame – *bez styda*

Exercise 9: Completing Sentences

1. *On poekhal otdykhat' odin,* **bez druzej.**

2. *Ona pozvonila materi* **pri mne.**

3. *U menia* **dlia tebia** *est' podarok.*

4. *Ia* **protiv** *kureniia.*

5. *Ia liubliu vsekh russkikh pisatelej,* **krome Tolstogo.**

6. *Davajte pogovorim* **o politike.**

7. *Ia* **za ravnopravie.**

8. **Dlia nego,** *kazhdyj den' byl prazdnikom.*

Exercise 10: Completing Phrases

1. *nesmotria na* **dozhd';** in spite of the rain

2. *v zakliuchenie* **seminara;** at the end of the seminar

3. *v sviazi s* **pogodoj** ; because of the weather

4. *vo izbezhanie* **neschastnogo sluchaia;**
   in order to avoid an accident

5. *v silu* **prikaza;** according to the policy

6. *v sled za* **proisshestviem;** following the incident

7. *nedaleko ot* **teatra;** not far from the theater

8. *nesmotria na* **slaboe zdorov'e;** despite the poor health

Exercise 11: Completing Sentences

1. *Moia kvartira nakhoditsia* **nedaleko ot** *universiteta.*

2. **Vo izbezhanie** *pozhara, ne kurite v posteli.*

3. **V techenie** *chasa on vstaval, sadilsia, i snova vstaval.*

4. **Nesmotria na** *zharu, oni poshli v pokhod.*

5. **V zakliuchenie** *svoej rechi dokladchik poblagodaril slush-ateley za vnimanie.*

6. **V sled za** *vojnoj nachalsia golod.*

7. **Za iskliucheniem** *Leny, vsem fil'm ponravilsia.*

8. **V sviazi s** *remontom, biblioteka zakryta.*

Exercise 12: Joining Clauses

1. *I Lena, i Misha rabotaiut v teatre. (Lena i Misha rabotaiut v teatre).*

2. *Lena rabotaet v teatre, a Misha rabotaet v ofise*

3. *Lena rabotaet v teatre, no ona sobiraetsia uvol'niat'sia.*

4. *Ni Lena, ni Misha ne rabotaiut v teatre.*

5. *Lena rabotala to v teatre, to v ofise*

6. *Lena rabotaet v teatre, no ona ne aktrisa.*

7. *Lena rabotaet v teatre, a Misha ne rabotaet.*

8. *Lena rabotaet i v teatre, i v ofise.*

Exercise 13: Composing Sentences

1. *Ni Olia, ni Andrej ne govoriat po-ital'ianski.*

2. *I mama, i papa rabotaiut v bol'nitse.*

3. *Brat uchitsia v universitete, a sestra – v shkole.*

4. *Ia prishiol na kontsert, no zabyl bilet.*

5. *Turisty poekhali v gostinitsu, a gid – domoj.*

6. *I mersedes, i kadillak — khoroshie mashiny.*

7. *U nikh net ni faksa, ni kseroksa.*

8. *On igraet i na skripke, i na pianino.*

Exercise 14: Translating into Russian

1. *I Natasha, i Dania rabotaiut zdes'.*
2. *Ni Vera, ni Boris ne znaiut otvet.*
3. *Mama spit, a papa rabotaet.*
4. *Ni on, ni ona ne chitali etu knigu.*
5. *Turisty prishli v muzej, no muzej byl zakryt.*
6. *On zhil i v Moskve, i v Sankt Peterburge.*
7. *Ona ne byla ni v Anglii, ni vo Frantsii.*
8. *Ona obychno ezdit v London, no bol'she liubit Parizh.*

Exercise 15: Joining Clauses

1. *Masha priekhala v Moskvu, chtoby sdelat' kar'eru.*
2. *Masha priekhala v Moskvu, potomu chto dolgo ob etom mechtala.*
3. *Masha priedet v Moskvu, esli najdiot den'gi.*
4. *Masha ne priedet v Moskvu, poka ne zakonchit institut. (Masha ne priedet v Moskvu, esli ne zakonchit institut.)*
5. *Masha ne priedet v Moskvu, tak kak ona ne mogla kupit' bilet. (Masha ne priedet v Moskvu, potomu chto ona ne mogla kupit' bilet.)*
6. *Masha priedet v Moskvu, chtoby najti svoego brata.*

Exercise 16: Matching Clauses

1. *Galileo Galileia sozhgli na kostre, **potomu chto on skazal: "Zemlia vertitsia!"***
2. *Liudi stroiat rakety, **chtoby letat' v kosmos.***
3. *Ia pojdu na kontsert, **esli smogu kupit' billet.***
4. *Vasia ne mozhet najti rabotu, **tak kak on ne zakonchil universitet.***
5. *Professor pokazal fil'm ob obez'ianakh **dlia togo, chtoby ob"iasnit' psikhologiiu liudej.***
6. *On poluchit rabotu, **esli projdiot sobesedovanie.***

Exercise 17: A Story about Dasha

*Dasha zhiviot **v** gorode Novorossijske, **na** ulitse Karamzina. **U** neio doma chasto sobiraiutsia gosti, **chtoby** pogovorit' **o** muzyke **i** literature. Dasha khorosho razbiraetsia **v** iskusstve, **tak kak (potomu chto)** ona sama – khudozhnitsa. **I** Dasha, **i** eio druz'ia chasto khodiat **na** vystavku **i na** kontserty. Oni by khodili **i v** teatr, **no v** Novorossijske net khoroshego teatra. Dasha dolzhna ezdit' **v** Moskvu, **chtoby** skhodit' **v** teatr.*

Exercise 18: Translating into Russian

1. *Lena zhiviot nedaleko ot ofisa.*
2. *On prishiol domoj poobedat'.*
3. *Ia zhivu v kvartire, a moj drug zhiviot v dome.*
4. *Ia videl (videla) i more, i okean.*
5. *Eto podarok dlia vas (tebia).*
6. *Kartina visela nad divanom.*
7. *Na proshloj nedele my rabotali v sadu.*
8. *V mae my edem v Moskvu.*

Part 13

Exercise 1: Asking Questions

1. What is your name?
2. Where do you live?
3. Where did you come from?
4. How old are you?
5. Where do you work?
6. What are you interested in?
7. Is it your first time here?
8. Do you like it here?

Exercise 2: Answering Questions

Answers may vary.
1. *Da, mne nravitsia izuchat' russkij iazyk.*
2. *Da, ia liubliu izuchat' inostrannye iazyki.*
3. *Mne kazhetsia, russkij iazyk – trudnyj.*
4. *Ia liubliu puteshestvovat' v …*
5. *Net, ia nikogda ne byl v Rossii.*
6. *Po professii ia …*
7. *Da, mne nravitsia moia rabota.*
8. *Ia uvlekaius'…*

Exercise 3: Reading the Text

1. *Toni edet v Rossiiu v iiule.*
2. *Net, Toni nikogda ne byl v Rossii.*
3. *Toni zhil v Germanni i puteshestvoval v Italii.*
4. *Toni volnuetsia, potomu chto on ne ochen' khorosho govorit po-russki.*
5. *Toni izuchal russkij iazyk v universitete i u sebia doma, v Chicago.*
6. *Net, u Toni ne bylo dostatochno praktiki.*
7. *V Rossii Toni khochet posmotret' Moskvu i Sankt Peterburg.*
8. *Toni khochet poekhat' na Kavkaz, potomu chto on liubit gory i interesuetsia istoriej.*

Exercise 4: Completing Sentences

1. *My uvideli **bol'shuiu rybu**.*
2. *Lena sidit v parke s **liubimoj knigoj**.*
3. *U nego nikogda net **khoroshikh otsenok**.*
4. *Moia sem'ia zhiviot v **krasivom dome**.*
5. *Mal'chik poslal pis'mo **starshemu bratu**.*
6. *Eto kabinet **glavnogo inzhenera**.*
7. *Ty liubish' smotret' **starye fil'my**?*
8. *My chasto razgovarivaem o **daliokikh stranakh**.*

Exercise 5: Talking about an Apartment

1. *Vika i Kirill ishchut novuiu kvartiru.*
2. *Vika khochet krasivuiu i svetluiu kvartiru.*
3. *Vika khochet bol'shie okna i vysokie potolki.*
4. *Kirill ishchet deshiovuiu kvartiru.*
5. *Vika khochet rozovye ili oranzhevye steny.*
6. *Kirill predpochitaet zelionyj i goluboj tsveta.*
7. *Kirill khochet bol'shuiu kukhniu.*
8. *Vika khochet najti kvartiru vozle Letnego sada.*

Exercise 6: Describing Appearance

1. *U Mariny dlinnye chiornye volosy.*
2. *U Natashi korotkie svetlye volosy.*
3. *U Mariny karie glaza.*
4. *U Natashi golubye glaza.*
5. *U Mariny ne ochen' sportivnaia figura.*
6. *U Natashi sportivnaia figura.*
7. *Natasha liubit nosit' serye svitera i briuki.*
8. *Marina liubit nosit' krasnye plat'ia i iubki.*

Exercise 7: Which Verb?

1. *Direktor **zakryvaet** magazin kazhdyj den' v deviat chasov vechera.*
2. *Ia **khozhu** na rabotu peshkom kazhdyj den'.*
3. *Oni **poznakomilis'** na vecherinke v proshlom godu.*
4. *On **poletit** v komandirovku na samoliote.*
5. *Moia sestra **rabotaet** v biblioteke.*
6. *Zavtra my **poedem** v Moskvu.*
7. *Vy **mozhete** segodnia prijti?*
8. *Ia ochen' **liubliu** morozhennoe.*

Exercise 8: Listening to Chekhov

1. *Kazhdyj polden' oni vstrechalis' na naberezhnoj, zavtrakali vmeste, obedali, guliali, voskhishchalis' morem.*
2. *V Oreande oni sideli na skam'e, smotreli vniz na more i molchali.*
3. *Kazhdyj vecher oni uezzhali kuda-nibud' za gorod.*
4. *Ona budet o niom dumat', vspominat'.*
5. *Potom, kogda oni vyshli.*
6. *U neio v komnate pakhlo dukhami, kotorye ona kupila v iaponskom magazine.*
7. *Ona skazala: "No khorosho, Vy zhe pervyj menia teper' uvazhat' ne budete."*
8. *Po sluchaiu volneniia na more parokhod prishiol pozdno.*

Exercise 9: Dasha's Schedule

2. 7:30 a.m. – ***Dasha vstaiot***
3. 8:00 a.m. – ***Dasha prinimaet dush i chistit zuby***
4. 8:30 a.m. – ***Dasha zavtrakaet.***
5. 9:00 a.m. – ***Dasha nachinaet odevat'sia***
6. 9:30 a.m. – ***Dasha vykhodit iz kvartiry***
7. 9:45 a.m. – ***Dasha saditsia na avtobus***
8. 10:30 a.m. – ***Dasha priezzhaet na rabotu***

Exercise 10: How Is It Done?

1. He came early.
2. She draws better than anyone else.
3. My brother runs very fast.
4. They've been living here for a long time.
5. Will you be walking in the park for a long time?
6. He was walking along the street and singing loudly.
7. She can speak Russian wonderfully.
8. I drive poorly.

Exercise 11: No Names Mentioned

1. *Ona rabotaet v teatre.*
2. *On pozvonil ej.*
3. *Vecherinka budet u nego doma.*
4. *Eto eio plat'e.*
5. *Oni vsegda dumaiut o nej.*
6. *My pojdiom segodnia v kino.*
7. *Ona lezhit na podokonnike.*
8. *Eio zovut Zhuchka.*

Exercise 12: What, Who, and Why?

2. *Gde **rabotaet Misha?***
3. *Pochemu **Natasha doma?***
4. *Kogda **Dasha vstretila Lenu?***
5. *Kuda **zavtra edet brat?***
6. *Kto **napisal mne pis'mo?***
7. *Otkuda **priekhala Vera?***
8. *Zachem **papa prishiol domoj?***

Exercise 13: Little Words

1. *My idiom **v** kino.*
2. *Ona znaet **i** anglijskij, **i** nemetskij iazyk.*
3. *Tebe nuzhno pojti **k** doktoru.*
4. *Oni dolgo guliali **u** moria.*
5. *Chto ty znaesh' **ob** etom dele?*
6. *Ia khotel pozvonit', **no** ne smog.*
7. *Natasha priekhala **iz** Moskvy.*
8. *On vsegda delaet zariadku **pered** zavtrakom.*

Index

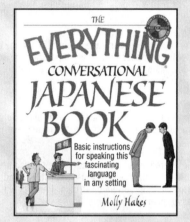

Software License Agreement

YOU SHOULD CAREFULLY READ THE FOLLOWING TERMS AND CONDITIONS BEFORE USING THIS SOFTWARE PRODUCT. INSTALLING AND USING THIS PRODUCT INDICATES YOUR ACCEPTANCE OF THESE CONDITIONS. IF YOU DO NOT AGREE WITH THESE TERMS AND CONDITIONS, DO NOT INSTALL THE SOFTWARE AND RETURN THIS PACKAGE PROMPTLY FOR A FULL REFUND.

1. Grant of License
This software package is protected under United States copyright law and international treaty. You are hereby entitled to one copy of the enclosed software and are allowed by law to make one backup copy or to copy the contents of the disks onto a single hard disk and keep the originals as your backup or archival copy. United States copyright law prohibits you from making a copy of this software for use on any computer other than your own computer. United States copyright law also prohibits you from copying any written material included in this software package without first obtaining the permission of F+W Publications, Inc.

2. Restrictions
You, the end-user, are hereby prohibited from the following:
You may not rent or lease the Software or make copies to rent or lease for profit or for any other purpose.
You may not disassemble or reverse compile for the purposes of reverse engineering the Software.
You may not modify or adapt the Software or documentation in whole or in part, including, but not limited to, translating or creating derivative works.

3. Transfer
You may transfer the Software to another person, provided that (a) you transfer all of the Software and documentation to the same transferee; (b) you do not retain any copies; and (c) the transferee is informed of and agrees to the terms and conditions of this Agreement.

4. Termination
This Agreement and your license to use the Software can be terminated without notice if you fail to comply with any of the provisions set forth in this Agreement. Upon termination of this Agreement, you promise to destroy all copies of the software including backup or archival copies as well as any documentation associated with the Software. All disclaimers of warranties and limitation of liability set forth in this Agreement shall survive any termination of this Agreement.

5. Limited Warranty
F+W Publications, Inc. warrants that the Software will perform according to the manual and other written materials accompanying the Software for a period of 30 days from the date of receipt. F+W Publications, Inc. does not accept responsibility for any malfunctioning computer hardware or any incompatibilities with existing or new computer hardware technology.

6. Customer Remedies
F+W Publications, Inc.'s entire liability and your exclusive remedy shall be, at the option of F+W Publications, Inc., either refund of your purchase price or repair and/or replacement of Software that does not meet this Limited Warranty. Proof of purchase shall be required. This Limited Warranty will be voided if Software failure was caused by abuse, neglect, accident or misapplication. All replacement Software will be warranted based on the remainder of the warranty or the full 30 days, whichever is shorter and will be subject to the terms of the Agreement.

7. No Other Warranties
F+W PUBLICATIONS, INC., TO THE FULLEST EXTENT OF THE LAW, DISCLAIMS ALL OTHER WARRANTIES, OTHER THAN THE LIMITED WARRANTY IN PARAGRAPH 5, EITHER EXPRESS OR IMPLIED, ASSOCIATED WITH ITS SOFTWARE, INCLUDING BUT NOT LIMITED TO IMPLIED WARRANTIES OF MERCHANTABILITY AND FITNESS FOR A PARTICULAR PURPOSE, WITH REGARD TO THE SOFTWARE AND ITS ACCOMPANYING WRITTEN MATERIALS. THIS LIMITED WARRANTY GIVES YOU SPECIFIC LEGAL RIGHTS. DEPENDING UPON WHERE THIS SOFTWARE WAS PURCHASED, YOU MAY HAVE OTHER RIGHTS.

8. Limitations on Remedies
TO THE MAXIMUM EXTENT PERMITTED BY LAW, F+W PUBLICATIONS, INC. SHALL NOT BE HELD LIABLE FOR ANY DAMAGES WHATSOEVER, INCLUDING WITHOUT LIMITATION, ANY LOSS FROM PERSONAL INJURY, LOSS OF BUSINESS PROFITS, BUSINESS INTERRUPTION, BUSINESS INFORMATION OR ANY OTHER PECUNIARY LOSS ARISING OUT OF THE USE OF THIS SOFTWARE.
This applies even if F+W Publications, Inc. has been advised of the possibility of such damages. F+W Publications, Inc.'s entire liability under any provision of this agreement shall be limited to the amount actually paid by you for the Software. Because some states may not allow for this type of limitation of liability, the above limitation may not apply to you.
THE WARRANTY AND REMEDIES SET FORTH ABOVE ARE EXCLUSIVE AND IN LIEU OF ALL OTHERS, ORAL OR WRITTEN, EXPRESS OR IMPLIED. No F+W Publications, Inc. dealer, distributor, agent, or employee is authorized to make any modification or addition to the warranty.

9. General
This Agreement shall be governed by the laws of the United States of America and the Commonwealth of Massachusetts. If you have any questions concerning this Agreement, contact F+W Publications, Inc., via Adams Media at 508-427-7100. Or write to us at: Adams Media, an F+W Publications Company, 57 Littlefield Street, Avon, MA 02322.